French Populism and Discourses on Secularism

Critiquing Religion: Discourse, Culture, Power

Series editor: Craig Martin

Critiquing Religion: Discourse, Culture, Power publishes works that historicize both religions and modern discourses on "religion" that treat it as a unique object of study. Using diverse methodologies and social theories, volumes in this series view religions and discourses on religion as commonplace rhetorics, authenticity narratives, or legitimating myths which function in the creation, maintenance, and contestation of social formations. Works in the series are on the cutting edge of critical scholarship, regarding "religion" as just another cultural tool used to gerrymander social space and distribute power relations in the modern world. *Critiquing Religion: Discourse, Culture, Power* provides a unique home for reflexive, critical work in the field of religious studies.

Christian Tourist Attractions, Mythmaking and Identity Formation,
edited by Erin Roberts and Jennifer Eyl

Spirituality, Corporate Culture, and American Business:
The Neoliberal Ethic and the Spirit of Global Capital,
James Dennis LoRusso

Stereotyping Religion: Critiquing Clichés,
edited by Brad Stoddard and Craig Martin

French Populism and Discourses on Secularism

Per-Erik Nilsson

BLOOMSBURY ACADEMIC
LONDON • NEW YORK • OXFORD • NEW DELHI • SYDNEY

BLOOMSBURY ACADEMIC
Bloomsbury Publishing Plc
50 Bedford Square, London, WC1B 3DP, UK
1385 Broadway, New York, NY 10018, USA

BLOOMSBURY, BLOOMSBURY ACADEMIC and the
Diana logo are trademarks of Bloomsbury Publishing Plc

First published in Great Britain 2019

Cover image © Yi Lu/EyeEm. Getty Images

A catalogue record for this book is available from the British Library.

A catalog record for this book is available from the Library of Congress.

ISBN: HB: 978-1-3500-5582-7
            ePDF: 978-1-3500-5583-4
            eBook: 978-1-3500-5584-1

Typeset by Integra Software Services Pvt. Ltd.

To find out more about our authors and books, visit www.bloomsbury.com
and sign up for our newsletters.

Contents

Preface

In March 2017, I was invited to have lunch with the secularist activists Pierre Cassen and Christine Tasin, and a small number of individuals with ties to Cassen and Tasin. The location was a brasserie in central Paris, close to the river Seine. The restaurant was completely empty, except for a bartender. I approached this bartender, most likely with some confusion in my eyes, and asked him if the address that Cassen had given me a couple of days earlier was correct. The bartender gazed at me for a couple of seconds, and then said: "They're upstairs." I found Cassen and Tasin sitting at a table behind lush red curtains in a corner of the large, empty second floor.

After small talk and the arrival of ten or so invited guests, most notably Cassen's lawyer, we all ordered lunch. The menu was set: the choice was traditional Alsatian sausage or French rump steak, not ideal for a vegetarian and aspiring vegan like me. As we waited for the food, the discussion turned to the reason we were there. Cassen was to appear, a couple of hours later, in the 17th chamber of the *Tribunal de grande instance*, a French court specializing in questions related to the press. The prosecutor had summoned him to answer allegations of "public provocation of racial or religious hatred."[1] On the plaintiff's side was the joint ministerial delegation against racism and antisemitism, the *Délégation Interministiriélle à la lutte contre le Racisme et l'Antisémitisme* (DILCRA), and a number of anti-racist organizations.[2] Cassen was first acquitted of the charges, but later the same year he was convicted to a three-month suspended prison sentence.[3]

This was not the first time Cassen had appeared in court, and probably not the last. Since he launched the web-based journal *Riposte Laïque* (which translates as *Secular Retaliation*), he and his co-writers' texts have provoked many in France and abroad. *Riposte Laïque* even became a topic of heated debate during the 2016 primary elections within the conservative party, *Les Républicains*. The publication had been driving a campaign against one of the top candidates, Alain Juppé, mockingly nicknamed Ali Juppé, for being the puppet of Islamists aiming to take over France, and in favor of the hard-liner François Fillon, a candidate *Riposte Laïque* later abandoned to solemnly favor the radical nationalist and populist Marine Le Pen and her party, *Front National* (FN).[4]

Similarly, Tasin has seen the inside of a court room for her activism within the *Riposte Laïque* sibling organization, the *Resistance Républicaine* (Republican Resistance). Cassin and Tasin portray themselves, and are portrayed by their supporters, as the leaders of an avant-garde movement in the fight against what they see as a war playing out in the midst of France. It is a war driven by "Islamo-fascists" who are supported by a corrupt political elite and a gullible and politically correct left: all central ingredients in contemporary European radical nationalist and populist discourse.

The general purpose of this book is to inquire into the recent changes in how French secularism *la laïcité*, as discourse, is articulated and practiced by populist modes of identification. This purpose is to be understood in relation to the shift that occurred in how secularism was talked about in public speech in 1989. Previously, during the Fifth Republic (1958–), debates about secularism (although from time to time a hotly debated issue) mainly concerned the school system, and whether or not religious private schools should be funded by the state, or even allowed; however, post-1989 secularism started to appear in debates about integration and national identity, and about the place of Islam in France.

In this book I use *Riposte Laïque* as a magnifying lens to focus on the conspicuous intersections between the appropriation of the category of secularism by the political mainstream, and the radical nationalist and populist groups and parties. This includes Marine Le Pen's FN, the French Identitarian movement, radical nationalist and populist groups and movements, the post-1968 "new-reactionary" intelligentsia, and certain hard-line secular politicians and public spokespersons from the left.[5] Here, issues relating to alterity, degradation, pride and resistance are central: alterity in terms of a fearful and hateful condemnation of that which is deemed foreign; degradation in the sense of an a claimed deterioration and deterritorialization of the French society and nation; pride with regard to a vainglorious love for those who qualify as being one's own; and resistance in relation to overcoming the acclaimed problems related to alterity and degradation.

As I will show in this book, the issues of alterity, degradation, pride, and resistance are tied up in a populist logic of identification, where secularism is turned into an emblem in the designation of the responsible agents for the degradation of both French society and nation, as well as the emblem for the true French people and their path to restoration. It should be noted that *Riposte Laïque* is not the most extreme or the most radical nationalist, secularist, and anti-Muslim populist voice in France; however, it is an exemplary point of convergence regarding these issues.

The timeline of the book was from 2007 to 2017, from the first publication of *Riposte Laïque* to its ten-year anniversary. During these years, a number of events have touched French social and political life, all focusing in one way or another on secularism, national identity, and Islam. These include the electoral success of the nationalist and populist party FN; *le Printemps Français* (the French Spring), during which millions of conservative and reactionary voices took to the streets to manifest their contempt for the legalization by the Socialist government of same-sex marriage; the rise of the current president Emmanuel Macron and the coupled dissolution of the French Socialist Party, the *Parti Socialiste* (PS); the large-scale jihadi-style attacks in Paris in 2015 and the declared state of emergency that lasted two years; the revelation of corruption and nepotism plaguing the corridors of the French state; and the many highly mediatized *affairs* and *gates* in which issues of alterity, morality, public order, and security have been channeled through fierce debates on what secularism in France entails. These debates include the Islamic Veil Affairs leading to the banning of *hijabs* in public schools in 2004, and of *niqabs* in public spaces in 2010; Burkini Gate during the summer of 2016, when national media focused on a dozen women wearing Islamic full-body coverage on public beaches, leading to local bans that were later lifted due to their unlawfulness; the Chocolate Bread Affair in 2012, when the then candidate for the Union for a Popular Movement (UMP) presidency, Jean-François Copé, declared that young white French citizens could no longer eat chocolate pastries during Ramadan due to a general anti-white racism driven by Muslim thugs; and finally Couscous Gate, revolving around Marine Le Pen's right-hand man, Florian Philippot, who during a visit to Strasbourg chose to eat couscous, causing an outcry among radical nationalist web-channels and mockery of the whole debacle by journalists and anti-FN activists on the web. These events and affairs are symptomatic of more large-scale developments, such as the obsession of French politicians and public spokespersons with issues of national identity, secularism, Islam, integration, securitization, and gender; increasing economic competition in the global marketplace; France's role in a changing European Union (EU); social and economic inequality along the lines of class, gender, and race; the precarization of the labor force (the process of rendering the labor force's lives precarious); and the changes in political communication brought about by the web and social media.[6]

Previously published research in English, with an empirical focus, can be divided into three categories: secularism, the far-right and populism, and anti-

The first chapter, "Under Siege," serves as an introduction to the central analytical topics of the book, namely secularism, nationhood, and populism. The analyzed material is introduced and contextualized by discussing the history and organization of *Riposte Laïque* in relation to other similar journals, movements, and political parties in France. Moreover, I present the methodological and theoretical starting points for the analysis: anti-foundational analysis of populism, national identity, gender, racism, and secularism; plus discourse theory and ethnographic fieldwork on street and web-based social and political movements.

In the second chapter, "A Green Cancer," I analyze how the national "we" is contrasted and juxtaposed to perceived others and the enemies of imaginations of what the French nation and the European civilization are. I focus on what *Riposte Laïque* perceives as culturally, religiously, and ethnically different enemies of the nation, i.e., Muslims. I present the publication's construction of Muslims as enemies and their theory of Islam as a fascist ideology. Finally, I contrast and compare *Riposte Laïque* constructions of Muslims and Islam with those of similar movements, intellectuals, and established political parties in France.

The third chapter, "Collaborators and Traitors," analyzes how a national "we" is contrasted and juxtaposed to perceived others and enemies within the *Riposte Laïque* notion of what the French nation and European civilization entail. The chapter focuses on "others" that are classified as culturally, religiously, and ethnically similar; but politically and by gender, the opposites of their concept of "we." I show how *Riposte Laïque* portrays the alleged political and societal elite as agents that have feminized and castrated the French nation, making it vulnerable to an imagined, ongoing Islamization of France. As with the previous chapter, I compare and contrast the *Riposte Laïque* vision with that of similar movements, intellectuals, and the established political parties in France.

In the fourth chapter, "The Real People," I show how *Riposte Laïque* constructs an exclusivist French identity based on traits and customs that are channeled through particular conceptions of nation, religion, secularism, politics, ethnicity, and gender. I also compare and contrast the *Riposte Laïque* vision of a populist national identity with both historical and current conceptions of national identity among similar French movements, intellectuals, and established political parties.

In the fifth and last analytical chapter, "*Reconquista* or Death," I tie the analysis together by analyzing the *Riposte Laïque* publication's theories and methods for coming to terms with the enemies of the nation. I show how *Riposte Laïque* uses such republican and liberal tropes as secularism, freedom, and democracy to formulate what they call a *reconquista* [re-conquering] of the nation, by expelling or converting the perceived enemies of the nation to construct a homogeneous, monocultural nation. I contrast the *Riposte Laïque* program for *reconquista* with the French far-right's appropriation of secularism and the political mainstream's different versions of secularism.

The final chapter, "Echoes from the Past," serves as a concluding discussion based on a comparative outlook. I compare and contrast *Riposte Laïque* and the French radical nationalists' take on secularism to that of other, similar groups, movements, and political parties in Europe.

1

Under Siege

Approaching Secularism, Populism, and Nationhood in France

The year is 2010. It is a grey and rainy December day in Paris. I am walking in the 12th *arrondissement*, one of Paris's twenty districts. My destination is the *Assises contre l'islamisation de nos pays* [Conference against the islamization of our countries], located in the *Espace Charenton*, a large venue. The conference flyer I am holding in my hand reads: "Defend secularism, defend our civilization's values." The main organizer is the French secularist and web-based journal, *Riposte Laïque*. They organized the conference together with an ensemble of twenty-five web-based journals, and social and political movements, some of which are: *Résistance Républicaine* [Republican Resistance], *Bloc Identitaire* [Identity Block], *Novopress, l'Obsérvatoire de l'islamisation* [Islamization Observatory], *Parti de l'Innocence* [Innocence Party], and *Ligue de Défence Française* [French Defense League].[1] On the list of invited speakers I see, among others, Oskar Freysinger from the Swiss *Union Démocratique du Centre* (UDC) [Democratic Union of the Center]; Tommy Robinson from the English Defence League (EDL); Renaud Camus from the *Parti de l'Innocence*; Fabrice Robert from *Bloc Identitaire*; Jean-Paul Gourevitch, an acclaimed international expert on immigration; Timo Vermuelen from the Dutch Defense League (DDL); Anders Gravers from Stop the Islamization of Europe (SIOE); Giselle Litman, the Eurabian author also known as Bat Ye'Or; and, finally, Pierre Cassen, the founder of *Riposte Laïque*. These groups and individuals conspicuously draw on contemporary radical nationalist, populist, identitarian, and anti-Muslim discourses; and they relate in one way or another to a European counter-jihad movement: a network of journalists, politicians, and web-based and street activists.[2] The network is heterogeneous, and actors within it draw eclectically on a wide variety of discourses that are adapted to their specific national and local arenas; however, according to Egil Asprem, they converge with regard to three aspects:

(a) Islam is seen as a new form of totalitarian ideology rooted in Europe and, as such, is seen as a great threat to European civilization;
(b) the political and cultural establishment is held responsible for the ongoing Islamization of Europe; and
(c) European civilization and Europe's nation-states thus face two enemies: Islam and the political and cultural establishment.[3]

There had been some buzz about the conference in the news media during the preceding days. Major news channels had denounced the conference for being a meeting of the European extreme right. According to *Riposte Laïque*, the organizers were the victims of a "mass-media misinformation worthy of the Soviet press back in the day."[4] Moreover, the mayor of Paris, Socialist Betrand Delanoë, and the first deputy mayor of the 12th *arrondissement*, Communist Alexis Corbière, as well as the antiracist organization *Mouvement contre le racism et pour l'amitié entre les peoples* (MRAP) [Movement against racism and for friendship between peoples], had tried in vain to ban the conference.[5] Regardless, the Parisian police had granted the organizers the right to hold the conference by referring to the French law of 1881, guaranteeing French citizens the right to hold public meetings. As I approach the conference, I notice that the police are actually present on site and have enforced a considerable security perimeter around the venue. As I reach the perimeter, two policemen ask me where I am heading and ask to look in my bag. I enter into a secured and desolate street. After a couple hundred meters, I see the entrance. A dozen white men and women stand outside. At the entrance, I am greeted by two large men with shaved heads who are wearing black bomber jackets and black knee-high leather boots. I later learn that security had been provided by one of the organizers, *Bloc identitaire*.

The inner entrance of the hall is narrow and packed with people. The walls are covered in posters portraying a woman wearing a *niqab* with a judge's mallet in her hand, a not so subtle depiction of an imagined Sharia Court. The poster reads: "No to Sharia!"

I pay my entrance fee of ten euros and enter the major hall. Nearly all of approximately 200 seats are full. The walls are draped with French flags: blue, white, and red. The white middle section is decorated with the Cross of Lorraine, the symbol of Free France, the exiled government during the Nazi occupation of France, the cross being the resistance movement's answer to the Nazis' swastika.

I was to learn during the day that the resistance movement is sitting in this hall, and their enemy is no longer the Nazis: it is the Islamists. France is under siege. While I am still standing at the entrance, a woman asks me if I am hungry. I realize that I am next to a food stand where she is selling ham sandwiches and wine. A large piggy bank for tips is standing in the middle of the table. The ham and the piggy bank are small symbols, but significant for French and other anti-Muslim movements: to eat pork functions as a technique of inclusion and exclusion, as it is seen to symbolize traditional French food, helping to designate the true French from the Semitic "others," as it is not part of halal or kosher food.[6] In 2006, French identitarians organized a *soupe au cochon*, a soup kitchen for homeless people which used and served pork, with the aim of excluding Muslims and Jews.[7]

Before I take my seat, I walk around the large hall and observe the many cameramen who are finalizing their set-up. The whole conference is being broadcast live. While approaching a book stand in one corner of the hall, I run into the person who invited me: a member of the *Riposte Laïque* editorial board. Up to this point, we had met on a couple of occasions for interviews. He is excited and tells me about what is to come. He is especially excited about the presence of Oskar Freysinger. I quickly learn that he is something of a star to the *Riposte Laïque* editorial staff. Freysinger, from the Swiss populist right-wing UDC, is one of the instigators behind the popular initiative to ban the construction of minarets in the country. During the campaign, Freysinger's party published a poster portraying a woman dressed in a black burqa standing in front of the Swiss flag, which is pierced with black missile-like minarets. My host then guides me over to a book stand to show me a new and "important" book by Joachim Véliocas, who had listed all the mayors in France who, according to him, betray the secular principles of France by paving the way for Islamists.[8] The book was published by the Tatamis publishing house, which, as I was about to learn, has filled its shelves with anti-Muslim literature and takes pride in printing books that are refused by the more renowned publishers.

The conference is about to start and I take a seat. A video starts playing on the large screen in front of the audience. An ancient map of France fills the screen, accompanied by the slogans "defend our secularism" and "defend our civilization." This is replaced by images portraying a mosque and then Muslims praying on three streets in northern Paris (rue Myrha, rue Leon, and the Boulevard de Barbès). This is followed by a sermon from Amar Lasfar, the long-term public face of the biggest French Islamic organization, *Union des organisations islamiques de France* (UOIF) and since 2013, its president. These images are meant to illustrate an ongoing Islamization of France. The video then turns to show resistance against it. First, there is an intervention by some seventy people wearing pig's masks at a Quick (French version of McDonald's) serving halal meat in the city of Villeurbanne. Next are images of the EDL, accompanied by the text "British patriots, taking to the streets to say no." The video ends with the slogan: "Defenders of secularism and the values of our civilization. You are no longer alone!!" The audience applauds the video; the mood in the room is vibrant.

Pierre Cassen takes the podium. He starts by thanking *Espace Charenton* for not giving in to the "politico-religious groups who think they are in Iran; that Sharia law rules in France." The audience shows its agreement by applauding any positive identification with France and booing as soon any connotation of Islam is mentioned. He continues to thank the police for resisting the pressure put on them by the mayor of Paris when he was "insulting the organizers and thus the participants of this conference by classifying them as haters, extreme-right wingers, and racists." Cassen leaves the podium and a long series of lectures follow on the ongoing Islamization of France and the fundamental incompatibility of Islam and Western civilization. A couple of days later, *Riposte Laïque* summarized the conference: according to them it was a great success, with over 600,000 viewers of their broadcast:

> During the conference, the speeches leaned both towards the left and the right. All the testimonials were very rich and touched upon different themes, such as: feminism, syndicalism, immigration, identity, secularism, and the Republic. All the participants gathered with love for our civilization's principles and the refusal to see our countries lose their democratic conquests to an increasingly violent and threatening Islamism.[9]

In the articles in *Riposte Laïque,* the conference was seen as the starting point for a larger avant-garde movement rooted in the core values of the French republic and secularism. *Riposte Laïque* and its co-organizers had laid the foundation for a self-acclaimed avant-gardist patriotic resistance against a perceived onslaught on the French nation and its people: an Islamic onslaught that had led to the development of a corrupt political elite, a politically correct and gullible political left, and a far-reaching feminization and castration of the nation's virility. This discourse on secularism has far-reaching echoes within contemporary French radical nationalist and populist milieus, most notably within *Front National,* with its leader Marine Le Pen. I was stunned by the participants' passion and professed love for France, as well as their unyielding conviction that

Islamists were waging a full-blown war of conquest against France, Europe, and Western civilization. To them, we were standing at a threshold. It was either them or us. It was a dire situation where one had to choose sides, to resist or perish.

Another aspect of *Riposte Laïque* and this conference was how secularism, this conspicuously multifaceted aspect of French politics and social life, appeared as an emblem, as a symbolic bridge, to unite, create, and reshape previously diverse and dispersed political and social voices around one cause. This cause was to purify France of all facets of Islam. But there was more to it. The cause was guided by a culturalist idea of who the real people of France were: those with a professed love for freedom, equality, and the nation-state. As Cassen said in his introductory speech, the Parisian Socialist mayor and the anti-racist organization MRAP had accused the organizers of being hateful and racist; but, in the eyes of *Riposte Laïque*, it was the other way around. The Socialist mayor and MRAP are the ones who hate; they are the ones who are blinded by racism: a racism targeting the white French population. On the other hand, *Riposte Laïque*, by their own logic, are the ones who love; they are the ones who see the order of things for what it is; they are the ones who are courageous enough to tell the truth; and they are the Republican avant-gardists standing up for the French people in the emerging apocalyptic battle between secular democracy and Islam.

A new media is born

Pierre Cassen founded *Riposte Laïque* in 2007. He describes himself as an old Trotskyist. He has been a member of the revolutionary communist party, *Ligue communiste révolutionnaire* (LCR) [Communist revolutionary league], editor of the republican leftist online journal *ReSPUBLICA*, and national spokesperson for the secularist organization *Union pour un movement laïque* (UFAL). Cassen's aim was to create a new journal to function as a forum for the defense of secularism against what Cassen and his co-editors saw as the most urgent threat against the Republic, a threat that Cassen's earlier political allies did not take seriously: "*Riposte Laïque* was founded because we think that the gravity of the offensive brought about by political Islam in France, in Europe, and around the world, has been dramatically underestimated by a large section of the left and by the secular movement."[10] The naming of the journal was not self-evident, but *Riposte Laïque* was chosen because it was thought to "speak to the left," as Cassen puts it.[11] The ambition was to "reunite republicans all over the political field," to "encourage patriotism among ordinary people," and to be "as little sectarian as possible and open to all."[12] Cassen is adamant, as are the articles in the journal, that the *Riposte Laïque* editorial staff is not a homogeneous group and that they do not agree on a large number of political issues, for example, on same-sex marriage or the Israel–Palestine question.[13] Cassen believes that, after almost ten years of existence, the ambition of *Riposte Laïque* to unify and awaken the left to these issues has not so far played out as planned: rather, the contrary. According to him, the left unjustly treats him and his fellows as "bastards," "extreme-rightists," and "all these sorts of derogatory terms."[14] Indeed, *Riposte Laïque* is frequently portrayed as being part of a blogosphere called the *fashosphère*, or the fascist-sphere, by left-leaning media channels.[15] However, when it comes to getting the message out to the general public and making French citizens understand that Islam is incompatible with the Republic and its values, Cassen sees his endeavor as a success: "We have constructed a war-machine against the islamists and the islamo-collaborators, a war-machine that re-informs the media's misinformation."[16] According to Cassen, this war-machine seeks out the truth, and refuses to confine itself to any "politically correct" or "secularly correct" conduct. It is seen as the continuation of a revolutionary, enlightenment-based republican heritage. Voltaire, for example, is frequently cited in *Riposte Laïque* publications; and especially the statement, incorrectly ascribed to Voltaire: "I disapprove of what you say, but I will defend to the death your right to say it."[17]

Another sign of the self-acclaimed heritage of *Riposte Laïque* is the frequent reference to Savinien de Cyrano de Bergerac, a seventeenth-century modernist and freethinker. All the *Riposte Laïque* editorials are signed "Cyrano." According to *Riposte Laïque*, Cyrano's satirical writings "assembled individuals skeptical of rules and conduct imposed by religion, morals, or tradition."[18] Yet another great historical figure that *Riposte Laïque* appropriates is Jean Jaurès, the early seventeenth-century leader of the French Socialist Party, the *Parti Socialiste Français* (PS), and has adopted his belief that "courage is to seek out the truth and to tell it."[19]

When *Riposte Laïque* began in 2007, it was published just once a week. Ten years later it has become a daily, with a few interruptions during holidays. *Riposte Laïque* has published over 700 editorials signed "Cyrano," tens of thousands of articles, and hundreds of videos on YouTube, has continuous postings on Facebook and Twitter, and publishes books through its own publishing house. Some of these will be presented in the analysis. In terms of followers and clicks, their articles generally have between a couple thousand and 10,000 readers; they have about 30,000 followers on Facebook; 12,000 on Twitter; and 8,000 course of history.[44] During the immense public demonstrations after the attacks against *Charlie Hebdo* and Hyper Cacher in January 2015, 4 million people all over France were reported to have gathered with chants, songs, and signs proclaiming "Freedom, equality, brotherhood, and secularism."[45] Shortly after the attacks, the Socialist Minister of Education, Najat Vallaud-Belkacem, stated that students and teachers needed to be thoroughly educated in the "Republic's values."[46] The minister declared that over 300,000 teachers would be given special education in secularism; that students and parents were requested to sign a declaration stating that they were obliged to respect secularism; and that disciplinary measures would be taken against those students who were not living up to the Republic's secular standards.[47] Public spokespeople and intellectuals followed suit and stressed the importance of the school as a site in the "war against terrorism."[48]

In one sense, Belkacem's statements repeated what former state representatives had been talking about endlessly since 1989. Secularism is a value, an entity that is a prerequisite for proper republican conduct, and a path to a peaceful society. It is the fruit of a long historical unfolding of the West, with its roots in ancient Greece. The presidentially appointed commission that did the preparatory work for the law of 2004 that banned conspicuous religious symbols in schools, for example, concluded that secularism "relates to Ancient Greece, the Reformation, the Edict of Nantes, and the Enlightenment. Each one of these stages has, in its own way, brought about individual autonomy and freedom of thought."[49] When President Jacques Chirac commented on the commission's work, he declared that "secularism is inscribed in our traditions. Secularism is close to the heart of our Republican identity."[50] President Nicolas Sarkozy argued in 2007 that secularism is "the value base of France," composed of, on the one hand, "the separation between the temporal and the spiritual"; and on the other, "gender equality."[51] Statements of this sort have been flooding French public debate. Secularism has indeed become a hot topic, and a topic that sells. During the last decade or so, French book stores have filled their bookshelves with popular literature on secularism that seeks to explain its true meaning and how to live accordingly. The proliferation of secularism is seen in the publication of instruction books like *Laïcité pour les nuls* [Secularism for dummies]; the cartoon version of secularism's history in *Comprendre la laïcité* [Understanding secularism]; the guide book to how to implement and understand secularism in daily life, *La laïcité au quotiden: guide pratique* [Secularism in daily life: A practical guide]; and the guide for teachers and students in public schools, *Petit manuel pour une laïcité apaisée* [A small manual for gaining a calm secularism].[52] In *Le dictionnaire amoureux de la laïcité* [The dictionary of love for secularism], Henri-Pena Ruiz, a philosopher and public specialist on French secularism, refers to secularism as an emancipatory ideal that merits love: "Loving secularism is loving an ideal that applies to all."[53] Here, secularism becomes a desired something that inhabits the path to peace and prosperity. It is something that can be loved and betrayed, and it is also an object that gets ascribed a variety of meanings through epithets such as being "open," "inclusive," "peaceful," and "combative." The way of perceiving this newly found French essentiality echoes Charles de Gaulle's poetic love for France: "All my life I have imagined France in a certain way. This has been inspired by sentiment as much as reason. The emotional side of me tends to imagine France, like a princess in the fairy tales or the Madonna in the Frescoes, as dedicated to an exalted and exceptional destiny ... France cannot be France without greatness."[54]

The image in *Charlie Hebdo* is also symptomatic of how this teleological development is seen as embodied in the French Republic: as a unified something, even personified, often presented as manifest in a bundle of laws and decrees.[55] The law most frequently referred to in this regard is the Law of 1905, separating church from state.[56] The legislative complexity concerning this law and its amendments has been visible in its unequal and ambiguous application on the French mainland, as in the colonies, and is visible today in the many various interpretations of it. This concerns, not least, the principle of state neutrality in relation to religious practice that is most often taken as one of the main outcomes of the law. During the debates preceding the laws of 2004 and 2010, state neutrality was a central theme. For example, the parliamentarian commission that conducted the preparatory work for the Law of 2010 stated that secularism "conditions the access to republican citizenship for all French by assuring state-neutrality vis-à-vis spiritual and religious choices."[57] However, the Law of 2004 that prohibited students in public schools from wearing conspicuously visible religious symbols turned the principle of neutrality on its head. If secularism embodied in the Law of 1905 prescribed state neutrality, which is highly debatable, it had now turned from the neutrality of state institutions and representatives to citizens.[58] Moreover, since the Islamic headscarf was the focal point of the debate, secularism specifically targeted Muslim citizens, as was the case with the Law of 2010.[59] When the aforementioned commission stated that secularism was a "foundational principle" leading to "peaceful coexistence," it implied that French Muslims needed to be pacified.[60]

One attempt to pacify Islam and Muslims has been made under the slogan "Islam of France," compared with "Islam in France."[61] The institutionalization of must be inconsistent with its 'true' meaning)."[90] Secularism is, in this regard, a spectacular category; it becomes a desired object as well as the projection surface for a wide variety of political and social struggles. Whatever secularism is, it is emblematically void of content, or, conversely, overdetermined with meaning.

Categories and discourse

In this book, besides my observations from the field, I present an analysis of more than 700 published editorials from *Riposte Laïque*. These editorials usually comment upon current events and both the publication and *Résistance Républicaine*'s activism. They are written in a satirical, sardonic tone and often contain cartoons and memes, links to videos, articles, and books by activists, politicians, scholars, and intellectuals that *Riposte Laïque* cherish. In my analysis, I used these editorials as a window into the counter-jihadist and radical nationalist inter-referential network, of which *Riposte Laïque* is a part. While this is representative of the general outlines of the journal, it does not cover the pluralism found in the tens of thousands of other publications. This analysis was carried out through careful reading of the material, which I have thematically and theoretically structured and then analyzed, mainly relying on post-structuralist discourse theory.[91] This is, as Jacob Torfing explains, an approach that asserts an anti-essentialist ontology and an anti-foundationalist epistemology.[92]

An anti-essentialist ontology sets out from the premise that "there is no pregiven, self-determining essence that is capable of determining and ultimately fixing all other identities within a stable and totalizing structure."[93] I see discourse as the result of articulatory practices that seek to give social and political categories a specific meaning;[94] however, given the anti-essentialist ontology that informs discourse theory, discourse is by necessity to be seen as a contingent and partially fixed meaning-making system.[95] Moreover, while the basic premise in discourse theory is that there is an independent reality outside discourse, in discourse theory it is argued that the way this reality is made sense of is through our conceptualizations of it. As Torfing puts it, the "contention is merely that nothing follows from the bare existence of matter. Matter does not carry the means of its own representation."[96]

Discourse theory is thus both realist and materialist: realist as it sees reality as independent of human thought, materialist because it argues that matter and form cannot be independently separated.[97] What interests the discourse theorists is the social and political actors' will to know reality: those who claim that they have broken through discourse and found the truth.[98] Now, if locally articulated discourse bound to time and space is the ultimate horizon for human conduct, are human beings simply able to invent reality as they see fit? From a discourse theoretical point of view, the answer is no. Discourse and hegemonic horizons can be, and are, continuously challenged; but, and this is the point, human beings are not seen as omnipotent. Even if the logical conclusion from the premise is that there is no universal truth or direct access to reality, society could potentially always be configured differently, and truth always be something else. Even if discourse theory highlights the potential for social change, human action is constrained by discourse. Hence, discourse is both enabling human action and constraining it. Thus, discourse theorists seek to understand how certain articulations of discourse have been ascribed the status of truth or objectivity, and the logical conclusions for human conduct that follow.

A case in point: In the human and social sciences it is commonplace to mention that the central analytical categories of the specific analysis are contested, that there is no single definition, and that the field is burdened by heterogeneous and sometimes contradictory definitions. Indeed, the central categories for my analysis (populism, secularism, and nationhood) are contested not only in academia, but also in many arenas that mark out social and political life. I have already touched on some aspects of the multitude of usages of secularism in France and the definition struggles surrounding the category in relation to what the French nation is. While populism is also a contested category, the appeal of it for political and social actors is more ambiguous. It is well known that politicians have used populism as a way to label political opponents and their policies as elitist. For example, both Marine Le Pen and the leader of the radical left party *Les insoumise(s)*, Jean-Luc Melenchon, have embraced populism. Le Pen has explained that the "way I see it, populism is a way to defend the people against the elites, to defend the forgotten ones against the elite which is strangling them. Yes, in this sense, I'm a populist."[99] Melenchon has, in polemical fashion, declared that "the beautiful, the satisfied, their griots and all those who are giving lessons from a moral high ground can suffocate themselves of indignation. They can dispel their pathetic red card. Populism! Misconduct! I accept!"[100]

The point here is that these categories are not just contested by politicians, since there is currently an ongoing debate on how to conceptualize them in the academic and political arena.[101] They are by necessity contested, because there is no one true meaning lurking behind their contingent use (i.e., relational, contextual, and historical). *Riposte Laïque*, FN, the political mainstream, and scholars are all part of an antagonistic social and political struggle in which

A Green Cancer

The Construction of an External Enemy

On a sunny December day in 2013, *Résistance Républicaine* led a march from the 'Place Denfer Rochereau' to the 'Place d'Italie,' in southern Paris.[1] The call to march was a poster depicting the face of a joyful Marianne, visible behind a transparent French flag. The poster read: "For secularism and our traditions. Don't touch our Christmas! Don't touch our Christian holidays." Christine Tasin, dressed in bright red, led that march with a couple hundred or so demonstrators, holding a banner with the text: "Don't touch the Law of 1905." I will note that here, secularism is explicitly tied to Christianity, which, as articulated in traditional and nationalist terms, is an essential part of what it means to be French. This shows how secularism is articulated as an emblem for, specifically, a national and Christian identity, an identity which is juxtaposed with Islam. During the march, the participants chanted slogans like: "Islamists, racists, fascists, and murderers!" and "Fascism get out! Sharia get out! This is our home!"

These slogans are directly related to the writings in *Riposte Laïque*, where Islam is depicted as a "political ideology," as "the Islamist extreme-right," as "fascist," "racist," and as a colonizing force on the verge of taking root in Europe. Islam is, moreover, articulated as being an enemy combatant; it is "the armored spearhead," "a Trojan horse," "a militia," and "an onslaught." It is also seen as a disease plaguing the national body as "a green pest" and "a cancer." Muslims are portrayed as "fifth columnists," "murderers," "soldiers of Allah," and "barbarians." These are fundamental notions in *Riposte Laïque's* diagnosis of the ills plaguing the French nation and society.

The anti-Muslim discourse in *Riposte Laïque* is an eclectic mixture of orientalist fantasies and counter-jihadist theories that need to be read in relation to the broader spectrum of national identity and its intertwined articulations of alterity through race, religion, and gender. In this chapter, I present the specific language and grammar employed by *Riposte Laïque* to articulate how Islam and Muslims are an enemy of the French people, along the horizontal axis of populist identification. I have read these articulations through the analytical lens of orientalist knowledge production.

Herein, I aim to show how the anti-Muslim discourse of *Riposte Laïque* articulates conceptualizations of religion, culture, and gender in relation to populism, nationhood, and secularism. What follows is an analysis that is structured along the central themes found in the anti-Muslim discourse used in *Riposte Laïque*. Throughout this chapter, I discuss the publication's material in relation to French radical nationalist and populist, and mainstream, articulations of anti-Muslim discourse. The chapter ends with a discussion of what function the *Riposte Laïque* anti-Muslim discourse has in relation to populism, nationhood, and secularism; and also how to understand and place the publication's anti-Muslim discourse in relation to the dominant discourses on Islam and alterity in France.

Islam is not a religion

During the first years of publication, *Riposte Laïque* published several editorials dealing with the state of religion in France. According to Cyrano, there is an ongoing "general religious" offensive in France.[2] "Religious people feel the wind at their backs" and they are multiplying "their attacks against the seculars and society as a whole."[3] Cyrano describes a situation where religious Jews claim special arrangements for Saturdays in public schools, and evangelicals and scientologists want to put an end to Article 2 in the Law of 1905, stipulating that the Republic does not recognize or subsidize any religious association. Moreover, "religious spokespeople qualify us as 'secularists,' they prohibit us from criticizing the harmful influence of religions and some of their texts."[4]

Riposte Laïque is especially critical towards "the three monotheist religions," which, as Cyrano states, "are representatives of a patriarchy that proclaim the superiority of men and the exclusion of women."[5] The publication affirms, "To us, when religion is lifted to the state of dogma, when it puts on the mask of obligation, prohibition, and sexual discrimination and spreads anathema, even death sentences, it can never expect mercy."[6]

One of the examples Cyrano brings up is when, in 1998, representatives from Muslim, Jewish, and Catholic communities demonstrated against the *Pacte Civil de Solidarité* (PACS), a gender-neutral civil solidarity pact, ratified in 1999 as being between two individuals, providing legal status for non-married couples.[7] This, according to Cyrano, "reveals the homophobic ecumenism of the three religions of the Book."[8] While the PACS was widely contested by the French right, to Cyrano it was the religious actors' condemnation of the union that was homophobic and an expression of patriarchy.[9]

Cyrano's view on monotheistic religion appears critical. He declares, for example, that "religion is always situated next to political power, a power that wants to guide and constrain conscience."[10] Cyrano also declares that "we know that religions rarely contribute to peace and are often the source of fanatical wars. We know of the Catholic fundamentalist's reactionary discourse, fundamentalist Jews, creationists, and certain sects."[11] Most significantly, "we have not forgotten our ancestors' ferocious battle to force the Catholic Church to accept the separation of church and state."[12] In editorials in *Riposte Laïque*, the separation of church and state is also seen as the separation of religion and politics; and Cyrano is, in this regard, rather ambivalent. He was critical when Catholic spokespeople attempted to cross the line of separation, as during the PACS debates in 1998, but it was a good thing when the Catholic Church supported the marches against same-sex marriage in 2013, as it defended "our values." What is less good, however, is that the Catholic Church appears as a collaborator with Islam, as it allegedly allows veils in private Catholic schools, which make up almost 20 percent of the French educational system. In editorials in *Riposte Laïque*, Christianity and the Catholic Church are sometimes articulated as being ancient, patriarchal, and part of a religious onslaught on France; and sometimes also cherished and defended. As seen during the protest organized by *Résistance Républicaine* in 2013, Christianity, regardless of its homophobic ecumenism, is part of the French *us*; "our Christian traditions" appear as an integral part of the French way of life. While Christianity and Catholicism might transgress the boundaries of the separation between religion and politics, this is merely "a straw" compared with the "Islamic beam."[13]

If articulations of religion, Christianity, and Catholicism in *Riposte Laïque* are ambiguous and sometimes contradictory, the articulations of Islam are rather more straightforward. Islam is not a religion like the others. Using a sardonically satiric tone, Cyrano declares that "of course, Benedict XVI is not our cup of tea"; and adds, "it is without doubt fanatical Christians who impose their illegal prayers on public streets, in Paris and in other cities, every Friday," "it is without doubt Parisian Christians who refuse to accept a house of worship because it is not facing Rome," "it is fanatical Christians who have, during the last ten years, caused over 17,000 deadly attacks around the world."[14] Thus, the mission of *Riposte Laïque* is to "virulently denounce the Muslim religion's offensive."[15] While *Riposte Laïque* sees this mission in the light of the quarrels of "the two Frances" [*les deux France*] when "the Catholic religion sought to impose its law throughout society," the situation today is different, as is the religion in question.[16]

To *Riposte Laïque*, this articulated return of religion is the result of what is referred to as "postcolonial immigration."[17] By employing this term, the publication signals that there has been a shift in the composition of immigration to France. As Cyrano states, "France should be proud to be a country of immigration where one out three French citizens has a non-French grandfather."[18] France was founded on the "ideal of the Republic as a melting pot [*creuset républicain*]: an egalitarian conception of the nation, and the refusal to see ethnicity or origin as the basis of identity."[19] This is what has made immigrants "full French citizens, equal before the obligations and rights" that France demands and gives.[20] Former immigrants, "Polish, Italians, Spanish, Portuguese, Algerians, Moroccans, Tunisians, Armenians, etc., were proud to become French."[21]

According to *Riposte Laïque,* during the 1970s and 1980s this changed. One of the journal's most cited references on this topic is the controversial media pundit and author Eric Zemmour. According to him, France is currently experiencing an invasion reminiscent of "the fall of Rome"; but today, the Huns and the Goths have been replaced by "Chechen gangs, Roma, Kosovars, Maghrebins; and Africans who steal, assault, and strip [*dépouillent*] the French population."[22] To Cyrano, this postcolonial immigration is a question of "migratory colonialism" that is becoming "more and more troublesome," as these migrants "have no respect for the values and the laws of their host country."[23] He continues, "via demographic pressure and ethno-religious violence, they have launched a civil war to disintegrate the values, the culture, and the economy, meaning the elimination of the host country's civilization."[24] Because of these new migrants, Cyrano believes, "France, the country of the Enlightenment, will disappear."[25] Cyrano is clear on this point: "a civil war is waging in France: that is a fact."[26]

To substantiate these claims, Cyrano quotes Laurent Obertone's *La France Orange Mécanique*, in which the author refers to Stanley Kubrick's *A Clockwork Orange* (1971), depicting a violent and hedonistic gang of British urban youth spreading terror and violence wherever they go. Cyrano refers to the book and concludes that "every day in France, there are 13,000 thefts, 2,000 violent assaults, and 200 rapes, numbers that no one has contested."[27] In the book, Obertone locates this violence in the metropolitan suburbs, in "the lost territories of the Republic," referencing an edited book published under the name of Emmanuel

Brenner.[28] In that book, French Maghrebi youth are held responsible for antisemitism, racism, and sexism that are said to be exploding in the suburbs.

The term "lost territories of the Republic" was picked up in a presidential speech by Jacques Chirac in 2003; and media pundit Alain Finkelkraut proclaimed in 2013 that the book addressed the "sad reality of stigmatized neighborhoods," issues that "neither journalists, nor sociologists, talk about."[29] Finkelkraut himself pursues these issues in the book *L'Identité Malheureuse*, published in 2013, where he claims that immigrants refuse to integrate; and concludes that "the more immigration increases, the more society fragments."[30]

This type of alarmist literature, with its harsh tonality, makes up the referential library at *Riposte Laïque* in terms of immigration and violence. In it, for example, Obertone proposes higher sentences and even the death penalty for assaults against the police, in order to come to grips with the violence that is described as plaguing France. Referring to offenders with an immigrant background as "dogs," he states: "We need to remind ourselves that dogs are normally classified according to their level of dangerousness: those who bite are euthanized."[31] Obertone's book created debate when it was published in 2013, and its views were contested. Sociologist Laurent Mucchielli, a specialist in the politics of security and crime, claimed that the book "is evidently not a scientific work, it is a marketing coup and propaganda book that serves the ideology of the extreme right."[32] Regardless, it was the fourth best-selling book on Amazon and it echoed hugely among the French radical nationalist milieu. It was cherished by such intellectuals and politicians as the aforementioned Zemmour, Robert Ménard (the independent but FN-supported mayor of the city of Beziers and the co-founder of the association called Reporters Without Borders, who in 2015 revealed that his administration was, contrary to French law, keeping statistics on the number of Muslim students in schools[33]), and Marine Le Pen. Marion Maréchale Le Pen, Le Pen's niece and strongwoman in southeastern France, advised the French people to read the book and spread it around.[34]

If postcolonial immigrants are a menace to society, Muslims are the worst sort of new migrant. Cyrano asks, "The Muslims, have you seen them? Have you seen them with their turbans and djellabas? You clearly see that they are not French."[35] Applying a satirical tone, Cyrano asserts that "the great majority of violent offenders, thieves, rapists, and murderers, are descendants from post-colonial migration, a large number of them are Muslims who call upon the religion of love, tolerance, and peace."[36] References to postcolonial immigrants and Muslims are often couched in ironic terms, drawing on what *Riposte Laïque* sees as politically correct lingua, such as "descendants from diversity."[37]

To substantiate his claims, Cyrano draws upon yet another frequently cited authority, the criminologist Xavier Raufer, a hardliner with a background in the French radical nationalist and post-fascist movements of the 1960s and 1970s.[38] In the northeastern Parisian district of Seines-Saint-Denis (*le 93*), where the 2006 riots started, it is accordingly "as dangerous to go for a walk there as it is in the worst zones of Baghdad or in the Afghan valleys where jihadists rule."[39] Raufer does not hesitate to call things by their alleged proper name: we are dealing with "urban guerrillas," and not "riots."[40] In these lost territories, the cause of the situation is "not social, economic or urban;" it is "cultural," where "populations on the margins of a normally functioning Republic reproduce the lifestyle they have in their homeland and bring in their customs and their laws."[41] "Religious fascists" have taken over and, hand in hand "with the islamicized trash," they are turning France into "Frankistan."[42]

White French citizens have no place in these territories: *Riposte Laïque* decries a rampant new type of racism among these descendants of diversity. *Riposte Laïque* especially targets a young generation of French rappers, who publicly show their Muslim background and often criticize secularism and racism in France.[43] According to Cyrano, the situation is serious: "A new type of barbarians with a very limited vocabulary cry out their hatred against the 'sons of whores,' referring to the French, Jews, whites, women, and homosexuals. This often takes the form of ultra-violent assault."[44] Among these types of racism, there is one that is particularly severe: anti-white and anti-French racism.[45] Cyrano explains that the rise of Islam in France "is accompanied by random, hateful, and violent assaults against all that look like a French person of European origin."[46] In editorials, several caricatures illustrate the *Riposte Laïque* vision of these lost territories, where black and Arab youngsters attack white French citizens. One of them depicts a white French male lying in a pool of blood, surrounded by fire. Six young men of the Islamic trash and fascist kind, one holding a bloody knife in his hand, are kicking the man. These men are screaming: "Do it! He disgusts me with his chalk face [*face de craie*]! We're not respecting your shitty laws! We're respecting Islam and the law of the strongest!"[47]

The *Riposte Laïque* imagery of anti-white racism is shared by many in the radical nationalist mileu, and is shared on other alternative news sites like *Novopress* and *Fdsouche* and by French identitarians.[48] FN has, since the late 1970s, depicted a France where it is the French who are victims of racism.[49] Jean-Marie Le Pen started to publicly denounce the supposed reality of anti-French racism just when anti-racist social movements like the *Marche des beurs*, the events of 1983, and organizations like *SOS Racisme* were gaining traction.[50] Marine Le Pen and FN started to articulate this in terms of whiteness, to the point that it sounds almost identical to the words in *Riposte Laïque*. During an interview with several news outlets in 2012, Marine Le Pen declared that racist slurs like "dirty white, chalk face, etc., were thrown at millions of our compatriots every day."[51]

The idea of a spreading anti-white or anti-French racism is not restricted to the radical nationalist camps. As mentioned, when François Copé was campaigning for the conservative party (UMP) presidency, he declared that young Muslims were prohibiting young white French from eating chocolate pastries during Ramadan, a story that no journalist or researcher has managed to confirm.[52] In a political manifesto published in 2012, Copé also wrote about the spread of anti-white racism in France.[53]

During the run-up to the 2017 presidential election, François Fillon, a candidate for the conservative LR, declared that he was against all sorts of racism, including "anti-French racism."[54] When in 2009 the parliamentary commission was investigating the reality of burqas in France, one of the heads of commission, the communist MP André Gerin, talked about "the venom of anti-French and anti-Christian racism" that was gaining ground among Islamists in France.[55] Up to now, a couple of people have been convicted for anti-white racist slander;[56] however, no research and no statistics exist that support the statements about anti-white racism, or systematic structures that exclude and discriminate against white French in terms of social distribution of rights, welfare, or access to the labor market. Regardless, according to *Riposte Laïque*, this is the reality of today's France. I have reason to return to this issue in Chapter 4.

Islamo-Fascism

Riposte Laïque articulates that Islam is a religion that differs from the other monotheisms of the "Book." This gives rise to the question of what exactly the publication sees in Islam as being quintessentially different from Christianity and Judaism. To *Riposte Laïque*, one of the fundamental problems of Islam is its imagined theological nature that prohibits "rational debate," and where "critical thought is a horrible sin."[57] Here, Cyrano refers to a quote attributed to Mustafa Kemal or Atatürk, the leading figure behind the creation of the Turkish Republic in the 1920s: "Islam, an absurd theology founded by an immoral Bedouin, is a rotten carcass that poisons our lives."[58] This immoral Bedouin (what he said of the prophet Mohammed) is also referred to as a "pedophile," which is seen as an intrinsic part of Islamic theology.[59] Islam is, moreover, seen as violent and imperialist: "As we explain, Islam is a religion of war and conquest with the objective of imposing Sharia on its disciples as soon as Muslims are in a position to do so."[60] This supposed violent impulse for conquest is inscribed in the sacred texts of Islam, Cyrano asserts, and "the Quran teaches Muslims, at a very young age, that infidels, Jews, Christians, and all those who are not Muslim, are enemies to combat, convert, or eliminate."[61]

As testimony to this, Cyrano quotes verses in the Quran. The first is Surah 8:12, which states: "Your Lord revealed to the angels: 'I am with you: give the believers firmness; I shall put terror into the hearts of the disbelievers: strike above their necks and strike all their fingertips.'"[62] The second verse is Surah 47:4, which is only partially quoted: "When you meet the disbelievers in battle, strike them in the neck."[63] Cyrano concludes: "this is what Islam is all about."[64] These verses are used as a lens to scrutinize violent acts and attacks that are committed in the name of Islam.

To Cyrano, Daesh or Isis is merely the logical outcome of real Islam. Cyrano paraphrases Oriana Fallaci, a standard reference in counter-jihadi circles, to give an historical explanation of Daesh: "The Islamic State's barbarism is nothing more than the continuity of fourteen centuries of war waged by Allah's soldiers against all those who are not Muslim, and its cruelty is sanctioned in the sacred texts."[65] Cyrano states, "All over the world, Islam shows its real face: hateful, violent, murderous, barbaric, and destructive."[66]

According to *Riposte Laïque*, Islam is certainly different from the other monotheistic religions, and not only in its violent nature. The publication frequently quotes the British anti-Muslim vlogger Pat Condel, who has stated that "Islam without violence is like an omelet without eggs,"[67] and that "we will respect Islam when Islam respects us; the problem is that when this happens, we are no longer dealing with Islam."[68]

In the logic of *Riposte Laïque*, "Islam is not merely a religion"; it is "first of all, a totalitarian political project"[69] in which "violence is inherent";[70] it is a "culture of death,"[71] "a murderous ideology,"[72] and a "mortal danger."[73] Hence, Islam and Islamism are seen as two sides of the same coin: "Islam is not different from Islamism, Islam is merely dormant Islamism, and Islamism is Islam in action."[74]

Cyrano cherishes Guillaume Faye, one of the leading figures of the French New Right and GRECE, for his lucidity, and assumes his argument: "Our country is facing a gigantic assault. France's problem is not Islamism, it is Islam."[75] Frequent allusions are made to equate Islam with fascism and Nazism. Cyrano states, for example, that Islam is a "political-religious fascism"[76] that "threatens, beyond any reasonable doubt, the secular, progressive, and feminist conquests."[77] To talk about secularism today without mentioning Islam "is like talking about capitalism in the 1930s without mentioning the rise of Nazi Germany."[78] Thus Cyrano, referring to the writer René Marchand, another acclaimed specialist on Islam frequently quoted in the publication's texts and a frequent lecturer in their gatherings, declares that "there cannot be any pacific cohabitation between Islam and Europe."[79] This statement is hammered out throughout writings in *Riposte Laïque*: "We confirm that Islam is incompatible with the secular Republic! We consider that Islam is not only a religion, but first of all a totalitarian political-religious project; it is a green pest that threatens our country."[80] Cyrano concludes: "France is in danger from Islam."[81]

Even what are seen as peaceful Islamic customs are incompatible with Europe and modern society. During a *Riposte Laïque* press conference held in Paris in 2009, one of the writers, Alain Rubin, declared with "humor" that "when a camel rider in the seventh century fell asleep on the back of the camel leading to the camel to taking another route, it caused no harm. But, if a truck driver, fourteen centuries later, falls asleep behind the wheel during Ramadan, it has other implications."[82]

If Islam is incompatible with the Republic, how does *Riposte Laïque* regard the place of Muslims in France? A common perception of Islam and Muslims is that there is a good and peaceful version of Islam to which the majority of Muslims adhere, and a violent and archaic version that appeals to a minority.[83] *Riposte Laïque* rejects this division, and calls it a "fable."[84] By quoting the anti-Muslim writer Wafa Sultan, whose book, *L'Islam, Fabrique de Déséquilibrés?* [Islam, a factory of the disturbed?], *Riposte Laïque* had published, Cyrano asserts that "the Muslim is an irrational creature dominated by its instincts."[85]

Cyrano ponders upon why Muslims are the way they are. He seeks an answer in the comic world of Tintin: "You ask yourself if Islam is like a poison that makes you crazy, like the Blue Lotus in the famous Tintin stories, a poison that, when injected in the neck, instantly makes your victim lose its mind."[86] Are, then, all Muslims injected by this poison? In a few editorials, *Riposte Laïque* declares that "all born Muslims are not Jihadists."[87] In fact, on the *Riposte Laïque* editorial board and at their public gatherings, there are some *born* Muslims present, most notably Pascal Hilout. They often reference people who, like Ayaan Hirsi Ali,[88] are also *born* Muslims. What they have in common, in the eyes of *Riposte Laïque,* is that they are no longer Muslim; they have either converted to Christianity or refuse to take any religious identity. As such, they become voices from within, those who have seen the truth about Islam, but also those who have seen the light of freedom.

By this logic, those who still claim to be Muslim are doing so actively; and thus, have chosen a path other than that of the secular Republic. Cyrano states, for example, "no, in this country there are not 99% 'moderate Muslims' who adhere to secularism and the Republic, and who reject 1% of the 'radicals' that supposedly have not understood the prophet's real message. No, you cannot be a French Muslim, a patriotic Muslim, or a secular Muslim; because then, you are no longer a Muslim."[89] To the critics of this, Cyrano retorts, "if you are not blind nor deaf, you cannot fail to observe that Islam is seeking to conquer Europe and France."[90] Muslims are presented as a unified collective, all guided by principles; by a twisted political, totalitarian, and religious ideology.

Occupation

Riposte Laïque articulates that Islam is a hateful, conquering, and totalitarian political project driven by Allah's crazies, incompatible with France and with Europe. It is seen, as Marine Le Pen inferred in 2010, as an occupying force seeking to colonize France. It is a contemporary form of Nazism. The category of occupation is itself an allusion to Nazism. In its editorials, this image is constructed by *Riposte Laïque* through the usage of photos from occupied Paris accompanied by sarcastic comments.

One image, for example, depicts Nazi troops marching along the Champs Elysées, who are being equated with today's migrants.[91] There is, however, one important difference between Nazi Germany and contemporary Islam. Cyrano explains that, while the Nazis' obsession with a "Jewish conspiracy was delirious" and based on racist "fantasies," "the project to impose a universal Islamic caliphate is not."[92] As proof of this, *Riposte Laïque* brings up the Cairo Declaration on Human Rights in Islam (CDHRI) accepted in 1990 by the Organization of the Islamic Conference (OIC). While this non-binding declaration and its guiding principles have been heavily criticized by human rights lawyers, scholars, and activists, especially in terms of gender equality, freedom of expression, and apostasy, the *Riposte Laïque* claim that it would be a path to a universal caliphate has been so far an unsubstantiated claim.[93]

Notwithstanding, the category of an Islamic conquest in the making is heavily influenced by the Eurabia thesis.[94] Gisèle Littman (aka *Bat Ye'Or*, or the Daughter of the Nile), published a seminal piece as her thesis, in 2005.[95] In an interview with the *Washington Post*, Ye'Or proclaimed that "Europe is no longer Europe; it is 'Eurabia,' a colony of Islam, where the Islamic invasion does not proceed only in a physical sense, but also in a mental and cultural sense." She continued: "The increased presence of Muslims in Italy, and in Europe, is directly proportional to our loss of freedom."[96] According to *Riposte Laïque*, Ye'Or "explains perfectly" how Europe is the scene for an Islamic conquest with the goal of "imposing Sharia through immigration and demography, which will turn non-Muslims into Dhimmis, even if this will take some time."[97]

While immigration, as was discussed earlier, is seen as the portal between the Orient and the West, or the link between Europe and Asia, demography is what will make that portal unnecessary when the French white and Christian or secular population has been replaced by Muslims.[98] Here, *Riposte Laïque* explicitly refers to the category of "the great replacement" as coined by the journal's close affiliate Renaud Camus, who is also close to FN.[99] *Riposte Laïque* uses demographic statistics and opinion polls on religious practice that are creatively interpreted. In 2008, *Riposte Laïque* stated that "67% of French citizens declare they are catholic; in 2007 it was 51%."[100] This is problematic, as they claim that "the Muslim religion is the only one that progresses; in fifteen years it has gone from two to four percent."[101] In 2010, the estimated number of Muslims in France was 5 million, and what is worse, even if one were to believe that "98% of the Muslim population is moderate, this means that 100,000 are ready for Jihad!"[102] In 2012, the number estimated was "10 million born Muslims,"[103] to which is added an annual arrival of 440,000 immigrants a year, of whom the majority are supposedly Muslim.[104] Thus, "things are getting clearer. In France, more than in other European countries, Allah's soldiers have perfectly accomplished their massive settlement" and "they use this ratio of power to weaken the Republic and to strengthen their ideology."[105]

Cyrano quotes Oskar Freysinger: "If you let Muslims reach 50% of the population, we are screwed [*c'est foutu*]!"[106] To which Cyrano adds, "even now with ten percent, they are already making our politicians retreat."[107] Cyrano fears that the philosopher and media pundit Michel Onfray might well be right in assessing that "within fifty years, France and Europe will be controlled by Islam."[108] Onfray has published numerous books on the decline of the French nation and European civilization, in which Islam is continuously articulated as being incompatible with modernity and reason.[109] On national television, Onfray has declared that "in the Quran, you won't read that you should love the other, but that you should behead him."[110] Cyrano concludes that immigration and demography are used as strategies of war: "a war of extermination waged against our civilization and our people."[111]

In a cartoon, *Riposte Laïque* illustrates a worst-case scenario where the Parisian Statue of Liberty, standing on the Île aux Cygnes, has been replaced by a jihadi holding up a scimitar instead of a torch, with a Quran under his left arm. The statue is surrounded by men in djellabas and women in burqas. The Eiffel Tower in the left of the caricature is covered with an Islamic banner.[112]

Alarmist calls about national decline through racial and cultural dilution brought about by external others is a long-running theme in radical nationalist discourse.[113] The category has been rearticulated in various forms within the ranks of the FN. Former president Jean-Marie Le Pen has warned that "we are running the risk of replacing our people with this massive immigration,"[114] and MP Marion Maréchale-Le Pen has expressed concerns about "seeing the French people disappear."[115] Marine Le Pen, in the national news media, publicly distances herself somewhat from this thesis, by stating that "the concept of a great replacement supposes an established plan. I do not share this vision of conspiracy."[116] While she distances herself from the thesis, she acknowledges its core precept: a great replacement is in the making, but it is not a great conspiracy. Regardless, the ambiguity of this statement appears less cryptic when Marine Le Pen is speaking in less public settings: "The numbers show that immigration in France is not slowing down, but that it is accelerating at a crazy rate, which makes you wonder if this is not part of a pure and simple objective to replace the French population."[117]

To *Riposte Laïque*, this replacement is being carried on throughout French society. Cyrano proclaims that "beyond doubt, the most radical are advancing every day … millimeter by millimeter, centimeter by centimeter, meter by meter."[118] "They" are "fifth columnists" and "internal enemies of France."[119] In the book *Musulmans: Vous nous Mentez* (Muslims: You Are Lying to Us), written by Hubert Lemaire and published in 2014 by *Riposte Laïque*, this theory is developed in detail. Cyrano describes the book as a "bomb," as it "has the courage to reveal what Islam is really about," and "most importantly, Muslims' duplicity, their *taqiyya*, and their deliberate lies to mask the dangerousness of their dogma."[120] *Taqiyya* is described as a manipulative strategy used by moderate Muslims to infiltrate and eventually overthrow society;[121] to turn "dar el harb," or the house of war, into "dar al islam," the house of Islam.[122] One of the worst foes in this sense is the Swiss public intellectual and scholar Tariq Ramadan.[123] Ramadan is accused of employing "double speech," through which he presents a "soft" version of Islam on prime time television, and an "aggressive version in the suburbs," where he calls for "war against our progressive and emancipatory values."[124]

According to *Riposte Laïque*, Ramadan has disciples all over the world "that with a violent fanaticism, no longer hide their hatred of the West and its democratic values."[125] "If you are secular," Cyrano declares, "you have to say that

Ramadan is a soldier of Islam on a mission to colonize France."[126] In publications of *Riposte Laïque*, the word *taqqiya* also refers to how Muslims are manipulating the French and their benevolence, and how "communitarian Muslims are assuming the role of victims."[127] According to Cyrano, when they are legitimately criticized, they cry "racism" and "Islamophobia" and use the fear of white French being called racist as "blackmail," taking advantage of French "postcolonial guilt."[128] Cyrano asserts: "We are living in a period when Islamists silence the resistance [such as *Riposte Laïque*] that tries to awaken people's awareness."[129]

The supposed occupation of France is manifested through a number of reoccurring obsessions in texts in *Riposte Laïque*. The most common ones are mosques, halal food, and headscarves: "Jihad's arms against France."[130] Mosques and the demands by French Muslims for places of worship are articulated as a strategy to take over public space. *Riposte Laïque* is stupefied by the increased number of mosques in France to approximately 2,000; with the majority being simply places of worship rather than full-blown mosques with domes and minarets. Regardless, Cyrano often returns to an alleged statement by the Turkish president Recept Tayip Erdogan: "Mosques are our barracks, the minarets our bayonets, the domes our helmets, and the believers our soldiers."[131]

While immigration is articulated as a portal for the orient, the mosque appears as a perpetual pathway to it, where Muslims are forged into soldiers of Allah. In France, mosques have been a heated topic of debate over the last decades, especially in the wake of the 2015 jihadi attacks. These debates often have a double-sided focus.[132] On the one hand, mosques are seen as a step in creating an Islamic France, as a way of controlling Islam, and lately as important locations to combat radicalization;[133] while on the other hand, they are treated with suspicion, as locations of foreign theological and ideological influence, and as sites where radicalization can take place.[134]

Halal food, another obsession, has become increasingly popular in France. During Ramadan, large supermarket chains run commercial campaigns for halal food, and it is an option in several restaurant chains, such as Quick (a French hamburger chain) and even Kentucky Fried Chicken; also at butchers' and in school canteens. To *Riposte Laïque*, this is a sign of the Islamic "conquest of public space."[135] It is a matter of a "food chain colonization" that "is imposing itself on French society."[136] In a cartoon reminiscent of the Swiss UDC's anti-minaret campaign in 2009, a map of France is displayed with the Quick restaurants looking like minarets of a mosque.[137] According to Cyrano, halal has assumed "monstrous proportions," and as with "icing on the cake, every one of us probably eats it without knowing or without wanting to"; and even worse, "we are thus financing the Muslim religion."[138] Besides the imagined implicit financing of the Islamic occupation of France, halal slaughter is articulated as being "particularly inhumane."[139]

Parallels are also drawn between the televised jihadi throat slittings and decapitations and halal slaughter, which is understood as a particular Islamic fascination that is prescribed in the Quran.[140] *Riposte Laïque* mocks halal food in several images and cartoons. For example, the publication applies a twist to a commercial poster by the company Isla Delice, in which different animals are depicted under the headline "proudly halal," by adding "proudly butchered [*égorgé*]." The focus by *Riposte Laïque* on halal food has made wide-ranging echoes throughout French society, and has been a topic of heated debate.[141]

French identitarians, like Nice-based *Nissa Rebela*, have been running campaigns denouncing kebabs under the slogan: "Yes to socca, no to kebab!"[142] In 2012, Marine Le Pen claimed that all meat sold in the Paris region was halal.[143] In 2014, she declared she would reinstate pork in school canteens.[144] In 2012, during the run-up to the presidential election, Nicolas Sarkozy, members of government, and leading figures in the Sarkozy party UMP also used this idea.[145]

In texts in *Riposte Laïque*, headscarves (i.e., *hijabs*) are interchangeably mentioned with the burqas, which no one has been able to confirm exist in France, and with *niqabs*, face-covering veils. Headscarves are articulated as being sexist and patriarchal practices that "steal women's identities," as an "archaic manifestation of oppression against women."[146] Cyrano declares that these women, "by wearing a stigmatizing symbol, discriminate themselves."[147] By choosing to wear the headscarf, these women actively distance themselves from the Republic: they "attack secularism."[148] In numerous editorials, Cyrano ponders upon the nature of the headscarf. To him it is "not only a religious sign. It is a sexist emblem, an emblem to display a refusal to integrate, and a communitarian withdrawal."[149] The headscarf is the "tip of the iceberg," the most conspicuous sign of the occupation; it is "an open defiance against the Republic's laws and flaunting symbol of a political-religious ideology that has declared war against our values."[150]

What is more, the headscarf excludes white French men from access to Muslim women. Cyrano explains that by wearing this type of garment, "the veiled woman conveys a message" that "she is reserved only for Muslims."[151] As such, she is viewed as manipulative, as the only way to access her body is to convert to Islam. Hence, the *Riposte Laïque* take on Muslim women in headscarves as being a "Belphegor" should come as no surprise (Belphegor, in Christian demonology, is the incarnation of the deadly sin of sloth. He rules over misogyny and governs riches. When he ascends from hell, he takes the form of a young girl, to seduce and tempt men).[152]

During the parliamentary debates preceding the Law of 2010, similar statements were made by republican MPs. Conservative Yves Albarello, for example, declared that "beyond being an offense against women," the integral veil was "an aggression towards everyone crossing its path," and especially so to "Western men," who in his logic "are said to be impure and sexually obsessed"; and this implies also that their women, who do not wear headscarves, "are prostitutes."[153] In fact, the statements on headscarves in *Riposte Laïque* draw excessively on dominant articulations on Muslim women's headscarves in the French political arena.[154] Expression of a headscarf as being the "tip of the iceberg" was used, for example, by the head of the parliamentary commission of the law, André Gerin.

Similarly to how the previous Headscarf Affair played out in the media, former Muslim women were brought into the media spotlight to testify about the nature of the garment.[155] *Riposte Laïque* does the same thing. Women such as Chahdortt Djavann, Ann Pak, Ayaan Hirsi Ali, and Fadela Amara are frequently referred to as witnesses from within the totalitarianism of Islam. By referring to these women's stories about veils in Iran, Saudi Arabia, Somalia, and France, *Riposte Laïque* is supposedly safeguarding itself from making any racist statements.[156] While these women's stories are surely important, what *Riposte Laïque* does is to use them to conflate Islam and Muslims into a timeless, universal, monolithic mass, being everywhere the same and always the same.

At any rate, the reoccurring imagery reminding one of the category "occupation" is heavily sexualized: the Republic is being raped by uncontrollable oriental men and led on by deceivingly seductive Belphegors. One cartoon portrays three women, two wearing *hijabs* and one a burqa, who are holding down a knocked-about version of Marianne. Marianne is wearing a torn red dress and the Phrygian bonnet; one of her breasts is showing. A green sticker covers her naked breast. It says "*haram*." She screams in agony as a turban-wearing man with an AK47 on his back is stabbing a massive syringe into her arm. The syringe contains a green liquid marked "Veil, Sharia, jihad, submission."[157]

Racism and religion

In anti-Muslim discourse in *Riposte Laïque,* Islam functions as a structural feature in the construction of an internal enemy that is joined by a broad range of other categories into a logic of equivalence that inform one another; e.g., as halal food is articulated as the equivalent of jihadi beheadings, anyone who eats halal food thus is seen as agreeing with beheadings; as Muslims eat halal food, they are all potential jihadis. This is framed into a grand conspiracy theory that, as Matt Carr points out, resembles "the antisemitic conspiracy theories of the first half of the twentieth century and contemporary notions of the 'Zionist Occupation Government.'"[158] It is well known that anti-Muslim discourse guided by this logic has become a core element in contemporary European radical nationalist and populist movements, groups, and parties.[159]

While it draws heavily on counter-jihadist and Eurabian knowledge production, this should be understood as a contemporary version of orientalism.[160] As Moustafa Bayoumi argues, there is a "twist to an old doctrine," in that the geographical distances between East and West have somewhat collapsed, or at least have been redrawn.[161] In contemporary orientalist imagination, the Orient has migrated from over there to here, in the midst of the former colonial centers.[162] Secondly, orientalist knowledge production has been increasingly popularized. This is manifested not least in the counter-jihadist networks. During the last decades, a plethora of self-proclaimed experts have emerged; ranging from journalists, academics, and politicians, to bloggers and activists. They present selective readings of the Quran to explain a supposed timeless truth of Islam by which they seek to legitimize an imagined universal cleavage between Islam and Christian, secular Europe.[163]

The articulation of anti-Muslim discourse at *Riposte Laïque* through populist identification is surely radical in many ways, but the point I would like to make here is that their articulation of otherness, along the horizontal axis of populist discourse, is not a species on its own; rather, it is related to and entangled with a broad-ranging history of discursive articulations on alterity through race, blood, gender, and belonging. I believe it is important to read this discourse in the light of a broader spectrum of nationhood and alterity, because discourse that constructs others as enemies or threats is not restricted to radical nationalist and populist movements.[164] The formation of the modern nation-state is also the history of the production of enemies external to the national body, and works to bring unity to the people. This has taken many forms and been shaped by a wide variety of discourses and techniques.

Of special interest is how alterity has been channeled through the concepts of religion, race, and gender. For example, David Goldberg argues that "race is integral to the emergence, development, and transformations of the modern nation-state."[165] With the formation of the modern nation-state in fifteenth- and sixteenth-century Spain, there followed a normalization and naturalization of "racial thinking and racist articulation," which spread "throughout modern European societies and their spheres of influence."[166] During the Spanish *Reconquista*, the idea of pure blood as a way to distinguish between Christians of pure ancestry and converted Jews was institutionalized by a doctrine of pure blood, known as *limpieza de sangre*,[167] which became the underlying prism for classification, organization, and hierarchization of the New World during the colonial conquest, carried out through the theological and emerging scientific discourse of the time.[168]

Fantasies about somatic attributes as essential tell-tale signs of an individual's or group's inner nature, however, existed before the formation of the modern nation-states and cannot exclusively be attributed to Jews.[169] As Nasar Meer points out, the Prophet Mohammed has, since Islam's early encounters with Christian Europe, been depicted as a "dark-skinned, satanic menace."[170]

The category of blood purity channeled through perceptions of race and theology emerged centuries before the biological study of race had its breakthrough. This has bearing on how to understand and analyze contemporary anti-Muslim discourse, in relation to the ideas of post-racism or any achieved colorblindness in terms of race.[171] In contemporary anti-Muslim discourse, ostracizing Islam and Muslims echoes Ernest Renan's assumption "that racism is simply a matter of only biology and origins, and not of culture."[172] This assumption is often used by anti-Muslim spokespeople to legitimize anti-Muslim discourse, by stating that because Islam is not a race, there can be no anti-Muslim racism, merely a critique of religion. "Race is not a static event," as Matthew Hughey states, "but a process of patterned events that demonstrate a larger cultural system that continually re-racializes certain objects, habits, rituals, words, and people."[173] Similarly to the *convertidos* (the converted) of fifteenth-century Spain, born Muslims are in this logic still carrying their Muslim identity with them, either as witnesses from within, where their Muslim identity is what grants them a legitimate voice, or as false-moderate Muslims, who at any moment might develop into full-blown jihadis.

Another equally important aspect regarding the analysis of anti-Muslim discourse in *Riposte Laïque* is to see it through the analytical lens of orientalism and gender. To paraphrase Jacqueline Hogan, while the racialization of national boundaries is crucial for an understanding of how the politics of inclusion and exclusion is channeled through alterity, it is equally important to recognize that they are gendered.[174] To quote McClintock: "Gendered imagery has ... been used to emphasize essential differences between Occident and Orient."[175]

In colonial conquests, the other woman has been an object of fear, desire, amazement, control, and conquest. When Columbus wrote home from the

Caribbean, he asserted that men were wrong to consider the earth as round; rather it held the shape of a woman's breast, crowned with a nipple, portrayed as the final destination. As McClintock describes, "Columbus' image feminizes the earth as a cosmic breast, in relation to which the epic male hero is a tiny, lost infant, yearning for the Edenic nipple."[176] In fantasies of this sort, "the world is feminized and spatially spread for male exploration, then reassembled and deployed in the interests of massive imperial power."[177] During the French subjugation of Algeria, Joan Scott asserts that it was "often depicted by metaphors of disrobing, unveiling, and penetration."[178] A gendered cartography emerges where fantasies about oriental women delineate the borders of the known and unknown.

Similar depictions of women have been articulated in relation to national identity. For example, the foundational work of Nira Yuval-Davis and Floya Anthias shows that national boundaries have been negotiated through the prism of biological and ideological reproduction, where the female body has often been articulated as being a sign of ethnic and national differences.[179] The oriental woman has continuously been positioned as both an object of desire and a threat: desire in the sense that to unveil her is to make her understandable, accessible, and the way to conquer; a threat as she is this demonic and seductive Belphegor, whose sexuality and reproductive powers need to be controlled.

Collaborators and Traitors

The Construction of Internal Enemies

In the French presidential election, it was clear that two candidates had made it to the second round by the eve of April 23, 2017. These candidates were FN's Marine Le Pen and a very young Emmanuel Macron (born in 1977), who later won, representing the party *La République en Marche!* Earlier, Macron had been the Minister of Economy in the government of Prime Minister Manuel Valls, but had left in August 2016 after some discord with Valls and President François Hollande. Macron is, in many eyes, success incarnate. He holds diplomas from two of France's most prestigious schools, *Science-Po* in Paris and *École Nationale d'Administration*, the latter a training school for the French political elite.

After graduating in 2004, Macron was given high-up positions in the French Elysée Palace, in economy and finance. In 2008, he joined the investment bank Rothschild & Co for a highly paid position that, by all accounts, he appears to have managed with success. Back in the service of the Republic in 2012, by 2014 he was offered the position of Minister of Economy. When he resigned two years later, he had already laid the ground for his coming electoral victory in the presidential elections by founding, in April 2016, the party *En marche!* Seen as a traitor by many in the socialist ranks, but also as a breath of fresh air, his rise was viewed as a contributory factor in the Socialist Party tearing itself to pieces.

When it was clear that Benoit Hamon, from the party's left flank, had beaten his main contender Valls in the second of the party's primaries in January 2017, leading figures broke with the party line and openly began to support Macron.[1] With a disintegrating PS and rising opinion polls, Macron had the wind in his sails. A mixture of liberal economic policies and proclaimed liberal values made his presidential program a bit unusual in France. Macron's many philosophically framed statements on French history and its values, notably secularism, created controversy. For example, in an interview with the Algerian TV channel Echourouk News in February 2017, Macron called French colonization "a crime against all of humanity" and "real barbarism."[2] Macron made several statements regarding secularism that seemed to echo the dominant discourse, by referring to the Law of 1905 and its sacrosanct status, without explaining exactly what it actually entails. In one of the many televised presidential debates, Macron declared that "secularism is what protects and allows us to believe or not to believe"; that the Law of 2004 "protects our children from all forms of manipulation"; and that it fully respects the laws of the Republic.[3] In addition, however, Macron declared that secularism is "not an arm to point fingers," and suggested that it was sometimes used to discriminate against or exclude those who "believe in one religion or another."[4] Moreover, Macron has stated that France is partly responsible for the jihadi attacks carried out on French soil. In an interview in the *Journal du Dimanche* (March 19, 2017), he stressed that the Kouachi brothers, who attacked *Charlie Hebdo* on January 7, 2015, "were born and raised among us, they did not come from Pakistan!"[5] He also asked, "what does it take for the Republic's children to turn like that?"[6]

Ironically, as president, Macron was quick to propose new laws that target French Muslims and minorities in the interest of national security. Patrick Weil, a French historian on immigration and national identity, referred to a French-type Patriot Act as being the "the first time since the age of de Gaulle that French law will enshrine a provision that will de facto target French minorities."[7] Regardless, Macron's many statements, by which he has problematized dominant views on secularism and French history, do not sit easily with many of his adversaries. In radical nationalist and populist milieus, Macron is seen as an outright traitor to the French people, especially so by *Riposte Laïque*, which had been running campaigns against Macron since he announced his candidacy.

Between April 23 and May 7, it became increasingly clear that Macron, and not Le Pen, was heading for the Elysée Palace. This made *Riposte Laïque* intensify its campaign against him. Five days prior to the final election, the publication posted a video on YouTube by Maxime Lepante, the main video journalist at *Riposte Laïque*, titled "Macron: The Muslim's candidate who wants to Islamize France."[8] This video presents a bundle of arguments supporting the claim that Macron is silently seeking to turn France into Frankistan. For example, the voice-over states: "Even when Muslim attacks are raging in our country, Macron has the audacity to pretend that none of the religions pose a problem!" The voice also refers to the aforementioned statements by Macron; and concludes that, with Macron, "Muslims will feel encouraged and will have their hands free to

Islamize France even more!" The video ends by displaying an image of a skull and cross-bones with the text: "Danger-Macron." The voice follows suit, by stating that: "on May 7, we have the occasion to vote in the second round of the presidential election to defend our country against the anti-French Macron! Let's vote to throw Macron in the trash-bin!"

To *Riposte Laïque*, the election of Macron confirmed their conviction that the political system is corrupt and ruled by a malevolent elite that seeks to destroy the French people and the French nation, by allowing the Islamization of the Republic. This elite, then, consists of the major segments of the political establishment, but also the major news media channels, academics and intellectuals, anti-racist organizations, and LGBTQ movements and individuals. Together, they are lumped under such names as "collaborators," "liars," "islamo-leftists," "pro-Islamists," "the real extreme-right," "anti-republican," "cockroaches," "red fascists," "pink Khmers," and "traitors."

In this chapter, I show how *Riposte Laïque* articulates alterity and the enemies of the French nation, through the vertical axis of populist identification. I present thematic readings of these enemies: the Gullible Collaborators, the Secularly Correct, the Thought Police, and the Pink Khmers. In the *Riposte Laïque* articulations of them as enemies, emotions are a central theme in a twofold sense; first of all, these enemies are hateful: they hate the French people, the French nation, and Western Civilization as such; secondly, while the external Muslim-body represents an imagined biological threat, both in terms of demography and as a sickness plaguing the national body, the internal enemies are, according to the publication, responsible for having removed the national soul from the Republic and turned it into a bleak shadow of its former glory, in particular by depriving it of masculinity and virility. Chapter 3 ends with a discussion of how the Eurabic conspiracy theory of *Riposte Laïque* is linked with a major theory suggesting that this is only a part of a much more sinister and far-reaching conspiracy, seeking to reshape the global economy and the national system.

The political elite

According to *Riposte Laïque*, the political elite is made up of the two longstanding major parties in France, the PS and the UMP (later renamed the LR or *Les Republicains*). Up until the UMP changed its name, *Riposte Laïque* used the neologism UMPS (the UMP plus the Socialists), which is also commonly used by leading voices within FN. As Cyrano states, "there are surely nuances between Sarkozy and Melenchon" and the political center, "but they all share the same societal project," which is used to keep what *Riposte Laïque* considers to be legitimate politicians, such as Marine Le Pen, out of politics.[9] They believe UMPS has monopolized the political arena; and, according to *Riposte Laïque*, is what is destroying France through its policies on immigration, interpretations of secularism, and control over the justice system, to the detriment of the French people. In terms of integration, Cyrano holds that UMPS has "for twenty years definitively transformed our country through irresponsible immigration politics"; and continues to explain that "work-related immigration has been replaced by an immigration of colonization [*peuplement*], predominantly from Islamized countries."[10] This change in immigration policy has also meant that the "demands of integration are no longer required, and there is much less assimilation; instead, claims for particular rights and identity politics [*repli identitaire*] is encouraged."[11]

The political elite "refuse to face the reality of the new immigration," which, according to *Riposte Laïque*, is "totally underestimated" by the National Institute of Statistics and Economic Studies (INSEE) and the government; which "is silent about the worrying progression of the Islamization of France."[12] It also masks "the reality of youth crime, largely committed by individuals arising from post-colonial immigration."[13]

As a step in this process, following the logic of *Riposte Laïque*, the UMPS actively encourage the Islamization of France: "They deliver the secular Republic to Islam!"[14] One recurring category that is used to exemplify this is the political mainstream's wish to create an Islam of France.

According to Cyrano, the political mainstream has built up the false idea that Islam and Islamism should not be confounded: " 'Islam of France', 'Republican mosques', 'the headscarf is my right'; we all know these slogans that, with the help of politicians, seek to make us accept the idea that the Islamic religion 'is an opportunity for France.'"[15] Cyrano asks us rhetorically how the government, then led by Sarkozy and PM Fillon, could have "such ruthless policies against the Roma and continue to close their eyes against Muslims praying in the street and other signs of the occupation of public space."[16] Cyrano adds that, by referring to the Roma in France, the publication has no intention to "suggest a do-gooder [*angélisme*] approach to the Roma," but is merely pointing out that "Muslims should be treated in the same way."[17]

According to *Riposte Laïque*, instead of tackling the Muslim problem in France, the political elite uses its influence to "polish statistics on criminality, to make us believe that it is in decline."[18] Similarly, the national opinion poll institute "lies to the French regarding the reality of immigration and its new nature."[19] *Riposte Laïque* believes that the political elite is using secularism as a tool to speed up the Islamic colonization of France through immigration. Examples of this are when politicians publicly display their religious convictions, partake in non-Christian ceremonies and festivities, and when they allow what the publication refers to as compromises in the Law of 1905 to accommodate Islam and accommodate Muslims.

It was not just Charles de Gaulle, the acclaimed founder of the Fifth Republic, who spoke publicly about his Catholic vocation; Nicolas Sarkozy, throughout his presidency, has referred to his Christian faith and how it guided him in life, plus how it could guide the French in general. For example, Sarkozy stated that "a school teacher could never replace a vicar or a priest in teaching morality, in teaching children to distinguish between good and bad."[20] To *Riposte Laïque*, Sarkozy was the epitome of a president interfering in religious affairs. "The situation is very serious for secularism," Cyrano states; "never has a president of the Republic been so close to putting secular principles in danger and displaying a will to reinstate the Church within the midst of French society."[21] In a *Riposte Laïque* caricature, Sarkozy's head is placed on Pope Benedict XVI's body, accompanied by the text "*Habemus Papum*" [We Have a Pope].[22]

Another politician criticized for her statements is the former Minister of Interior Michèle Alliot-Marie, who stated in 2007 that: "In a world that has seen the majority of its moral and ideological points of reference collapse, religions have more than ever [become] a vocation to enlighten society." To Cyrano, this is an "appalling" statement that "discreetely undermines" secularism;[23] however, it does seem to escape *Riposte Laïque* censure that, during the presidential election of 2017, Marine Le Pen declared herself to be religious,[24] and that the FN in general cherishes France's Christian past and even has a Catholic Saint, Jeanne d'Arc, as one the party's emblems.[25]

For *Riposte Laïque*, the problem with Catholicism is not doctrinal; it is the Catholic Church and most notably Pope Francis's statements on equality and immigration. This concept is also shared by Marine Le Pen, who explains, in the journal *La Croix* [The Cross], that she is "extremely irritated with the Catholic Church," as it "sometimes intervenes in questions that are not of its concern."[26] Le Pen referred to the Pope's tweets calling for solidarity with migrants, and stating that "welcoming a migrant is to welcome God in person."[27] Thus, the problem with the Catholic Church (and politicians speaking in its name) is when Christianity is used to legitimize politics that are contrary to the ideals of *Riposte Laïque* and FN.

In the eyes of *Riposte Laïque,* the worst treason against secularism is when the political elite seek compromises in the Law of 1905, in order to accommodate Islam and Muslims. One example of this concerns the reservation of public swimming pools for women in the city of Lille. According to Cyrano, the Socialist mayor of the city, Martine Aubrey, has given in to Muslim demands and created a "communitarian swimming pool" reserved for Muslim women.[28] It is clear that, between 2000 and 2009, a swimming pool was reserved for women for one hour a week: the reason was, according to Aubrey and the City of Lille, to give those women who felt uncomfortable displaying their bodies publicly, mainly due to excess weight, the chance to swim.[29] According to *Riposte Laïque* and sibling sites like *FdSouche* and *Boulevard Voltaire,* this was just a pretext to give in to the Muslim community.[30] Thus, *Riposte Laïque* declared that "we do not fight against Aubrey based on rumors, but on her politics …." *Riposte Laïque* added, "this woman is the incarnation of all that we reject … she and her friends in PS are the worst adversaries of our republican, secular, social, and civilizational model."[31] A cartoon in the publication portrays Aubrey in a headscarf in the colors of the French flag, accompanied by the ironic statement: "The candidate of diversity and of cohabitation."[32]

The issue of public swimming pools being reserved for women was not a topic reserved for the radical nationalist news channels; it became a national, heatedly debated topic. For example, during a 2012 presidential election rally, President Sarkozy declared: "I am sorry to say, Madame Aubrey, in the swimming pools on the Republic's territory, we want to see the same hours for men and for women."[33] In *Riposte Laïque* content regarding Sarkozy, this one swimming pool turned into a symbol of the ongoing compromises of secularism, and the unjustifiable compromises vis-à-vis French Muslims, that could lead to a society divided along gender lines.

When Sarkozy and many of the politicians from what *Riposte Laïque* calls the political elite tap into and reproduce the same categories as the publication uses, it is, according to *Riposte Laïque,* part of their manipulative nature. Commenting on Sarkozy's often hard-line statements on secularism, security, and immigration, *Riposte Laïque* argues that Sarkozy is practicing double speech and that it is all a charade to appeal to the French people, when in reality he is aiding Muslims in their colonization of France.[34] In this vein, Cyrano asks rhetorically if there is any difference between Nicolas Sarkozy, Socialist Mayor Martine Aubrey, and all the other "mason-communist mayors who reach deep into the wallet … to finance new mosques?"[35] In numerous cartoons, political leaders are depicted as "slipper-lickers," submissively licking the Moroccan slippers of representatives of

Islam like Tariq Ramadan.[36] They have the audacity to attend Islamic festivities, like the *Eid al-Fitr*, which is yet more proof "of the political elites' treason and their capitulation" to Islam.[37]

According to *Riposte Laïque*, the reality of the Islamic onslaught is ignored and even encouraged, not only by the UMPS but also by large segments of France as a whole: "No lesson has been learned from the irresponsible attitude of UMPS; there is no lucid criticism of the suicidal politics brought about by those politically responsible"; and thus, the Republic stands "incapable of dealing with the rise of communitarianism, led on by the iron spearhead of Islam, which has destroyed the republican link with the nation."[38]

The people of France, the nation, have been detached from the Republic. Following this logic, any politician not fervently denouncing Islam as whole is a political dupe, who is "either blind or a collaborator." Cyrano concludes: "By now it is clear, the entire political class has sold out to Allah's crazies and the scum,"[39] and "the Republic's elected [politicians] are all complicit in the Jihad against France."[40] He then refers to the Munich Agreement of 1938, when Great Britain, France, Italy, and Germany made an agreement that was meant to appease Germany and secure peace in Europe. The difference, according to Cyrano, is that today Nazi Germany and Fascist Italy have been replaced by Islam: "In France and all over Europe, liberty is slowly being humiliatingly compromised by Islam. In 1938, Chamberlain and Daladier made the same mistake in Munich. Does this remind you of something?"[41]

This supposed sellout of the Republic took on even greater proportions during the Hollande presidency, during 2012–17. After his election in 2012, *Riposte Laïque* ponders upon the new president's path. For example, Cyrano questions whether Hollande would choose "suicidal immigrationism [*immigrationisme*] or a return to a republican common sense?"[42] The answer: "To Hollande and his peers, one no longer speaks about problems related to immigration, insecurity, Islamization, and even less about national identity!"[43] Hollande's future "conception of France" is a "multicultural one," supposedly illustrated in press photos from the annual Christmas Tree Festivities at the Elysée Palace in 2014.[44] These depict Hollande standing in front of the Palace's Christmas tree, surrounded by a dozen or so children. For *Riposte Laïque*, the problem is that "there are no Gauls."[45] Gaul, or *gaulois*, a term frequently used by that publication and other radical nationalist milieus as a synonym for someone of a supposed pure French heritage and whiteness, is often implicitly articulated through the category. I will return to this issue in more detail, in the following chapter.

For *Riposte Laïque*, Hollande is a traitor to France. The nomination of two particular government ministers by Hollande, the PM François Ayrault (serving 2012–14) and his successor Manuel Valls (serving until 2017), is seen as particularly heinous, as they are "Francophobic" ministers who "hate France."[46] The first is Najat Vallaud-Belkacem, first the Minister of Women's Rights and then Minister of Education and Research, who was born in Morocco and given French citizenship in 1995, while still keeping her Moroccan citizenship. She is seen by *Riposte Laïque* as an "Islamic agent, as a cog in the Global Caliphate's offensive against France."[47] "Certainly," Cyrano admits, she "has not killed anyone," but adds, "that is not her role"; instead, "she and her complicit traitors in government are preparing the ground" for the Islamization of France.[48] To add to this image, *Riposte Laïque* made a photo montage depicting her as a lobotomized and stupidly smiling rat.[49]

For *Riposte Laïque,* the other target is the Minister of Justice, Christiane Taubira, who held office during 2012–16. Taubira was born in French Guiana and not the French mainland, and is black. Her loyalty to France and the French people is repeatedly questioned by *Riposte Laïque*. Cyrano declares that Taubira's taking office "is a nightmare to our people," that "this woman has nothing but hate for our country," and that she "rejects whites."[50] *Riposte Laïque* argues that her real objective is to liberate French Guiana and to take revenge on the French. Emblematic of this is the Law of 2001, which was named after her as she was heading the preparatory commission that recognized French slavery and crimes against humanity during the colonial era.[51] This law, in the eyes of *Riposte Laïque*, is "racist" and an attempt to put guilt, blame, and shame on the French.[52]

In a *Riposte Laïque* cartoon, a grossly overweight Taubira gives the finger and says: "I take advantage of my ministerial position to settle my scores with France and the French!"[53] According to *Riposte Laïque*, Taubira's work to raise awareness of racism and anti-Jewish discourse in France, and to equate hate speech on the internet to that in the public space, is proof of her hatred for the French.[54] *Riposte Laïque* contends that Taubira uses the race card to express her hate on those who "defend France:" *Riposte Laïque* and the FN.[55] This makes *Riposte Laïque* question whether Taubira and her like, who seek to "gag the Freedom of Internet," have "a fascist attitude" towards the French people.[56] Taubira is, in this sense, depicted as the mastermind behind all the legal proceedings against *Riposte Laïque;* and in another cartoon, she is turned into a symbol of all the threats hanging over France, as she declares that the old prison for political dissidents, the *Bagne de Cayenne*, will be reopened as a place to which "to deport the whites who criticize my justice."[57] In yet another cartoon, Taubira and Valls are seen wearing Nazi costumes; behind them is hanging a painting of Hollande. They give instructions to not only the representatives of the French justice system, but also the suburban Muslim youth and journalists, declaring: "You have a free card to burn all those who resist us. If not, we are all fucked."[58]

The attacks on the French left should be seen in light of where *Riposte Laïque* positions itself on the political scale. In the eyes of the publication, the left has betrayed the journal by "stabbing us in the back."[59] The left has abandoned its republican ideals and the defense of secularism. Cyrano explains: "yesterday, being left was to fight for emancipation, to fight against religion, the opium of the people that masked social injustice. Today, it is to defend Muslims who illegally occupy public space. Yesterday, being communist was to defend the symbols of the working class and the peasantry. Today, it is to defend the burqa and the kufiyah."[60] What is worse is that, by doing so, the left, guided by the "dogma of diversity," has also betrayed the people and the Republic: "A left that looks down on the people is no longer the left."[61]

The left has supposedly betrayed its cause to such an extent that *Riposte Laïque* qualifies it as the "new extreme right."[62] The publication picked up this idea from the author and activist Jean Robin, who in 2010 published a book using the phrase as the title.[63] According to Cyrano, Robin "boldly shows how a new extreme-right governs this country," and how it "totally responds to the criteria of the old extreme-right; like the refusal of democracy, authoritarianism, a racist view on society, and complicity with religious fundamentalists."[64] Moreover, *Riposte Laïque* declares that the left is "Stalinist" and suggests that it uses the same measures as Stalin to silence its political adversaries.[65]

The members of the political elite "hate France," they are "traitors," "collaborators," some of them are even "Islamic agents"; and they have "led France into an apocalyptical impasse."[66] In short, the political elite lies to and manipulates the French electorate, as is depicted in a cartoon with the elite's party leaders opening champagne bottles, while declaring: "We screwed the stupid French voters again!"[67]

The political elite, socialism, and communism have been articulated as categories of enmity within radical nationalist circles since the nineteenth century.[68] Peter Davies refers to this as blame-allocation: those responsible for the nation's degeneration are known and embodied in various figures of hateful enemies.[69]

Marine Le Pen of the FN sometimes adds "pseudo" to "elite," to emphasize what she sees as its illegitimate claim to power. As she said in 2015, "Our fight is against the pseudo-elites that do not serve the people."[70] She frequently ridicules the UMPS. To FN, this is not haphazard. Since the entrance of the party into the political arena, various strategies have been used by the socialists and the conservatives to keep the FN out of power. For example, in 1986, when the Fifth Republic saw its first and only legislative election where proportional representation was employed, the FN received almost 10 percent of the votes and thus, 35 places in the National Assembly. To secure a conservative majority in parliament, Prime Minister Jacques Chirac called on his party members not to work with the FN. Jean Marie Le Pen referred to this move as a *"cordon sanitaire"* and argued that the difference between Chirac and the Socialist president François Mitterrand was negligible, and that "changing government was doubtless not worth the effort."[71] In 1992, Jacques Chirac won the presidential election's second round against Jean-Marie Le Pen with 82 percent of the vote, with an electoral turnout of nearly 95 percent: Le Pen only managed to raise his score by 1 percent from the first round, while Chirac raised his score by over 60 percent. Hence, it seems both traditional left and right wings had rallied behind Chirac. On the eve of the election, Chirac declared the election had "transgressed the traditional cleavages"; and had interpreted this as a "choice to renew the republican pact."[72] This *cordon sanitaire* or republican pact is also employed in local elections, where, when relevant, the left wing and the right wing typically rally around the candidate who has the greatest chance of winning against FN representatives.

In the regional elections of 2015, Marine Le Pen was looking to take control of Nord-Pas-de-Calais-Picardie by receiving 40 percent of the votes in the first round and against her nearest contender, the conservative Xavier Bertrand (LR-UDI); however, after the Socialist candidate Pierre de Saintignon, as well as Prime Minister Manuel Valls, had called upon Socialist voters to support Bertrand, Le Pen lost the second round. She later declared: "This is the unashamed workings of the UMPS."[73] During a 2015 meeting for party members in Marseille, she also declared that she was fed up with the UMPS, referring to them as a "privileged elite" and "four-year-old children" who blame one another for the rise of FN.[74]

Marine Le Pen often portrays the political elite as completely "disconnected from the people," guided by self-interest and "clientelism," and responsible for all the ills that she argues are plaguing the country, notably Islam and immigration.[75] Similar statements are also made by other radical nationalist voices. In the Foreword to the French translation of Markus Willinger's Identitarian manifesto, Philippe Vardon, the co-founder of *Bloc Identitaire*, and in 2017 the vice-president of FN for the southeastern French region Provence-Alpes-Côtes-d'Azur, wrote that the political elite "imposed massive and uncontrollable immigration in all of Europe, to force the march towards a triumphalist multiculturalism and a global village."[76]

This type of populist articulation mentioning a corrupt elite that betrays the people and the nation is not reserved for radical nationalist circles. Approaching the presidential election of 2017, even a longstanding statesman, such as former prime minister and conservative candidate François Fillon, had decried the workings of the political elite and presented himself as the "anti-system" candidate.[77] At a rally in Besançon in March 2017, Fillon declared: "During the primaries, I was the candidate of national recovery. While I am still this, I have also become the rebel that the system won't stop."[78] Fillon's populist statements can be seen as a result of accusations of dubious handling of public funds and fictitious employment records regarding his wife, who had apparently been employed by Fillon, yet allegedly never done any real work.[79] According to opinion polls published in December 2016, Fillon was heading straight for the presidency, regardless of whom he would be facing in the second round; however, after the investigative journal *Canard Enchaîné* and news media site *Mediapart* revealed Fillon's closet skeletons, his popularity plummeted. This is not to suggest that Fillon subscribes to the anti-elitist discourse of *Riposte Laïque* and the FN, but it does show the flexibility and adaptability of populist modes of identification.[80] To quote Ernesto Laclau: "The language of populist discourse— whether of [the] Left or Right—is always going to be imprecise and fluctuating: not because of a cognitive failure, but because it tries to operate formatively within a social reality that is, to a large extent, heterogeneous and fluctuating."[81]

By dividing society into two homogeneous blocks (the people and its enemies), the radical nationalist voices and mainstream ones alike seek to downplay the heterogeneous fluctuation of social reality.[82]

The privileged class

The political elite is steering France into an apocalypse. At their side stand other members of the establishment: journalists, academics, and intellectuals. Together, they make up the "privileged class [*caste*]" that lives largely on the backs of the French people. Cyrano asks rhetorically: "What is a caste?" His answer: "they are the political careerists that live a comfortable life, the opinion manipulating media hacks and all the sociologists, pedagogues, researchers, and other bourgeois leftist [*gôche*] ideologues who cannibalize on national education, justice, and the media; and who withhold the power of this, our country."[83] *Riposte Laïque*'s disdain for the left is manifest here in the use of mocking slurs, like "bourgeois leftists." As Cyrano explains, "the real enemy is not the one who defends theories that are the most opposite to yours; it is the one whose theories are the most similar."[84]

Riposte Laïque especially targets intellectuals who frequently appear in national news media as experts and defenders of secularism, such as the feminist activist and writer Caroline Fourest, sociologist Emmanuel Todd, the activist and writer Mohammed Sifaoui, and the 2017 presidential candidate and leader of *Les Insoumis* (LI), Jean-Luc Melenchon. During the first year of the journal's publication, *Riposte Laïque* sought dialogue with, and even cherished, the work of Fourest and Sifaoui. *Riposte Laïque* holds that not everybody in the privileged class is guided by the will to overthrow the nation; however, when these voices started to criticize the publication for being close to the extreme right, it became more and more hostile towards the critics. Cyrano explains that by labeling *Riposte Laïque* as extreme right, Fourest and Sifaoui were being "sectarian" and sought to "defend their income base (in the media market) against competition."[85]

Cyrano states that "a lot of leftists show solidarity with Muslims, because they see them as the Republic's indigenous people, a left-behind group in a society."[86] According to *Riposte Laïque,* one group in particular is ridden with post-colonial guilt: academics and "self-avowed" sociologists.[87] "Researchers in the social sciences and sociologists are hateful defenders of a multicultural society. They hate the Republic and secularism, and they think that the little people are racist."[88] Cyrano further claims that they manipulate the people by a sort of "intellectual terrorism," "the argument of authority," which boils down to the truism: "I am correct, as I am a scholar (and you are not)."[89] The privileged class's interest in secularism appears to be partly guided by self-interest, as its members "overlook the Islamists' fascist, totalitarian, imperialist, and male chauvinistic projects to strengthen their ranks."[90] Yet it is also guided by a hatred for the Republic's history and postcolonial guilt, as with the political elite.

Cyrano refers to this as "masochism, even a hate of oneself"; it is "disgust for a country and its history that many of people see as admirable."[91] One of the problems of the privileged class is that it is "completely disconnected from any popular reality," which makes it blind to the reality of the Islamic onslaught.[92] The class is often depicted as *bobo*, a French slur for the bohemian bourgeoisie. To *Riposte Laïque,* the bobos are from, or are the descendants of, the 1968 generation; they are the "degenerate ones who still claim to be left."[93] The majority of the bobos "live in nice neighborhoods, and they are not disturbed by immigration, the Roma, and the clandestines, these they defend with their 'do-gooder' statements."[94] "While the majority of them claim social mixing," Cyrano continues, they place their children "in private schools, to protect them from trouble makers who are usually descendants of immigration."[95]

Nowadays, even if the privileged class is not aware of it, it is a mere puppet in the hands of the political elite. In one cartoon, Melenchon, Fourest, and Todd are depicted as string puppets manipulated by Sarkozy, Alliot-Marie, and Hollande. The cartoon reads: "They are invited by TV to spread the ideology of the UMPS."[96] In another cartoon, well-known French journalists like David Poujadas, Claude Askolovitch, Edwy Plenel, and many others are portrayed as the political elite's watch dogs: "aggressive and hateful."[97]

To spread the UMPS ideology, the privileged class's spokespeople package their message in a gullible "political" and "secular correctness" approach that is like "gangrene on the press."[98] *Riposte Laïque* has come to know any political correctness "by heart," and it means that one "must say that Islam is a religion of peace"; that "the current Islamicized immigration is an opportunity for France"; that "there are no problems related to insecurity in the suburbs"; that "positive discrimination" and "multiculturalism" are needed; and that "racism is only perpetuated by whites."[99]

The privileged class manipulates public opinion with its political correctness. An example of this is the attacks on Oslo by Anders Behring Breivik, and later his assassination spree against the Norwegian Socialist Youth Party members on Utoya in 2011. This was, according to Cyrano, a "divine surprise" to "gullible journalists, and of course to 'anti-racist' organizations" because "for once, the culprit was blond with blue eyes!"[100] All day long, the news media "hammered on that he was Christian, extremist, islamophobic, a patriot, and against multiculturalism."[101] According to *Riposte Laïque*, Breivik was used by the privileged class as a scapegoat for the faulty claim that terrorism by nature is not just Islamist. According to *Riposte Laïque*, Breivik was the epitome of the compulsion by the privileged class to treat anything remotely related to patriotism and nationalism, as racist and fascist.[102]

Similarly, according to *Riposte Laïque*, when the images of the four-year-old boy Alan Kurdi appeared in the news media in the summer of 2015, they were used, in a manner reminiscent of Nazi propaganda, to manipulate public opinion to open the French borders to refugees. It was, claimed Cyrano, "crazy media political propaganda, next to which Goebbels looks like an amateur," by which the privileged "accused the West, Europe, and above all France, of being responsible for this drama … the weight of a mere photograph was used as a weapon of war to call upon our countries, already submerged in a major Muslim migratory invasion, to receive even more newly arrived into their territories."[103]

According to *Riposte Laïque*, a politically correct wet blanket dampens public debate and allows journalists and politicians to silence political adversaries, and "to support the indefensible."[104] The political elite is lying, manipulating, and conspiring against the French people, and the privileged class is the elite's voice to the masses. This makes *Riposte Laïque* question whether or not the journalist hacks are "stupid or paid for by the Islamists."[105]

In the *Riposte Laïque* worldview, the third important group of actors is the anti-racist and civil rights organizations. Their function is to make sure that those who transgress the boundaries of the politically correct are condemned. As Cyrano states, "in Iran there is a Moral Police!" yet in France, "there is a Thought Police!"[106] This Orwellian "Thought Police" is mainly made up of the organizations Licra, MRAP, SOS Racisme, (*Collectif Contre l'Islamophobie en France*), and *Les indigènes de la République* [the indigenous peoples of the Republic]; plus the governmental bureau against discrimination, HALDE. *Riposte Laïque* declares: "we are well aware of their police methods, based on defamation and lynching, and won't let them go unchallenged."[107] According to Cyrano, they are generally students of the 1968 movements and are guided by politically correct, anti-secular sentiments, and a "pathological hatred for their country."[108] They are convinced that "the French are racist" and they find "racism where it does not exist," while refusing to see the "development of anti-French racism" in France.[109] And they are the "armed branch of the masters of censorship [that is, the privileged class] who in the media seek to impose a dictatorship of a monopoly on thought and a politically correct tyranny,"[110] which is, according to *Riposte Laïque*, "when freedom of expression is no longer possible, when you can no longer speak about security, immigration, and Islam without being classified as extreme-right."[111] Within this logic, the Thought Police are out to stigmatize and falsely classify *Riposte Laïque*. They are, to *Riposte Laïque*, "cockroaches on the Web that nitpick every word of our journal, and like snipers, wait for the right moment to shoot."[112]

Some of these "inquisitors of the politically correct" are indeed outspoken critics of *Riposte Laïque,* and have brought the publication and those it considers to be patriotic truth-tellers (e.g., Marine Le Pen, Eric Zemmour and Michel Houellebecq) to court for various accounts of hate-speech, defamation, and threats.[113]

Even if many of the cases against *Riposte Laïque* have not led to conviction, they are costly, and the publication sees this as a strategy by the Thought Police to "attack our wallets."[114] This strategy is doubly provocative to *Riposte Laïque,* because these organizations are "stuffed with national, regional, and local subsidies."[115] The worst is HALDE, which "costs us around 11 million euro a year." HALDE spends its time "looking for discrimination in school books" and seeks to "impose the veil everywhere in France."[116] Representatives of HALDE and the aforementioned organizations are frequently depicted in cartoons, wearing Nazi and Fascist uniforms and saying things like "In this exceptional situation, we need to silence Marine Le Pen, Eric Zemmour, and *Riposte Laïque*."[117] The situation is exceptional, as *Riposte Laïque* sees it, because the French people are on the verge of waking up and seeing reality for what it is, mainly because of *Riposte Laïque* itself. I will come back to this issue in more detail, in the following chapter.

Now, within the ranks of the FN, the news media is often attacked, not the least by Marine Le Pen, who frequently denounces it as unjust and guided by bipartisan interests. When, in April 2017, she presented her presidential program in Bordeaux, she began by declaring that the news media "unleashes themselves to try to strike us down with their venomous arrows."[118] Certain media outlets have been banned from interviewing FN representatives and have been barred from FN meetings. For example, the satirical news show *Quotidien,* hosted by star journalist Yann Barthes, is routinely denounced as anti-FN; and when journalists have tried, sometimes provocatively, to gain access to meetings, they have been thrown out by security personnel.[119] During the FN 'First of May' March, the FN minister in the European Parliament and party veteran Bruno Gollnish attacked journalists from Barthes' previous show, *Le Petit Journal.* Gollnish used his umbrella to hit the journalists and to steal their microphone, while reportedly also destroying their camera. When explaining his deeds in a press communiqué, Gollnish stated that the show had invaded his private life by publishing personal letters, and explained that "I always respectfully respond to journalists; however, I destroy the microphones of spies."[120]

A leading ideologue of the 1980s, Bruno Mégret, decried how Human Rights had become used as a "war machine against the nation";[121] and although the term political correctness was not employed, Mégret's statement captures how the FN has articulated a belief that the privileged class and the political elite, as inheritors of Enlightenment ideals, together seek to favor immigrants to the detriment of the French people.

Marine Le Pen also frequently associates the news media with political correctness and Islam. In a tweet from November 2014, she declared that "the politically correct must not slow down our fight against Islamic fundamentalism."[122] During a meeting in Haute-Marne in 2016, she proclaimed that the political right is "fundamentally obsessed by a fear of hurting the politically correct."[123] A curious statement, given that the right has long led the political debate on questions of secularism, Islam, integration, security, and national identity. Equally curious was when, in 2015, FN member of parliament Marion Maréchale-Le Pen attacked Roger Cukierman, the president of the French Jewish Council, the *Conceil répresentatif des institutions juives en France* (CRIF), for being blind to the reality of anti-Jewish discourse and being "grinded by the politically correct."[124] Cukierman had previously stated that as long as Marine Le Pen does not clearly distance herself and the FN from her father's anti-Jewish statements while continuously "accepting negationists, Vichyites, and Petanists" into the party, she is "neither respectable, nor irreproachable."[125] Maréchale-Le Pen accused Cukierman of also being blind to "the fact that Muslims are responsible for the majority of anti-Jewish acts committed in France."[126] Following up on these statements in an interview on national radio, Florian Philippot added that "antisemitism" in France is "linked to Islamism, not FN. FN is its antidote."[127]

During FN's annual *Fête de Jeanne d'Arc* [Joan of Arc party] and the Popular and Patriotic 'Banquette' of May 1, 2016, Marine Le Pen proposed a strategy to circumvent the news media and the politically correct hegemony that supposedly reigns over French political debate. She began by declaring that "a calm and peaceful [*appaisée*] democracy should secure a sane and pluralist functioning of the media; to free journalism from governmental, private, and politically correct influences."[128] While waiting for this to happen, she declared, "we can short-circuit the traditional media with social media"; and to achieve this, "every activist needs to seize social media to convince [the] people."[129]

The Pink Khmers

Another internal enemy identified by *Riposte Laïque* is the "Pink Khmers," a label used by the publication's writers to name specific LGBTQ movements and organizations, but also as a more generic term for the political left. The label "Pink Khmers" obviously alludes to Pol Pot's Red Khmers; and thus, continues to articulate that they are adversaries of *Riposte Laïque,* in terms of totalitarian and genocidal political regimes. In the eyes of *Riposte Laïque,* they have made the national body vulnerable to foreign colonization, and internally, aid the depletion of its masculinity and virility. According to *Riposte Laïque,* the epitome of this development is the legalization of gender-neutral marriage, which was ratified in France on May 17, 2013, and the Hollande administration's work on gender equality.[130] Cyrano states that gender-neutral marriage, or "homo-marriage," along with the Islamization of France, "is part of the same fight against our civilization."[131] It is seen as a Pandora's Box, leading France into a future where the family and the social fundament as a whole are undermined.

One of the leading governmental voices regarding these issues has been Minister of Education Vallaud-Belkacem, the alleged Islamic agent. *Riposte Laïque* states that she and the government are influenced by the "homosexual" and "LBGTQ lobby," and that they seek to impose "Gender Theory" in schools. Gender Theory is articulated by the publication as a way to "indoctrinate our children, showing homosexual couples with children, as if heterosexuality was merely an ideological condition!"[132]

The political left and the privileged class are, according to the logic of *Riposte Laïque*, trying to breed a new generation of soft and feminized French citizens that will stand helpless against the Islamic take-over of France. Cyrano declares that the elite and the privileged "love the development of a new youth of mindless idiots that lower their heads to the racist aggression that they live by daily," and that they "prefer a youth where men are no longer men; but instead, increasingly feminized."[133] Cyrano argues that "these mindless and idiotic youngsters quiver when a bearded transsexual wins Eurovision," here referring to the Austrian singer Conchita Wurst, "who is a symbol of European decadence which they cherish in a twisted logic of tolerance."[134] Gender Theory, and the supposed imposition of gender-neutral marriage on the French population, are described as "fascist," as is the experience of *Riposte Laïque* as being treated as "reactionary homophobes," for speaking frankly about these issues.

In one cartoon, Vallaud-Belkacem and her predecessor as Minister of Education, Vincent Peillon, appear as SS officers standing in front of a school blackboard. The cartoon reads "the new socialist order" and "obligatory- parent one and parent two," with a large cross over "forbidden- mother and father."[135] In other cartoons, *Riposte Laïque* attacks couples of mixed color, as when the journal turned a poster of Disney's *Beauty and the Beast* into what is framed as an interracial nightmare.[136]

Riposte Laïque paints the picture of a near future where gender roles are erased and homosexuality is the new norm; where heterosexual love and seduction "that have given meaning to our life on earth" are a thing of the past;[137] however, according to *Riposte Laïque*, there is an even more sinister part the story. Cyrano explains that "their claimed equality between men and women is nothing but a war machine to devirilize men, to deprive us of our male warriors, who would be capable of defending us against Islam's offensive and Allah's soldiers."[138] This is the strategy they see for Vallaud-Belkacem: "an incompetent parasite" and "an

Islamic agent in action."[139] This strategy has already started to bear fruit. The political elite is continuously portrayed as a feminized bunch of helpless men. France is "soft," and, Cyrano declares, the Hollande administration is a bunch of "Care Bears who give up France to the violence of those who hate it and who dream of imposing their law."[140] Hollande is often depicted as an emasculated, overweight, and crying puppet waltzing around cluelessly in the Elysée Palace, pampered by the leaders of the Socialist Party.

In one cartoon, Holland holds a sign reading: "Homo marriage is ratified!" To which he adds: "You see Segolène, I do have balls!" Segolène Royal is an abiding political face of the French Socialist Party, and was also previously married to Hollande.

In another cartoon, the then Minister of the Interior, Manuel Valls, is wearing a fez and holding a program on which is written "civil war, population replacement, Islamization, Koran, Sharia," to which he adds: "My method for security. No balls, no trouble."[141] In yet another cartoon, Valls is depicted as a transvestite belly dancer.[142] His successor as Minister of the Interior, Bernard Cazeneuve, is also extensively ridiculed. In one cartoon the journal refers to the burial of the citizen Hervé Cornara, murdered June 26, 2015 by the self-proclaimed jihadi freedom fighter Yassin Salhi, in southeastern France. During the ceremony, Cazeneuve cried. This is supposedly not what a man of stature does. In the cartoon, Cazeneuve stands in a white petticoat, he has female breasts, and he weeps. Behind him is written "burqa, terrorist, scum" and the caption reads: "A minister who cries. It is too embarrassing."[143] Cyrano concludes that "France is on the verge of becoming a country that is spiritually ruined, open for all sort of relavitisms and prepared to lie flat for the first one who arrives. To evade violence, the whole country kneels without violent resistance."[144]

The discourse by *Riposte Laïque* on alterity within the national body is not unique to the journal. For example, regarding questions of women's and LGBTQ rights, the FN is similar to *Riposte Laïque* in how it juxtaposes women's rights as a civilizational marker between secular Europe and Islam, where the latter is articulated as being eternally misogynistic and homophobic.[145] From the outset, however, two of FN's leading positions were occupied by a woman and an openly gay man, Florian Philippot.

In Marine Le Pen's autobiography, *À contre flots* (Against the current), published in 2006, she describes how she became a "quasi-'feminist'" after her time as a single mother of three.[146] She described how women suffer from a "double penalty": taking care of a "demanding job and the family, and all with a smile, please!"[147] She rebuts the critique of FN being a party "who wants to send women back to the kitchen and care-taking"; and describes how, "during my upbringing, my father told me and my sisters: 'Work! Do not depend on anyone else! Be independent!'"[148] In interviews with the press and TV, Marine Le Pen declared on several occasions that she is in favor of "total equality between men and women in all domains, in all circumstances."[149] Marine Le Pen's 2017 presidential program proposed "a national plan to instate equal pay between men and women."[150] She very selectively quotes French feminists, like Simone de Beauvoir and Elisabeth Badinter, applying their words to her discussion of Islam.[151]

In the official FN program there is no mention of, for example, equal pay; women's rights are mostly mentioned under the heading "family," where a number of measures are put forward to help women in their role as mothers and single mothers, including sections on nativist politics and the "freedom not to abort."[152] But the real problem lies elsewhere. In an interview on BFM-TV, during the run-up to the presidential election of 2017, Marine Le Pen proposed that the real problem concerning women's rights in France stems partly from "associations from the left who raise their voices against dangers that in my opinion do not exist, while shutting their eyes to a danger that does exist."[153] She continued by stating that "today, the gigantic danger against women's rights is, I believe, objectively, Islamic fundamentalism."[154] In her presidential program of 2017, under the heading "protect women's rights," the first initiative is "to fight against Islamism," which is then followed by the proposition about equal pay.[155] Thus, when she quotes French feminists, she uses them as a means to denounce Islam and immigration.[156]

While Marine Le Pen makes use of feminism in FN's strategy of normalization, she has been rather ambivalent regarding LGBTQ questions and gender-neutral marriages. The massive demonstrations in 2013 against same-sex marriage, and the possibility for same-sex couples to adopt, conceive, and bear children through a third party, rallied millions of French citizens and political leaders from the conservative right and the radical nationalists. The demonstrations were also called *la Manif pour tous* (the manifestation for everybody) and *le Printemps français* (the French Spring), symbolizing that an open and liberating revolution was in the making. While several high-ranking politicians from FN were present, Marine Le Pen chose not to participate. During the presidential election in 2017, she was also remarkably silent on the question, while stating in her program that these laws would be withdrawn if she won.[157]

Within the FN, anti-LGBTQ voices are not uncommon.[158] For example, in 2014, the president of FN's youth party *Front National de la Jeunesse* (FNJ), Julien

Rochedy, declared that he would like a law prohibiting "LGBT propaganda in schools" like in Russia, and added that this law could be extended to include "the streets and walls, as well."[159] On critical questions regarding homophobia in Russia, he retorted that the reports about this were exaggerated by the media, and instead the focus should be on Muslim countries: "Last week the President visited Saudi Arabia, where homosexuals are actually killed. Nobody said a thing."[160] In this sense, feminism and homosexuality take on two functions within the FN. On the horizontal axis of populist identification, they are a marker for the national body vis-à-vis the external other; but on the vertical axis, as Dimitri Almeida points out, they become a danger for "the demographic survival of the nation."[161]

Such discourse on alterity, targeting LGBTQ rights, is not reserved for the radical nationalist milieu.[162] For example, before taking office, the Minister for Budget and Public Accounts, Gérald Darmanin, who is from the conservative LR, made several anti-LGBTQ remarks. Echoing *Riposte Laïque*, he has tweeted that "homo-marriage," "voting rights for immigrants," and "euthanasia" are part of the *Parti Socialiste*'s "harmful social reforms"; and has also asked: "One has to accept everything"? "Homosexual marriage and adoption ... under the pretext of societal evolution?"[163] Since being in office, however, he has answered his own tweets, by stating that "marriage for all is part of the Republic's laws" and that he has "no intention of putting it into question."[164]

On the famous political debate program *C Politique*, the acclaimed writer Pascal Bruckner ridiculed the LGBTQ abbreviation and suggested that it belonged in the same category as pedophiles: "LGGBDTTTIQQAAP. That is to say, lesbian, gay, genders, queers, bisexuals, demisexuals, and transgender. But it seems that they have forgotten to add masturbators, fetishists, and pedophiles."[165] Cyril Hanouna, the talk-show host of the famous TV show *Touche pas à mon poste*, has even turned the ridiculing of homosexual men and women into entertainment, by luring them onto dating sites with fake ads to call him on live TV, while he impersonates what, according to him, is a stereotypical gay person.[166]

A global conspiracy and an abject nation

In an article quoted by Cyrano, Christine Tasin concludes: "For ideological and economic reasons, our national and local elected [personages], who are imposing upon us a complete civilizational change without saying so or even asking us, are sucking our blood, both from the inside and the outside."[167] Tasin added: "it is becoming more and more clear that the economic crisis [of 2008] and the national debt have been deliberately created, with the sole aim of forcing us to kneel to our Qatari saviors and their Islam; the new 'benevolent' masters of France."[168] Here, Tasin neatly summarizes the convergence of the Eurabic conspiracy theory and the roles played by the internal enemies of the people; however, this gives rise to the question of why it would be a desirable scenario for the political elite and the privileged class. The answer is to be found in a larger conspiracy, one which seeks to dissolve the nation-state within the EU, and impose global liberal governance.

Since its first publications, the idea of a grand conspiracy had started to develop in writings from *Riposte Laïque*; however, it was a couple of years later that the publication first began to spin it, and it appears as if the editors knew that they were heading into murky waters. In 2009, Cyrano declared: "Our journal is very careful regarding conspiracy theories ... We know all too well how the extreme-right, throughout our history, has employed hateful speech against immigrants and the Jews."[169] Regardless, the logic underlying articulations of alterity in *Riposte Laïque,* and enmity along the horizontal and vertical axes of populist identification, is guided by a great conspiracy theory.

Now, according to *Riposte Laïque,* the interest of the political elite, and especially the left, is to reassure their electoral base. According to the publication, more than 90 percent of French Muslims vote PS. By replacing the white French population with Muslims, PS would thus increase its electorate. In one cartoon, Aburey, Hollande, the former leading Socialist figure Dominique Strauss-Kahn, and the Green party's leader Daniel Cohn-Bendit declare that "these working-class bastards are no longer voting for us: we need to replace them with immigrants!"[170] According to *Riposte Laïque,* this supposed Muslim vote is not free.

Another cartoon depicts Muslims in burqas, beards, and *djellabas* standing together with the suburban scum holding Algerian, Moroccan, Tunisian, and Iraqi flags. They all proclaim: "Sir Hollande, you won because of us! Now we no longer want to see any cops! Now we want more cash for our mosques!"[171]

The devirilization of France is also explained as part of an elaborate political scheme to impose "*l'humanus unisexus*,"[172] "racial mixing,"[173] and to "humiliate" the white French people: "A humiliated people is less inclined to fight against an oppressive government, as it thinks first and foremost of its own and its children's survival."[174] Thus, the goal for the elite is to "put an end to France, to its people, its civilization, and to act in the same way in all the other European countries."[175] In one cartoon, the political leaders of the UMPS are gathered around a cooking pot. In it boils a soup with the main ingredient, France, slowly dissolving into a

European melting pot.[176] Cyrano explains that the major actor behind this plot is not François Hollande, but Jacques Attali, a high-ranking statesman, former presidential advisor, and leading figure within the socialist think-tank Terra Nova. "The dissolution of our country into a federal Europe" is only the first step in Attali's plan; the second is to make Europe part of a global village. In one cartoon, the conspiracy is displayed in full: Attali is depicted as a vulture with a human head, sitting on a nest made of money from major currencies around the globe. The nest is resting on a pillar with the words "finance" and "global governance." The pillar is planted in France, colored green with the Islamic moon painted on it, and it is drenched in blood and fire. Attali says: "Islamization is the best way to destroy France and to realize my dream: to be the major councillor of global governance–because I'm worth it!"[177]

As pointed out earlier, the Eurabic conspiracy theory is strongly reminiscent of anti-Jewish conspiracy theories and from the outset, this grander conspiracy was even more so; however, Attali is Jewish.[178] While *Riposte Laïque* never explicitly refers to Attali as a Jew, what the journal displays is more of a merger of anti-Jewish conspiracy theories with an anti-Muslim one. Another case in point is the book *Le Vrai Visage de Manuel Valls* [The Real Face of Manuel Valls], published by Emmanuel Ratier, a journalist and the former editor-in-chief for the weekly radical nationalist *Minute*. According to *Riposte Laïque*, the book shows "the real face of Manuel Valls, the enemy of France, the socialist imposter, and the agent of global capital."[179] In the book, the double citizenship held by Valls, Spanish and French, and the fact that he is married to a Jewish woman who is supposed to have great political influence on him, are all taken as evidence of his deceitful nature.[180] He is declared to be an "unreserved supporter of Israeli politics and of the Netanyahu government" and as having "liaisons" with Netanyahu through communitarian French and North American Jewish organizations, such as the CRIF and the American Jewish Committee.[181] This theory has gained widespread traction in radical nationalist news sites, like *Fdscouche* and *Novopresse*,[182] and was even debated in national news media when Roland Dumas, former Minister of Foreign Affairs during Mitterrand's presidency and previous President of the Constitutional Council, suggested on national television that Valls was under Jewish influence.[183] Jean-Marie Le Pen has commented on this book, describing it as being of "great interest" and pronouncing "Valls" with a German accent.[184]

Jean-Marie Le Pen is well known for his anti-Jewish statements; for example, calling the Nazi gas chambers an "historical detail."[185] Marine Le Pen's father surely cast a dark shadow over the party of today; one central feature in the party's normalization strategy has been to try to wash away her father's revisionist statements. When the party leadership voted to exclude Jean-Marie Le Pen in 2015, it appeared to be a step in this direction.[186] Marine Le Pen has also rebutted some of her father's statements. For example, she has declared that the Nazi gas chambers were "the sum of barbarism [*barbarie*]"; however, she arguably banalizes French anti-Jewish discourse and the Vichy Regime by equating the Nazi occupation during the 1940s with the street prayers of a couple of hundred Muslim men.

In addition, during the presidential campaign in 2017, she declared that France "was not responsible for the *Vel' d'hiv.*"[187] This was when the French police, during the Vichy Regime, rounded up approximately thirteen thousand Jews, children included, and handed them over to the Nazis. Criticized for reproducing her father's revisionism, she argued she had stated that "during the occupation, France and the Republic was in London, thus the Vichy Regime was not France."[188] While its clear that the FN has replaced the Jew with the Muslim as the emblematic projection surface for society's ills, it could be argued that statements of this sort are playing to FN's revisionist history, showing that the party's anti-Jewish discourse has not been entirely replaced by anti-Muslim discourse. Instead, this reveals how Marine Le Pen and the current FN leadership navigate between anti-Jewish and anti-Muslim discourse.[189]

As pointed out by Cécile Alduy and Stéphane Wahnich, one of the challenges Marine Le Pen has been facing since taking over the leadership of FN is to normalize the party, without losing its radical elements in the process.[190] Sociological studies suggest that anti-Jewish discourse still has deep roots within FN, within both the party's grass roots and the electorate.[191] Thus, as the party seeks to attract new voters, alluding to revisionist and anti-Jewish statements might be understood as a way of appealing to a wider audience. In this regard, both *Riposte Laïque* and FN appear to articulate an esoteric anti-Jewish discourse, whilst their anti-Muslim discourse is conspicuously exoteric.[192] Whatever the case, within *Riposte Laïque*, FN, and other radical nationalist groups, the conspiracy theories are a central feature in how they approach politics and society. Articulations of alterity that are tied to a great conspiracy are certainly not always identical within these camps, but they appear to follow a similar logic.

Social grievances are construed and projected onto the enemies of the people, and hence, the nation, and are articulated into one singular element, a chain of equivalence, where the different categories of alterity call upon one another.[193] In other words, they all constitute and embody the figure of anti-France.[194] For example, within this radical nationalist and populist logic, gender-neutral marriage becomes a sign for the political elite's nativist onslaught on the white

French nation, through the help of Islam and Muslims. Conversely, Attali turns into a symbol of the Islamization of France and the secret master of political correctness. Emotions and morality are employed as discursive strategies to paint the picture of a nation in decline, as an abject soul.[195] Abjection is a category taken from psychoanalysis. It designates, as Dino Franco Felluga puts it, "a reaction (horror, vomiting) to a threatened breakdown in meaning, caused by the loss of the distinction between subject and object or between self and other."[196]

Sandrine Sanos uses abjection as an analytical category, to describe the intellectual French radical nationalists of the 1930s in their "obsession with wholeness, purity, and regeneration." Sanos shows how this obsession was anchored "in a grammar of sex, gender, and race," where fantasies of "abjection, dissolution, and dissociation were translated into particular aesthetics where young far-right intellectuals reimagined nation, race, and bodies articulated in a gendered and sexual discourse of male identity, citizenship, and civilization." Abjection, as such, applies neatly to the diagnosis by *Riposte Laïque* of the current state of the French nation, as well as allowing the publication's writers to imagine ways of overcoming this abject situation. Thus, *Riposte Laïque* seeks to locate the true people of France and convince them to join the organization and their peers in the fight against Islam, the political elite, and the privileged class.

In the following chapter, I will show how the people writing *Riposte Laïque* construct themselves and people as the true people of France, through a negative identification with its enemies, so as to locate the agent who could resurrect the nation from its abject state.

The Real People

Identifying the True People of France

"People of France wake up, there is so much suffering in you; don't let anyone other than you decide your path."[1] This is the first verse in the marching song *Peuple de France!* The song was published on their YouTube channel by *Riposte Laïque,* in 2010. According to *Riposte Laïque,* it was sent in by a reader of the journal and was seen by them as "a great symbol." It lasts for a little more than four minutes, contains ten verses, and is sung by a male voice. The video projects the lyrics, as well as images symbolizing the alleged Islamic onslaught and what France is supposedly really about. The second verse depicts the French male national football team, *Les bleues,* lined up before a match to sing the national anthem. The lyrics read: "Your anthem is booed, your flag, for which so many brothers have fallen in battle, is burned." With the following verse, the video shows a woman wearing a *niqab* while the lyrics express the agony of a French man walking the streets and suddenly discovering that he can no longer flirt with women: "No more exchange of smiles when you pass by a pretty girl, from now on her face is covered: How can one integrate with a veil?"

If women walking the streets are no longer available for flirting, the fourth verse explains that it is hard to walk the streets of your neighborhood at all. The accompanying image depicts praying Muslim men on a narrow street: "Secularism in your neighborhood has slowly disappeared, with so many carpets for prayer creating a barrier on the sidewalks." The fifth verse states that the flagpoles at offices of mayors in France will soon see the French flag replaced by an Algerian one. The sixth verse, accompanied by a photo of socialist Martine Aubrey, complains about the current regulation at municipal swimming pools: "In your swimming pools one no longer has the right to swim as before; hours are now reserved for the purity of women in veils."

The seventh verse explains how canteens in public schools have replaced the "bacon that one loves so much" with halal food. The eighth verse shows an image of the writer Eric Zemmour and reads: "LICRA and CSA scrutinize your smallest mistake, but no one worries when we're called 'chalk-face'." The next verse displays a burning French flag accompanied by the lyrics, "France, your values are dissolved, you are being Islamized, your symbols are violated; goodbye to your identity." The final verse begins by showing a minaret, which is replaced by the image of a young man dressed in a blue-and-white striped pullover and a black beret. He is standing in front of the Eiffel Tower, with a baguette and newspaper (*Le Figaro*) under his arm: "Minarets will replace your deserted churches, no more baguettes under your arms; from now on it's the *burqa*." These verses capture the abject state of the French nation, having lost what was; but the refrain attempts to counter this state, to arouse the French people and the nation to reclaim and resurrect what has been lost: "People of France, the time has come to break the silence and make your voice heard; people of France, do not give up, resist the enemies of your laws!"

This song repeats the foundations of the supposed Islamic onslaught against France, and the role played by the political elite and the privileged class. But it also articulates a certain notion about the French people. The song is portrayed through the gaze of a heterosexual male and "the French people" articulated as group that, being French, likes eating bacon, going to the swimming pool, carrying baguettes under their arms, and wearing berets and striped pullovers. These rather mundane features are all central to the *Riposte Laïque* conception of who the French people are, and the reality they live by. They have become a forgotten, abject people who suffer, whose traditions are being taken away, and who can no longer roam freely in their own land.

While the category of "the people" is omnipresent in writings at *Riposte Laïque*, it is important to inquire into who these people are: how are they identified and what logic underpins their identification? This is key in understanding how *Riposte Laïque* and its peers understand the current state of France, and what to do about it. In this chapter, I show in detail how *Riposte Laïque* seeks to articulate that there is an exclusivist national identity, by mixing conceptions of cultural, religious, and ethnic belonging through the category of "the people" in relation to the horizontal and vertical axes of alterity in the publication's populist logic of identification. This chapter is structured in accordance with what I identify as the central features in this articulation: love, injustice, dissatisfaction, and its allies.

Loving the nation

As will become clear, love is a central category in articulating "the people"; however, before coming to the question of love, it is necessary to address who "the people" are, according to *Riposte Laïque*. When the publication refers to the "Real People of France"; they are the ones who:

> do not make any noise, it is the well-educated France that does not want to disturb; those who work and pay their taxes without protest, those who have never committed any crime except for spending their time politely standing in line; those who give up their places on public transport, and who help old ladies to carry their luggage on the train.[2]

Thus, they are helpful and quiet, merely seeking to live their lives in peace:

> This is the France that does not get talked about on the news, because their children do not deal drugs, do not burn cars, and do not hit their teachers. It is a France that no government seeks to domesticate, because it is known that they are docile, respectful of the established law and order. It is the gentile and familial France, Catholic or not.[3]

The Real People of France are the bedrock of France, and most importantly, they are French. The *Riposte Laïque* texts are very elaborative upon the question of the people and nationhood; and read together, they appear rather ambiguous and sometimes outright contradictory. Notwithstanding, Cyrano declares that "I am French because I have French nationality."[4] Cyrano declares, "Our concept of the nation is absolutely not ethnic; it is constructed on the basis of a contract and the acceptance of this contract. The rules are clear: you accept the rules of the host country and you become a citizen with the same rights and duties as everybody else. This is called assimilation."[5]

Riposte Laïque appears to argue for a *jus solis*-based citizenship, as Cyrano argues that it does not matter whether nationality is given by birth or attained through naturalization; however, obtaining citizenship is conditioned on the premise of assimilation, which means that the individual in question needs to see *him*self as "a son of a nation."[6] It is worth noting that citizenship is only discussed here in terms of masculine epithets. Moreover, given that *Riposte Laïque* continuously refers to the real French people as being Gauls and as white, their acclaimed non-ethnic conception of national identity is dubious, to say the least.

Notwithstanding, Cyrano ponders upon what a nation is, and describes it as: "an ensemble of human beings, united by/in a territorial community, a language, traditions, and ambitions."[7] Cyrano continues to describe the nation as a house:

"The territory is my house, the language is the key, the traditions the foundation, the ambitions the windows of my house."[8] Thus, the people living in the house need to share a common national identity. This identity is, according to *Riposte Laïque*, specific to France; but is also part of a European lineage "that starts with Homer up to Goethe and Victor Hugo, from Descartes to Newton, from a Judeo-Christian essence to the Copernican revolution, from Swiss reformist theologians to German philosophers, from Greek philosophy and Roman Law to the Italian Renaissance and to British industrialization."[9] The specificity of French identity is described as founded upon "centuries-long French *genius*" consisting of "our culture, our literature, our castles, our sculptures, our paintings."[10]

Riposte Laïque claims a number of historical figures as "heroes" to the nation: "Vercingétorix, Charles Martel, Charlemagne, Saint-Louis, Jeanne d'Arc, Clovis, Louix XIV, Napoléon, Clemenceau, de Gaulle, embody the grandeur of the nation."[11] This selective writing of history inscribes France in a Eurocentric historical narrative. The events and figures referenced are given little more than just a mention, except for one: Charles Martel. *Riposte Laïque* and other radical nationalist voices have turned Martel and the Battle of Poitiers in 732, when Martel's army allegedly fought back the Saracens marching up from the Iberian Peninsula, into the quintessential historical reference for how France has been engaged in millennia-long battles with Islam.[12]

After the attacks in Paris on January 7, 2015, when the hashtag *Je suis Charlie* [I am Charlie] was used throughout France, *Riposte Laïque* and French identitarians came up with their own version: "I am Charles Martel."[13] According to Cyrano, the grandeur of France only developed "because our country has escaped the barbarian Muslim hordes for over fourteen centuries."[14] While France has resisted for so long against these barbarian hordes, Cyrano believes that today, Muslims in France "were they the majority of the country, would destroy and burn it," like ISIS is doing at "this moment in Palmyra."[15]

The unifying category of the concept of national identity by *Riposte Laïque* is described as a will to react against those who threaten it. As Cyrano declares, "My identity is an action!"[16] He continues: "My identity is thus more than my identity card; it is the will to *be* that obliges me to react against those who do not want to participate in the French nation, even when they live in it."[17] Being a citizen is to be the inheritor of the "real Gauls and Asterix," referring here to the famous comic strip that tells the tale of a Gallic village that resisted Caesar's conquering of France.[18] According to *Riposte Laïque*, the French *genie* and the Gallic heritage translate to being "secular and republican," which is: "to favor the general interest; and thus, to be on the side of the oppressed."[19]

The situation described is one where minorities oppress the majority, which calls for a progressive and revolutionary awakening. This is why, according to *Riposte Laïque*, resurrecting the French people from its state of abjection is important: "Do we really need to remind everyone that throughout our history, the progressive and revolutionary movements always have reference to national identity?"[20] Cyrano goes on to explain that the mission of *Riposte Laïque* inscribes itself on the left side of politics: "We know that these conquests have never been driven by the right and far less the extreme-right ... to us, the *l'esprit* of the left is contained in values like solidarity, humanism, quality, feminism; values that we absolutely do not negate."[21]

Being a self-acclaimed feminist journal, *Riposte Laïque* decries unequal pay between the sexes, unfair labor conditions for women, the supposed rise in forced marriages in France; and, according to *Riposte Laïque*, the over 130 rapes committed each day.[22] As seen in the previous chapter, the responsibility for the state of women in France is tied to the Eurabic and global capitalist conspiracy headed by Jacques Attali; however, *Riposte Laïque* is vague in terms of explaining what gender equality means, exactly. For example, in the book *La Faut de Bobo Jocelyn* (2011), written by Cassen and Tasin, they explain that what women really want is real men who can pleasure their woman and stand up for the nation.[23] And while the people might be against gender-neutral marriage, this does not mean that they are homophobic. According to the journal: "The French are absolutely not homophobic, they do not care what happens in bedrooms" of gays or lesbians; but "they do not want see Bertrand marry Guillaume [male names] or Caroline marry Fiammetta [female names]."[24]

The *Riposte Laïque* texts are most often written through a masculine viewpoint, where women are discussed as objects of desire for sexual conquest, and also for securing a demographic feature of the French people as white. What *Riposte Laïque* appears to wish for is a return to what is an imagined state of natural gender roles.

Now, what really distinguishes the real people of France from the traitors and Muslims is a profound love for the nation. As Cyrano declares, France today is split "between those who love France and those who want to see it disappear."[25] *Riposte Laïque* "loves the beauty of democracy,"[26] which translates to "popular sovereignty."[27] *Riposte Laïque* also states that they, the editorial board and its readers, are guilty: guilty of "loving France too much."[28] As a left-leaning journal, *Riposte Laïque* does not want to abandon "the love for the Republic, the nation, the Republic, and secularism to FN, as has been the case the last 30 years."[29] Love unites, and love is what makes possible the unification of *Riposte Laïque* with identitarian, conservative, and reactionary political actors in France.

Commenting on joint work with *Bloc Identitaire, Riposte Laïque* states that "what unites us is the love for France, the Republic; and the secular, solidarity, brotherly, and humanist principles."[30] Moreover, *Riposte Laïque* describes how the letters they receive from readers talk about love and that the activists who join *Résistance Républicaine* do so out of "love for France and the refusal to see our country become Islamized."[31]

While emotional statements, in particular national romantic ones about loving France, are far from uncommon in French politics, the particularity of using love as a dividing category between the real France and the supposed false France has become a common practice for radical nationalist voices. For example, after the first round of the presidential election in 2012, when Marine Le Pen came in third with nearly 18 percent of the vote, she declared that the first round "was merely the start of a vast gathering of patriots, of the ones who love France's exceptionality: the battle of France has only just begun."[32]

In 2015, in the midst of handling her father's many troubling statements and in her effort to normalize the party, she called upon party adherents to join in a discussion of whether or not the party should continue to name honorary members. In that call, she declared that "my objective is clear; I want to make FN into the most-performing instrument in the service of the patriots and the ones who love France; with the goal of ending our country's desolation, decline, and disappearance."[33]

In a letter to the party members in 2015, the Secretary General of the FN, Nicolas Bay, similarly thanked all members for "having carried the voice of love for the motherland [*patrie*] throughout France."[34] These are examples of how articulations of national identity are used through the category of love, to make possible a unification of the people, or a national "we": it becomes its *raison d'être* [reason to be].

Injustice

Injustice is similar to love in how it structures the articulation of the people. As discussed, *Riposte Laïque* argues that the real people of France make up the large majority of the country, using various opinion polls to confirm their assessment. For example, polls show that 90 percent of the population were in favor of the Law of 2010 that prohibits face-covering headscarves: these are taken as proof of a total adherence to the political opinions of *Riposte Laïque*.[35] The publication also quotes a poll from 2010, showing that 74 percent of the French population "rejects Islam."[36] Therefore, *Riposte Laïque* is perplexed about the fact that the people do not vote for the FN: "We know that seventy percent of the 'castrated' say that they are hostile to the Islamization of our country and immigration; however, they vote for the traitors that impose these two cancers on us."[37] The reason for this is found in the abject state of the people. Cyrano declares that "our compatriots are facing a real feeling of abandonment."[38] They appear to have lost hope in the political system, worn down by political correctness and the injustice imposed on the people by the political elite and the privileged class.

Cyrano refers to how *Riposte Laïque* readers "are suffering from insults and defamation from the extreme-left and the "bobos" [*bourgeoisie bohème*], but also from people who pretend to be republican."[39] One of the seminal examples at *Riposte Laïque* is Fanny Truchelet, who in 2007 refused a woman wearing a veil a room in her guesthouse. According to Cyrano, "Fanny is a real girl of the people, raised in hard conditions; she understood early on the reality and harshness of life. She has raised four children. She is a country girl, deeply attached to the soil and the region."[40] Truchelet was later sued by the MRAP and also convicted of discrimination. This was the proof to *Riposte Laïque* of the great injustice that plagues the average white French citizen.[41] Another case that supposedly testifies to this injustice is about a middle-aged couple who threatened a group of youngsters with a rifle during Ramadan in 2012. "If your names are William and Monique," Cyrano states, "and if you are fed up with the provocations from those who fast, and you bring out your rifle [*carabine à plomb*] to get some respect, without hurting anyone, within 48 hours you are convicted to four years and two years of imprisonment, even though this was their first crime."[42]

Another injustice is apparently speed cameras on highways, which supposedly reveal the state's double standards in how it treats its native population. Cyrano asks, rhetorically, how "the average French are to understand the state's powerlessness towards these little fascist racists [suburban youth and Muslims], when honest citizens, who happen to drive slightly too fast, are shamelessly racketeered?"[43] What is worse is that the money collected from this type of alleged state-organized racketeering is used to "pay for two extra nights for illegal immigrants and to pay for family support for polygamous families!"[44] This double standard is, according to *Riposte Laïque*, engrained in the everyday life of the French: "Why do smokers, who are requested to smoke their cigarettes outside, obey laws that disturb their habits, whilst the religious do not?"[45]

Riposte Laïque also deplores how this double standard impacts the critics of Islam. When women like Wafa Sultan, Chahdhortt Djavann, Ayaan Hirsi Ali, or

Taslima Nasreen "equate Islam to totalitarianism," apparently "nobody has the courage to lecture them."[46] "When they say that we are living in a civilizational clash" between "obscurantism and democracy, everybody rightfully applauds."[47] According to *Riposte Laïque*, the problem is that "when a 'native French person' dares to say the same things, he is immediately suspected of being extreme-right"; he is "smothered and forced to make a distinction between Islam and Islamism."[48] This double standard of justice is depicted in a caricature of a dark-skinned Muslim man dressed in a green robe, who covers his eyes with one hand to display disgrace, while in the other hand he holds an issue of both *Charlie Hebdo* and *France Soir*, journals that had published cartoons of Mohammed. Beside him lies a white man dressed in a pullover and pants. He is covered in blood with a scimitar in his chest. The image is accompanied by the text: "Believer hurt by the nonbelievers. Nonbeliever hurt by the believers."[49]

If average citizens are being policed by political correctness, the case appears even worse for the police and for schools: "the Republic's two pillars."[50] Police officers and teachers are "despised, and treated in the worst possible manner."[51] Referring to the many revolts in metropolitan suburbs,[52] Cyrano declares that "the politically correct and the leftish demagoguery accuse cops, seen as racist and fascist, for being provocative and responsible for a 'legitimate revolt by the youth'."[53] "In schools," Cyrano continues, "the politically correct make teachers, who are daily victims of uproar and mayhem, [be] guilty: If students are not interested, teachers are told by the hierarchy that it is their fault!"[54]

Riposte Laïque argues that the responsible politicians blame the lower ranks, teachers and police officers, "to protect" themselves.[55] As these professions represent authority, *Riposte Laïque* ironically suggests, they are led to believe that it is "progressive to let oneself be insulted."[56] To *Riposte Laïque*, then, anyone who claims that minorities, and especially Muslims, are victims of structural discrimination and racism in France is gravely misled: "It is France, the social republic, secularism, and democracy that are the real victims."[57] Cyrano urges the people not to listen to the left, because "it is not the horrific skins with shaved heads that are multiplying."[58] This injustice is illustrated in a caricature depicting the political elite standing on the real people of France. The elite, Sarkozy and Aubrey standing in front, declare: "Let's accept everyone! All of the illegal immigrants! Let's be generous!" The people cry in agony: "What about us, France?"[59] Cyrano concludes: "our compatriots are attacked like never before, by its regime and its assistants."[60] Here, injustice emerges as a structuring category for, on the one hand, the reality that the real people of France are living in, but it is also a category that explains why the people do not act as they should:

Injustice has worn the people down into an abject state of being. They are the silenced majority, and their abject state of existence hinders them from fully acting out their love for the nation. This is depicted in a cartoon displaying a burning suburb. Masked men hold automatic rifles and bloody knives. White French citizens, that is, the people, stand in front of them. The masked men scream: "Fuck your race. We will kill all the white French [*céfrans*]!" The people cry for help: "We can't stand this any longer. Help us!"[61] Here *Riposte Laïque* enters as a clarion call, as freethinkers and the voice of the people.[62]

In addressing the people, *Riposte Laïque* wants to transcend any left–right divide: "We do not only want to serve the left, we want to trigger the awakening of the people of France."[63] According to *Riposte Laïque*, there are true seculars that "do not vote for the left, but that nonetheless fight to defend the separation between religion and politics, and the sense of the Law of 1905, with more belligerence than a lot of the elected socialists, communists, or ecologists."[64] *Riposte Laïque* is sure that "the public is with us."[65] "Why?" asks Cyrano. "Simply because they understand that we are the carriers of a real wake-up call in the face of the unacceptable."[66] This is why the publication "does not want its ideas to end up in a useless journal!"[67] To reach the people, *Riposte Laïque* refuses to "let the new *cogito* ['I think' definition] be: 'I think, therefore I shut up.'"[68]

According to the journal itself, the many articles and activist work by *Résistance Républicaine* are bearing fruit. Cyrano recounts numerous emotionally loaded anecdotes about ordinary French citizens who, thanks to their journal, do wake up; that, by reading *Riposte Laïque*, the citizens manage to see through the fog of political correctness.

Regarding anti-French and anti-white racism, Cyrano states that "this taboo is openly addressed at our meetings," and relates that "one of the speakers at one of our meetings told us an emotional story about a man who came to see her with tears in his eyes: 'Thank you for what you say; I started to doubt myself, to fear that I was becoming racist, but you gave me confidence.'"[69] In another anecdote, Cyrano tells the story of a reader who thinks that *Riposte Laïque* has managed to "to put all the pieces together."[70] According to Cyrano, there are "dozens of testimonies of this sort."[71] Just as French history is something to be proud of, so is one's Gallic skin and French customs. Thus, *Riposte Laïque* calls upon the French people: "All of you French people, wake up! Look at yourself and see what you are ..." "be proud ..." "do not let anyone pretend that you are worthless."[72]

Following this logic, instead of questioning whether one shamefully withholds racist thoughts, as the politically correct regime dictates, one should be proud of seeing reality for what it is. *Riposte Laïque* states that "evidently, none of the texts published by the journal contain even a minor racist statement."[73] Moreover, Cyrano declares that nobody, during public meetings at *Riposte Laïque*, has "raised an arm to cry out 'Heil Hitler!' None of the speakers has chanted: 'Throw the Arabs into the sea!' Nor, 'throw the Jews in the oven!'"[74] This image is apparently shared with the readers of *Riposte Laïque*: "None of our readers has said he has seen any trace of racism nor any call to violence."[75]

How, then, does *Riposte Laïque* see its countless anti-Muslim statements and the call to arms against injustice? According to the publication, denouncing what it sees as the hidden truth of Islam and Muslims is not racist, as Islam is a totalitarian, fascist, and religious political ideology, and Muslims are not a race. Instead, the act of denouncing Islam and Muslims is anti-fascist: "We reclaim the anti-racist struggle, we reclaim the anti-fascist struggle, and we reclaim republican values."[76] Here, *Riposte Laïque* picks up on a campaign driven by *Résistance Républicaine*, which revolves around Islamophobia, where *Riposte Laïque* and *Résistance Républicaine* proclaim themselves to be proud Islamophobes. This is illustrated by a poster depicting a Koran lying on a bed of blood. The text reads "Islamophobia is not a crime, it is a legitimate defense"; and "I am Islamophobic, and I am proud of it."[77] Hence, to *Riposte Laïque*, Islamophobia and secularism are two sides of the same coin in today's anti-fascist, anti-racist, and republican struggle. In their logic, *Riposte Laïque* and the people of France are fed up with the guilt imposed upon them by the political elite and the privileged class: "The voice of the people, yes, but on the condition that the people say exactly the same thing as the guardians of the temple. Jesus, Voltaire, Jaurès, and all of the fighters against hypocrisy and untruth are turning in their graves."[78] Cyrano quotes the "remarkable" Maurice Vidal, a writer and contributor to *Riposte Laïque*, who writes: "It is not by classifying statements, texts, or posters as 'racist' that a contradictor convinces; it is by proving that these statements, texts, and posters are 'racist.' But when the proof is founded on fraud, the task is deemed to have failed, and rage conquers!"[79]

To *Riposte Laïque* and the people, enough is enough. Rage here appears as a key to wake up and resurrects the people from abjection. Cyrano interprets for the people, that: "France has had enough of people spitting in its face!"[80] They have had enough of the "moralizers."[81] Cyrano reminds the people that the:

> free spirits of our time are here to remind and to help everyone to say no. We all have the right to say no. No to discrimination of women, no to public influence of religion, no to ghettos, no to inequalities, no to censorship, no to totalitarianism, no to this world that wants to make man a slave to production, consumption, and debt.[82]

Cyrano declares, ironically: "We no longer want this! We no longer want the Republic to cede to permanent harassment by the graceful religious Muslims."[83] Regarding headscarves, he states that the people "are increasingly exasperated by this discriminatory garment that insults women's struggles for equality and secularism!"[84] He continues: "It does not matter that the *burqa* is the norm in Muslim countries. We are in France as far as I know!"[85] Cyrano concludes by reframing the Spanish anti-fascist slogan: "*No pasarán!* [They shall not pass through!]"[86]

That France and its people have had enough is frequently heard by radical nationalist voices. The phrase "*on est chez nous!*" [this is in our land, our home!] has become a common slogan for FN spokespeople and activists. In meetings and during rallies, it is often chanted with an air of defiance, as a cry to action, to reclaim what once was. In 2012, FN's youth party created a poster for a publicity campaign, depicting a woman with a French flag painted on her face, crying in agony. The poster reads: "Enough with anti-French racism! This is our land!"[87] At a meeting for the 2017 presidential election, Marine Le Pen explained how she interprets the call: "This call, 'This is our land,' is a cry from the heart and of love." Moreover, she attacked the mainstream media for calling it xenophobic: "No, ladies and gentlemen, this cry is not xenophobic; it is a cry of love, because we belong to this country. Yes, this is our land!" She continued: "You are the proprietors of France. You do not rent it; you do not occupy it without right or entitlement."[88]

A shared cause

While *Riposte Laïque* sees itself as a voice of the large majority of the French, it also sees itself as part of a minority who actually hear the people; however, the publication does consider itself to have allies on the French activist and political scene, who inspire the journal and the people of France. *Riposte Laïque* states that they "support personalities from the right and the left when they take a clear stance against the politically correct," and that the publication will "go anywhere where we are invited to debate as free spirits and without compromise."[89] This does not mean that *Riposte Laïque* sees itself in perfect political alignment with all its allies. As Cyrano explains, while sharing "the same concern regarding the Islamization of France and proposing of a number of identical solutions to the problem" with French identitarians, "we hold different political opinions; but that does not stop us from working together against the Islamization of France."[90]

Commenting on one of the many debates that *Riposte Laïque* and *Résistance Républicaine* have had at Local, a now-closed neo-Nazi pub in the fifteenth district in Paris, the publication concludes that "we had a rich exchange, allowing us to sincerely debate legitimate questions that the people ask themselves."[91] At Local, "those who defend an ethnic idea of France sometimes severely contested Christine Tasin on the question of immigration and Islam; however, no chair was thrown and the debate remained respectful, where everybody had the time to listen to the other."[92] According to *Riposte Laïque*, no matter who the publication debates with, criticism follows:

> We agreed to speak at Local? We are neither more nor less than neo-Nazis! When we agree to debate on Radio-Courtoisie? We are called Catholic fundamentalists … We accept an invitation by secular organizations? Catholic fundamentalists shout out that we are anti-clerical and freemasons. We accept an invitation to Bnai Brith [a Jewish organization with its French seat in Paris], this time we have sold out to the Jews and are paid by the Mossad.[93]

The difference in how *Riposte Laïque* treats anyone who does not firmly reject all aspects of Islam, in relation to self-avowed fascists and Nazis, is noteworthy. Anders Behring Breivik is referred to as a "so-called Norwegian terrorist."[94] Another example concerns a 19-year-old Frenchman who had bought a Celtic cross flag that, in various forms, is used by white supremacists, neo-Nazis, neo-fascists, and in this case, French identitarians, to put on the back of his car. According to *Riposte Laïque*, "the question is not whether we are in agreement with the symbol or not;" the important thing is "that French police officers [*gendarmes*] stopped him, and that later on, this young man found himself in court, although he wasn't threatening anyone."[95] *Riposte Laïque* concludes: "This is a real inquisition by the Thought Police!"[96]

Another example is when *Riposte Laïque* defended, without hesitation, two skinheads and two members of the radical nationalist and revolutionary group *Troisième Voie*, later prohibited by the government, who had killed an anti-fascist activist in central Paris, in 2013.[97] The two skinheads were convicted of involuntary manslaughter; but according to *Riposte Laïque*, "they are only guilty of not letting the self-proclaimed anti-fascists massacre them."[98] *Riposte Laïque* turns these figures into martyrs, into real patriots who are victims of an unjust society. The most emblematic of such patriots is Dominique Venner. Venner was a writer and intellectual, co-founder of GRECE, and admired by many leading figures within the ranks of the FN. In 2013, Venner took his own life in the great cathedral of Notre-Dame, in Paris. *Riposte Laïque* interprets this as an act to "wake up our kind, and to encourage them to resist the image of a France without pride that passively suffers from immigration, Islamization, the replacement of the people, daily assaults, the devirilization of its men, the defeminization of its women; and that no longer defends its values, its traditions, and its civilization."[99]

For a self-acclaimed anti-fascist journal, the publication's bedfellows are indeed conspicuous; however, its logic is to recast the traditional political dividing lines between left and right, to argue that the traditional left is the new extreme right, and that radical nationalist patriots are the ones who incarnate the anti-fascist struggle of our times. As for the FN, during the first years of its publication, *Riposte Laïque* was critical of the party. In several articles, Cyrano declared that the FN was the extreme right, and that, "without the least ambiguity, the extreme right's thesis, abroad as in France, is dangerous to liberty, the status of women, to secularism, and to the foundations of our Republic."[100] Cyrano has stated that "at *Riposte Laïque*, we will never support Jean-Marie Le Pen's and other negationists' statements concerning the Holocaust," while adding that Le Pen's statements were close to the "Islamist extreme right."[101]

If anti-Jewish statements from FN representatives created a dividing line between *Riposte Laïque* and the FN, this all started to change with Marine Le Pen's rise to power within the FN. As early as 2009, *Riposte Laïque* started to see Marine Le Pen as a future leader of France: "Unlike her father, Marine Le Pen knows how to avoid pointless provocations and she has understood that the republican and secular discourse (in particular against Islam) can be a winner."[102] It is noteworthy that what *Riposte Laïque* really cherishes about Marine Le Pen's "new discourse" is that she knows how to avoid "pointless provocations," and that secularism and republicanism were seen as useful tools in the fight against Islam. "Of course," Cyrano states, "the extreme right knows the gains in using the legitimate worry against the reality of the Islamic onslaught," and adds: "we will not play along with the politically correct and say the opposite to what the daughter of Jean-Marie Le Pen says, simply because she is a member of FN."[103] Moreover, Cyrano declares: "We have the courage to say that Marine Le Pen does not speak with the usual language of the extreme right; and that she absolutely does not embody any fascist danger, as the leftists imply."[104]

From the beginning, support for Marine Le Pen from *Riposte Laïque* becomes more and more explicit. For example, in 2013 *Riposte Laïque* declared that even though "our journal has always confirmed a total independence vis-à-vis political parties, independence does not signify neutrality."[105] Indeed, Marine Le Pen's appeal to republicanism, secularism, and women's rights appeared to echo what *Riposte Laïque* had been writing about for nearly two years. "We have appreciated that Marine Le Pen is the only one that passes on *Riposte Laïque* campaigns on the illegal Muslim street prayers and on halal food."[106] In conclusion, Cyrano states: "it has to be acknowledged; to millions of the French, Marine Le Pen appears more and more as the only alternative to the suicidal politics of our country."[107]

Another cherished member of the party is Fabien Engelmann, FN mayor of the city of Hayange. Engelmann has on several occasions contributed to the journal, and he is deemed "courageous" for his many anti-Muslim and anti-immigration actions.[108] Among other things, Engelmann has installed an annual *Fête du cochon* (Pork Fest) to celebrate French traditions and a French lifestyle;[109] however, *Riposte Laïque* support for Marine Le Pen, Engelmann, and many others within the ranks of FN does not mean unequivocal support for FN. *Riposte Laïque* is fiercely critical of Marine Le Pen's right hand man, Florian Philippot, who is seen as weak on immigration and Islam: "We are often exasperated by the Islamophilic statements by FN's number two, Florian Philippot, and by his excessive prudence regarding the evident incompatibility between Islam and the Republic."[110] *Riposte Laïque* quotes Florian Philippot as saying: "I will never confound Islam and Islamism! If the Republic is weak regarding Islamization, it will allow immigration to create ghettos, and it will signal to the French that Islam is the problem."[111] According to *Riposte Laïque*:

> these statements are terrible because, first of all they are wrong, but mostly they are counter-productive. When the majority of the French has had enough with Islam, headscarves, *burqas*, halal, mosques, the violence connected to this ideology; the arrogance of its representatives; and of a fifth columnist no longer hiding its intentions; Philippot appears to call our compatriots to order ... telling them that Islam is not the problem.[112]

Cyrano then ponders whether Philippot's next step would be to say: "I forbid you to say that Islam is the problem?"[113]

Even though the texts in *Riposte Laïque* are critical of the major political parties, they do support a few individual politicians, from the left to the right. André Gerin, communist MP and the initiator of the Law of 2010, is, besides Marine Le Pen, the politician who is most frequently referred to. Gerin, who is "alone on the left" with a "touch of lucidity,"[114] is reported about as sounding "the alert on the reality of Islam's offensive."[115] As stated in *Riposte Laïque*, "we have a certain weak spot for him..." who "has exactly the same analysis as the FN" regarding Islam, immigration, and secularism;[116] however, *Riposte Laïque* is disappointed with his actions. After resigning his public mandate in 2012, instead of "joining the only political prospect that corresponds to his political opinions, he calls upon his comrades to rebuild the Communist Party!"[117]

From the right, *Riposte Laïque* cherishes the conservative mayor of the city of Montfermeil, Xavier Lemoine (UMP). *Riposte Laïque* states that "although we do not share the integrality of his statements, he has the courage to put his feet into the plate" and talk about the elephant in the room, to denounce "without compromise, the incompatibilities of the religion of Islam with democracy and the Republic."[118] *Riposte Laïque* quotes Lemoine as saying that the cause of suburban problems "is not social, economic, nor urban"; instead it is "cultural," if not "religious."[119] Moreover, *Riposte Laïque* quotes him as saying: "Secularism, one of the pillars of our republic, is a notion that does not exist within Islam. Equality between men and women does not exist, whilst it is the basis of our society. The same goes for freedom of conscience. The Republic is really in danger."[120]

Yet another politician who has gained the support of *Riposte Laïque* is Nicolas Dupont-Aignan, founder and president of the party *Debout la France*.[121] In 2016, Dupont-Aignan declared himself a candidate for the 2017 presidential election. Having relatively low scores in the polls, he joined Marine Le Pen in an alliance, in which he would be prime minister. During the run-up to the election he made several noteworthy statements. Among other things, Dupont-Aignon cherished France's "Christian roots, which are a constituting element of our identity." He referred to the thesis of the great replacement, and talked publicly about immigration as an "invasion" and a new type of "colonialism."[122] In his presidential program, Dupont-Aignon proposed measures to drastically cut immigration in France, stronger measures to control Muslims in France, and to make offences against secularism punishable by law.[123] As he is anti-EU, he wants to shut down Schengen and reintroduce border controls, and was an ally of the British UK Independence Party (UKIP) in the parliamentary elections in 2014.[124] According to *Riposte Laïque*, Dupont-Aignon apparently checks off the most important boxes for a competent politician. While Cyrano is often pessimistic and skeptical about the future of France, when he dreams of these politicians working together, a glimmer of hope is expressed: "Imagine the effect that it would have if André Gerin, with his past, his political statements, his *resistant* communist spirit, appeared together with Marine Le Pen and Nicolas Dupont-Aignan."[125] This dream team of "patriotic" politicians would be the "only possible alternative to the 40-year-long-catastrophe caused by UMP and PS."[126]

The way *Riposte Laïque* articulates its allies is simplified and reduced to the question of Islam, and turning the classical right–left political divide on its head. Thus, the real extreme right is the former republican left, whose spirit has been taken over by the new, real republicans, the patriotic defenders of the nation and its people, most notably the FN. This is illustrated in a cartoon where Cassen, Tasin, and Hilout stand in front of a French flag.[127] Hilout, who is a "born Muslim," as *Riposte Laïque* is adamant in pointing out, holds a sausage in his hand, as a symbol of his conversion to a French way of life, and behind them are four posters. The first one reads "forced marriages" and depicts an older, bearded Muslim man holding onto a much younger Muslim woman in a *hijab*. The second poster reads "women's inferiority" and illustrates women dressed in a burqa, *niqab*, or *hijab*. The third depicts a sheep being beheaded with a bloody knife, accompanied by the statement "halal beheadings." The final poster says "conquest of public space" and shows Muslim men praying in the streets. The trio asks: "Who are the allies of the extreme right? The culprits of the Islamist offensive? Or the resistance fighters?"

Populism and nation

In this chapter I sought to display how *Riposte Laïque* articulates nationhood through a populist logic of identification. The real people of France are conceptualized through a chain of equivalence that distills and reduces national identity into a single, graspable identity: the people, whose core feature is to love the French nation. The categories of the people and love are emblematically unstable, however, and they are in constant need of being rearticulated and relocated. As Laclau argues, this "is why an equivalent chain has to be expressed through the cathexis of a singular element: because we are dealing not with the conceptual operation of finding an abstract common feature underlying all social grievances, but with a performative operation constituting the chain as such."[128] Now, I am not suggesting here that "the people" and "love" have no meaning at all. To quote Francisco Panizza, what I argue is that the meaning "is determined by a process of naming that retroactively determines its meaning."[129] The singular, underlying category that gives meaning to the people's love for the nation, as well as secularism, republicanism, and feminism, boils down to being anti-Muslim.

France, the nation, is articulated as being home and a territory where love is the universal link between the people and its soil; however, this link is threatened by the haters of the nation, who have forced the nation-loving people into abjection. Reminding the people of its love for the nation is to give an imagined meaning to a bundle of heterogeneous historical events that, nonetheless, ties them together into a larger nationalistic unveiling. To paraphrase Lene Austad, nationalist discourse channeled through love makes "memories hang together, lending them a teleology, a link to a larger purpose."[130]

Love appears as a key in waking the people out of their abject state, because it reminds the people who they really are; love as the shibboleth for a true French national, versus a false one, someone who hates the nation. As is shown, this link is gendered. Abjection has divirilized and castrated French men, leaving the door open for Muslims to populate their territory. To quote Sarah Ahmed, restoring the nation is, thus, "tied to making love in the choice of an ideal other" (different sex/same race), "who allows the reproduction of the nation as ideal, in the form of the future generation."[131]

This is also how the populist logic of identification in *Riposte Laïque* merges with orientalism, since the processes of construing alterity also inhabit the function of reifying a sense of unity or alikeness. Thus, orientalism is also a mode of identification in a double sense: as a producer of alterity, but also as a producer of alikeness.

Said pointed out this function of Orientalist knowledge production by stating that: "the orient has helped to define Europe (or the West), and as such it is not merely imaginative ... The orient is an integral part of European material civilization."[132] Islam and Muslims function as constitutive outsiders for the production of an imagined Christian and European alikeness.[133] For example, Thomaž Mastnak argues that from the Crusades onwards, this joint production of alterity/alikeness has been informing and shaping European identity: "The construction of the Muslim enemy was an essential moment in the articulation of the self-awareness of the *res publica christiana*. The antagonistic difference between themselves and Muslims became, at this crucial point, a constitutive element of the Latin Christians' collective identity."[134] It is also through this logic that the *Riposte Laïque* articulation of national identity as being one based on *jus solis* and cultural belonging, rather than ethnicity, is muddled, as the publication seems to trace the origin of true Frenchness to the Gauls and whiteness. As Cyrano declares, "just to be clear, we are first of all a European people of the white race, deriving from Greek and Latin culture, and from the Christian religion."[135] Thus, race and soil are central to the articulation of the people as being universally French and universally anti-Muslim, where heterosexual love turns into a tool to overcome abjection, to restore the link between the people and its territory. In the following chapter, I will show by what tactics *Riposte Laïque* aimed to restore this link.

Reconquista or Death

The Exploration of Strategies to Purify the Nation

By September 2017, the time had come for *Riposte Laïque* to celebrate ten years of existence. The celebrations were to take place in the Espace Jean-Monnet, a large conference park located in the small city of Rungis in Val-de-Marne, south of Paris. The conference park is part of a vast commercial area housing one of the world's largest wholegrain food market. It is a convenient place to house meetings of this sort, as it is easily accessible by commuter train (approximately thirty minutes from the center of Paris). Then it is just a ten-minute walk from the station to the conference hall. Sitting on commuter train C, for one last time I read the event program, which promised speeches, social events, and festivities.

At the entrance, security personnel checked my ticket and directed me to the assembly hall. As I was running a bit late, they let me know that "it's already started." In the hall, I was met by the event co-organizers (*Riposte Laïque*'s sibling organization *Résistance Républicaine*, as well as *Souveraineté, Identité et Liberté* (SIEL) and *Synthèse Nationale)*. SIEL is a small political constellation, currently headed by Karim Ouchikh. After its foundation in 2011, SIEL had been a part of the *Rassemblement Bleu Marine* (RBM), a political coalition of far-right micro-parties and groups working for the election of Marine Le Pen as president. SIEL left in 2016. The party president Karim Ouchikh deplored the fact that the FN had diluted their politics, turned too much to the left, and were not interested in having any real allies, merely supporters.[1] Notwithstanding, Ouchikh and SIEL supported Le Pen in the 2017 presidential election.[2] *Synthèse Nationale* is an identitarian and radical nationalist review founded by Roland Hélie, a member of and close to the FN, in 2006. *Synthèse Nationale* has, since 2007, held annual meetings: the ones I visited have all been in Rungis. These meetings gather together various figures from the French radical nationalist milieu, such as the former leader of the FN, Jean-Marie Le Pen; the iconic figure among French skinheads, Serge Ayoub[3]; and the editor-in-chief of the counter-revolutionary weekly *Rivarol,* Jérome Bourbon, known for his anti-Jewish and revisionist statements.[4] As was previously mentioned, not all these actors are in perfect ideological alignment; their relations are muddled by discord and sometimes outright dispute. I've been sitting next to leading figures in *Riposte Laïque* and seen their unease when young skinheads have raised their hands in a Nazi salute during the *Synthèse Nationale*'s annual meeting. Notwithstanding, these are bedfellows of *Riposte Laïque.*

The co-organizers of the anniversary had put up tables displaying information and books for sale. In the hall, approximately 200 people were seated on brown plastic chairs, both men and women properly and very ordinarily dressed. The walls were covered in blue cloth decorated with a couple of large French flags. In front was a large podium; and above, a large screen displaying the program of talks, videos, and images. The day was filled with speeches, presentations, and social events like the Alsatian lunch that consisted of ham, sausages, and wine.

One of the most remarkable and appreciated speeches was made by Tatjana Festerling, former spokesperson of the anti-Muslim movement *Patriotische Europäer gegen die Islamisierung des Abendlandes* (PEGIDA), which had dropped her after her call to shoot Syrian refugees at the European border.[5] During the speech, Festerling declared that a "racist war" against the "white man" was playing out in Europe. Festerling also deplored the guilt that she argued was imposed on the German people and on Europeans in general:

> "We are guilty if we use our cars; guilty if we buy strawberries during the winter; guilty if we leave the lights on during the day; guilty if you, as a man, take a piss standing up; guilty if we earn more money than someone else; guilty if we eat sugar, eat fat or consume tuna; guilty if a glacier in the North Pole melts. All day long, we are told: guilty, guilty, guilty!"

She added: "The cardinal question that each and every one of us should ask is: 'Do I want to live?' 'To be or not to be?' This question has never been as clear as it is today."

Another noteworthy speech, given by Renaud Camus, drew on the idea that France was being colonized by Muslims and North Africans. He rounded off his speech by stating that "the time for democratic solutions is over," which was followed by rousing applause.

During the *Riposte Laïque* meetings and co-organized conferences, there is usually a certain tension in the air. It is a tension created by the audience and the organizers' sense of being among friends, sometimes uneasy, but nonetheless being among friends. It is the sense of being able to speak unhindered and unashamed, freed from the chains of a politically correct hegemony that, according to *Riposte Laïque*, lies like a wet cloth on public debate; of being unashamed to profess one's worldview. And it is the sense of having initiated a movement, of being the avant-garde in the midst of a war between civilizations. As *Riposte Laïque* has declared: "Secularists around the world, unite."

When Pierre Cassen, the main organizer of the event, took to the platform to summarize their ten years of web- and street-based activism, the audience showed its appreciation by cheering and applauding. After twenty minutes or so of speaking about how *Riposte Laïque* came into being and the struggles the journal had fought, Cassen declared that France was facing the end of an apocalyptic war between the people and its foes: the political elite, the privileged class, and the Muslims. The time for retaliation had come: "The collaborators will die. Either at the hands of the Islamists once they are in power, or they will be sentenced in Nuremberg-like trials when the patriots win." After this declaration, he added, "there will now be cake and champagne, and yes, we shouldn't forget to sing." The audience applauded and praised the speech, and then sang the Marseillaise.

This chapter presents the *Riposte Laïque* strategies for retaliation. I show how the logic of populist identification along the horizontal and vertical axes of enmity converges with the category of secularism. Secularism is, as revealed in the earlier chapters, the emblematic identity of the French nation and its people; but it is also a political and social strategy, a revolutionary overthrow of the current political establishment (excluding the FN, of course).

Three minutes to midnight

Given the diagnosis that *Riposte Laïque* makes of the state of France (that France is being colonized, war is being waged against its people, and the Republic has lost its potency), the publication's writers find that it is urgently necessary to act. According to Cyrano, "the French house is on fire"; thus, "it is urgent to gather our people around its ideals."[6] Cyrano declares that "France is finding itself at an historical turning point."[7] While it is important for *Riposte Laïque* to "make the obscurantists [Muslims] understand that the laws of the Republic are superior to Sharia law,"[8] he asserted, addressing the people, that "we need to accelerate to a faster pace, because the Islamist offensive (our most important battle) continues to progress and does so with the scandalous complicity of the majority of the political class, as well as large segments of the feminist and the secular movements that should be standing on the front line of the Resistance."[9] The people need to unite, as "it is time to gather behind the Republic's banner, to pass from individual resistance to a collective retaliation to save this secularism that our history has handed down to us."[10] Cyrano pulls no punches in describing the urgency of the situation: "It is futile to beat around the bush; the survival of France, the nation, the historical conquests, the Republic's historical glories, and above all, gender equality and secularism are at stake, nothing less!"[11] As he puts it: "time is of the essence ... to do nothing is to passively accept the slow suicide of our civilization."[12] All is not lost, however; "France still has the means to save its secular, social, feminist, republican" model and civilization "from the Islamist pest." Cyrano paraphrases Gert Wilders, the leader of the Dutch *Partij voor de Vrijheid* (PVV), known for his many anti-Muslim statements: "It is no longer five minutes to midnight as Gert Wilders said; it is three minutes to midnight."[13]

To *Riposte Laïque*, the doomsday clock is ticking; and to stop it, the people need to unite to put an end to the onslaughts upon France, its people, and secularism.[14] *Riposte Laïque* proclaims that the people, "lulled to sleep by the guilt-inducing and anesthetizing elite," need to wake up, for only then can "the universal values that exist in the West be saved."[15] The time has come to make a choice between "barbarian Islamism or the love of life; it will be one or the other ..."[16] "It will be us or them, the Islamists or the democracy; fascism or freedom."[17] This choice is described as a choice of "cowardice or honor,"[18] and it requires courage: "Will we finally have the courage to defend ourselves against the peril that grows each day, in France and all over Europe, and stop sugarcoating reality, which only plays into the hands of the fascists?"[19]

What, then, is this courage? According to *Riposte Laïque*, "we believe that we are courageous when we protest against this new type of fascism, against the racist scum that terrorize the population and impose their barbaric law ..., when we take on the question of immigration ..., and when we point fingers at the occupation of public space by veils, burqas, mosques, and the halalization of France."[20] Now, even if there are potential allies to the left of the political field, Cyrano explains that "we cannot have a common societal project with those who support the Islamist occupation, even if they say the right things on the distribution of riches and scandalous social inequalities."[21]

Once again, the dividing line between the people and its foes is drawn between those who reject Islam altogether, and those who, according to *Riposte Laïque*, support it. To Cyrano, any political "division" on the matter "is irresponsible."[22] Thus, responsibility lies in the creation of "a patriotic union."[23] The people need to be courageous "to preserve their values," and, in so doing, "they can only count on themselves."[24] The people need to realize their own potential; and to emphasize this, Cyrano incorrectly quotes Étienne de La Boétie, a French sixteenth-century writer and poet: "The tyrants are big only because we are kneeling."[25] *Riposte Laïque* is seemingly convinced that this sort of union would be a truly socialist one, and calls out to the people: "Once again you need to become seculars and republicans, and like Jaurès, become real socialists!"[26] As shown earlier, Jean Jaurès, the early twentieth-century leader of the French Socialist Party, is a key reference used for being a true socialist, republican, and secular patriot.

The call to the people by *Riposte Laïque* runs through a great number of their texts and intensifies with time. In one editorial, *Riposte Laïque* published an image of the French comic *Superdupont*, a caricature of American DC Comics and Marvel heroes like Superman and Captain America.[27] *Superdupont* was first published in 1972. The character *Superdupont* is a male, chauvinistic, patriotic super-hero who wears a black beret, has as his weapon a baguette, consumes only French food, heavily smokes French Gauloise cigarettes, and fights against "anti-France," an international terrorist group that attacks France and such emblematic symbols as wine, cheese, and the Eiffel Tower.[28] In the editorial in *Riposte Laïque*, Superdupont is pointing at the reader while saying in English with a heavy French accent: "Oui nide iou,"[29] as a parody of British and American recruitment posters during the first and second world wars. While Superdupont is a fictional parody of French romantic and radical nationalism, it is somewhat ironic that *Riposte Laïque* make use of a symbol that is a cartoon parody to try to express their own romantic views on nationhood (which appear just as black and white as the reality of the comic itself).

Superdupont was used, without the permission of the comic's creator Marcel Gotlieb, by Jean-Marie Le Pen in the 1980s; and more recently by radical nationalist Alain Soral, infamous for his anti-Jewish statements.[30] The appropriation of Superdupont is also indicative of how radical nationalist voices eclectically pick and mix symbolic figures and historical events. Regardless, *Riposte Laïque* uses Superdupont to call upon the people to urgently unite in the war against Islam. Thus, the categories of urgency and unity, coupled with the category of war, are central to *Riposte Laïque*.

Similar articulations are made by other radical nationalist voices. The whole manifesto of the Identitarian movement is a declaration of war: against Islam, against multiculturalism, against the political elite and the politically correct. In the video "A declaration of war," published in 2012 on the *Génération Identitaire* website and YouTube, and spread widely via social media, members of the movement can read the introduction to the manifesto, which ends with the words: "Do not be mistaken, this text is not a simple manifesto, it is a declaration of war."[31] *Bloc Identitaire's* response to the attacks of January 7, 2015, stated accordingly that: "nobody can pretend to fight against jihadism without putting into question the massive immigration and the Islamization of our countries."[32] In order to fight back, "what we need is not a national union behind the political leaders who have failed us thousands of times, but an awakening that removes them from power."[33]

Unlike *Riposte Laïque* and the Identitarians, Marine Le Pen has been adamant in not projecting all of society's ills onto Islam and Muslims. Thus, when Marine Le Pen responded to the January attacks, she declared that it was necessary to avoid "all conflation of our Muslim compatriots, attached to our nation and its values, with those who believe that they can kill in the name of Islam."[34] Furthermore, she stated that it was a matter of "fundamentalist Islam," of "a terrorist attack committed in the name of radical Islam, a murderous ideology that causes the death of thousands of victims all over the world."[35] Her statement was, moreover, a call for unity: "The nation is united to say that we, French of all origins, do not accept lives and freedoms being attacked."[36] But while she declared it important not to confuse Islam with "fundamentalist" or "radical" Islam, she stated that "the refusal of conflation cannot be an excuse for passivity [*inertie* or inertia] nor denial, which would be the worst favor we could do for the French."[37] Hence, Marine Le Pen announced that, "from now on, France should consider itself at war"; and the enemy was declared to be "fundamentalist Islamism."[38]

While Marine Le Pen has been careful about making the distinction between Islam and radical or fundamentalist Islam, other leading voices in FN have not. For example, one week after the attacks in 2015, the then FN Member of the European Parliament Aymeric Chauprade declared that: "France is at war with Muslims. France is not at war against *the* Muslims, but with Muslims."[39] Contrary to Marine Le Pen, Chauprade argues that "calls against associating ('*pas d'amalgame*' [not amalgamating]) Islam with Islamism are both wrong and dangerous."[40] As an echo of *Riposte Laïque*, Chauprade explained that "a powerful fifth column lives among us, and it can turn its back on us at any time." And he continued: "We are told that a majority of the Muslims are peaceful. Sure, but a majority of the Germans were peaceful before 1933 and the emergence of national-socialism."[41] Chauprade concluded: "In a firm and determined manner, we should take on the fight to de-Islamize our country."[42] This declaration caused Marine Le Pen to publicly distance herself from Chauprade.[43]

When Marine Le Pen stresses the necessity of separating Islam from Islamism, she safeguards herself from accusations of Islamophobia and Muslim racism, while at the same time she repeats what the French political mainstream have been saying for nearly thirty years. Neither Islam nor Muslims are essentially problematic; however, those Muslims who choose not to adhere to the values of the republic *are* (i.e., those wearing headscarves, eating halal, praying publicly, and of course those who take up arms). While Marine Le Pen has declared that "Islam is compatible with the Republic," Islam is still seen as a particularly archaic and pre-modern "religion" in need of "secularization through Enlightenment, as the other religions have already done."[44] Notwithstanding, even if the statements from FN on Islam are ambiguous, the party is united in its view on immigration.

In the 2015 political pamphlet "Migratory explosion: it is urgent to act!" FN states that a supposedly uncontrolled European migration policy is a "threat against the nations who are obliged to accept migrants without discretion"; thus, leaving the door open for "jihadists and criminals that pose as migrants [*s'infiltrent* (to infiltrate)]." The pamphlet's cover page displays the earth as a bomb; a lighter that is labelled "UMP PS" is lighting the fuse, and beneath that lighter is a pile of *cartes de séjour* (residential visas). The image is unambiguous: immigration and current immigration policies are threatening to blow up France and Europe.

A call to arms

According to *Riposte Laïque*, it is of the utmost urgency for the people to unite and reclaim their country. But how are the people to do this, and what logic underlies this unification? First of all, *Riposte Laïque* draws heavily on symbolism from the French Revolution and calls for a popular resistance. Cyrano declares that "the people of France need to prepare themselves for a new 1789."[45] In this vein, *Riposte Laïque* pays great attention to one article from the Declaration of the Rights of Man and Citizen from 1793. Article 35 states: "When the government violates the rights of the people, insurrection is for the people, and for each section of the people, the most sacred of rights and the most indispensable of duties."[46]

The current situation also calls for a proper insurrection. According to Cyrano, the people are ready: "All the signs show that France is in a pre-revolutionary situation; anger is rising everywhere."[47] Cyrano discusses how this anger can be mobilized, and quotes Christine Tasin and her call "to create a republican resistance network," where she stresses that success depends on "winning the battle of ideas" with the goal of "defining our national identity," which she coins as "strongly secular, feminist, democratic, and republican."[48] Cyrano adds that "after thirty years of the totalitarian dictatorship of narrow ideological conformism" (of *la pensée unique* [the unique thought]), the resistance will have to focus on "winning back freedom of speech, expression, and thought."[49] In many articles, *Riposte Laïque* writers ponder upon "all the possible initiatives that will allow for the construction of this secular, feminist, and republican resistance."[50] The journal concludes that it first will be necessary to concentrate the work in France, as "we cannot wait for the answer to come from anywhere else."[51] The activities at *Riposte Laïque*, its articles, books, debates, demonstrations, conferences, support for the people, patriotic eating and drinking, and sticker campaigns, are inscribed with this rationale. Thus, the journal states that, "with its modest resources, *Riposte Laïque* ... patiently constructs the conditions for a new secular and republican resistance that alone will allow our country to take the necessary leap to preserve our values."[52]

While symbolism from the French Revolution is central to how the *Riposte Laïque* writers articulate their resistance, symbolism from the Resistance Movement of the 1940s is also used in abundance: "With modesty, we reclaim the heritage of the resistance spirit of the 1940s."[53] The presentation of one initiative by Christine Tasin and *Résistance Républicaine* is noteworthy. In 2012, Tasin launched a radio show for the resistance fighters. In a drawing, she is sitting in a simple radio studio wearing headphones with a French flag as the backdrop. She is saying: "This is France. The resistant fighters are talking to the French people."[54] The imagery of the initiative alludes to Charles de Gaulle's call to resistance against the Nazi Regime that was broadcast by the BBC, given on June 18, 1940.

Another example concerns *Riposte Laïque* and *Résistance Républicaine*'s *Marche contre l'islamization fasciste* (the march against fascist Islamization), at the Place de la Concorde in Paris, on November 10, 2012. The march drew inspiration from a student demonstration in 1940: "November 11, 1940, young Parisian students managed to organize the first resistance demonstration against the Nazi occupation. Let us be inspired by their example, 72 years later."[55] As discussed earlier, by employing the category of war, *Riposte Laïque* further emphasizes the need for unity among the French: "new alliances that transcend the obsolete left-right divide need to be achieved."[56] *Riposte Laïque* and its peers are, according to themselves, the avant-garde of this alliance: "The Muslim extremists have declared war against us, we have to win it," and "as in all wars, there are resistance fighters who instantly rise to the task."[57] "Our model is a model of resistance," Cyrano declares and continues, "we are the children of an historical period when the French, no matter what tradition (Gaullist, communist, Christian, or atheist) united to defend their country against the Nazi invader."[58] As Cyrano states, the big difference from 1940 is, of course, that it is "the Islamists and their allies" who are invading France; "one needs to be deaf or blind to not realize this."[59]

Riposte Laïque resumes its call to the people in a "virile" style: "Are you ready to fight for your ideas? Time is of the essence, because demography does not wait!!! Gauls, fight or suffer in silence! Do you exist, yes or no?! Hurry up and think … history does not give second chances!"[60] In one image, *Riposte Laïque* paints a picture of mass resistance.[61] The French people stand united, holding French flags. The image reads: "Popular revolution against the Islamization of France." The people cry out: "We want to stay free! No veils, no mosques, no halal! No Sharia in France!"

Riposte Laïque described the emergence of a popular resistance movement working to change ideas and win back rights that had been taken away. In terms of changing ideas, the *Riposte Laïque* strategy echoes Alain de Benoist, and the long-term meta-political strategies of *La nouvelle droite* and the FN, to come to power through a hegemonic change (through FN's strategy of normalization and *lepenization* of politics) in the perception of reality among the general population in France (as discussed in Chapter 1). Regardless of actual cases brought against *Riposte Laïque*, which have seen the authors of their articles convicted of defamatory speech and incitement to racial discrimination, the publication continues to operate, as does its web-based peers. While French laws on freedom of expression are indeed restrictive in terms of racism, public slander and defamation, incitement and justification of terrorism, and denials of crimes against humanity,[62] it is unclear whether *Riposte Laïque* wants to change these laws; however, what the publication mostly targets is political correctness. Thus, when *Riposte Laïque* claims to win back freedom of expression, what the journal targets is its ideological foes; those who classify the journal as fascist, racist, and extreme right. This apparently disturbs *Riposte Laïque*, because these labels could create a negative connotation in the minds of the general population, and appear to shame *Riposte Laïque*. Getting rid of political correctness would allow *Riposte Laïque* to be unashamed of its statements. As discussed earlier, one strategy that the publication employs to circumvent this classification is to project these categories onto Muslims, the political elite, and the privileged class. In so doing, *Riposte Laïque* can logically portray their writers and followers as the real heirs of the Revolution, socialism, secularism, and the Resistance movement.

This frontal assault on political correctness is also practiced by the FN and Marine Le Pen. The clearest case is the many outbursts from Marine Le Pen against those who classify the party as extreme right. For example, in 2013 she declared: "we are absolutely not a right-wing party; thinking so is a total analytical error." Moreover, she stated that "I am even more concerned by the usage of the term 'extreme right.'"[63] Additionally, Marine Le Pen made clear that she would "take judicial action" if the party were to be associated with pejorative terms like racism in opinion polls.[64]

While the intertextual and interdiscursive links between *Riposte Laïque* and FN are many, theorization by *Riposte Laïque* of how to take immediate action to restore the nation fits badly within FN's normalization strategy. In 2010, the publication started to question how far they could reach by merely changing the minds of the people or by the ballot. Wrongfully attributing a quote to the nineteenth-century anarchist Mikhail Bakunin, Cyrano stated: "Do not forget this phrase: 'If elections could change lives, they would be illegal.'"[65] Cyrano asked: "Can we fight back the Islamist offensive by solely democratic measures?"[66] Drawing on the acclaimed revolutionary heritage, he turns to the national hymn to discuss a proper response, paying particular attention to the refrain: "To arms, citizens, form your battalions, let's march, let's march! Lest an impure blood soak our fields!"[67]

According to Cyrano, the first armed defense against an Islamic onslaught in France and the unjust political system should be with both the police and the army: "Do we have to state the obvious: the police, but also the army are the ultimate protection against this war that has been declared on our own territory."[68] For the police and the army to take action, however, the political elite needs to say so. According to *Riposte Laïque*, it refuses: "We were awaiting a clear address that would give clear instructions to the security forces [*forces de l'ordre* (forces of order)]: 'When you feel that you are threatened, or if you are being shot at, you have the right to shoot to defend yourselves and the properties of the local population.'"[69]

With an impotent political elite that refuses to give the police and the army instructions to safeguard the nation, "and when so many Muslims (not all of them, of course) are walking around armed in their neighborhoods, often concealing knives with blades that are twenty centimeters long … it is time for the government to facilitate the arming of our compatriots, whose lives are threatened daily, in certain areas."[70]

The same problem arises here: A government that is complicit in the Islamic onslaught needs to take action. While waiting for the government to act, *Riposte Laïque* states that patriotic citizens should "organize by joining patriotic groups or parties that are ready to take political action or take to the streets [the specific wording was *terrain* or territory]."[71] While doing so, "we can only encourage our compatriots to the utmost vigilance, to look over their shoulders when walking the streets, to avoid unnecessary crossing of paths with groups or threatening 'lone wolves.'"[72]

Riposte Laïque refers to Gandhi and his "civil disobedience," an inspirational source for the resistance, with this curious addition: "Of course, our disobedience will not be civil."[73] Gandhian non-civil disobedience is, in fact, described by *Riposte Laïque* as being a rather violent one. Patriotic citizens are encouraged "to start visiting shooting clubs; and in full legality, have a weapon at their disposal, and join a martial arts club."[74] While *Riposte Laïque* explicitly flirts with the idea of creating a paramilitary resistance movement here, it has not been theorized further during the period analyzed for this book. Regardless, during its years of publication, the journal has suggested that actions turn more and more violent. The journal wants to promote a key icon for the resistance against Islam in France: Charles Martel, the military commander who allegedly fought back a Muslim invasion at the Battle of Poitiers in 732, and to replace the bland "*Je suis Charlie*" with the identitarian "*Je suis Charles Martel*."[75]

Islamectomy

Riposte Laïque theorizes a strategy for hegemony of ideation, political and social organization; and as a last resort, arming the people to restore order. How does this turn into a program for social and political change, and what would a future France, rid of Islam, be like? *Islamectomie!*, a book written by Yidir Aberkane and Carole Maillac, published by *Riposte Laïque* in 2013, proposes a general concept of the publication's program. Cyrano explains that the term "*islamectomie*" refers to "a surgical removal of Islam from European and French bodies."[76]

If their strategy is coined in medical terms, it also draws on European history, with references to the Spanish *Reconquista*. In articles in *Riposte Laïque*, the *Reconquista* refers to the defeat of the last Moorish ruler of the Emirate of Granada, Mohammed XII, in 1492; and the conquest of the Iberian Peninsula by the Catholic monarchs Queen Isabella I of Castile and Ferdinand II of Aragon, to form Spain. After a treaty was signed between the parties, granting rights to the Moorish minorities, these new rulers of Iberia soon imposed a choice upon them: conversion to Catholicism or expatriation. The seminal reference of what a modern *Reconquista* would be like is found in the book *Reconquista ou Mort de l'Europe* (*Reconquista* or the Death of Europe) by René Marchand, who is the alleged specialist on Islam at *Riposte Laïque*. The book was published by *Riposte Laïque* in 2013. Marchand draws eclectically and selectively on European and Islamic history, mixing it with orientalist fantasies and radical nationalist discourse to make his case. He concludes that "the presence of millions of Muslims in Europe, who are, with total ease, waging a war of invasion through demography and *takkiya*, with the passive complicity of the people they target, is a totally absurd fact that cannot be allowed to continue."[77]

The last chapter captures what the *Reconquista* was all about: "The eradication of Islam in Europe."[78] Now, according to *Riposte Laïque*, "the *Reconquista* starts with a display of force; this display will also be measured on the streets."[79] Cyrano continues, "Islam and its fifth column need to be attacked head on, if we are to preserve the lives of the majority of our compatriots."[80] Supposedly, "things are getting more and more clear; if France does not eradicate Islam, it will become Muslim."[81] The measures to be taken need no limit, in the eyes of *Riposte Laïque*. Cyrano refers to Christine Tasin's statement, that if Muslims were to rise up against such an eradication, it might "be necessary for the army to open fire and shoot into the crowd [*tirer dans le tas*], to preserve France and its values."[82] Before reaching what is articulated as an unwanted but potentially necessary execution of Muslims, however, *Riposte Laïque* proposes a number of social and political policy measures, and declares that "we have resolutely decided to fight" for the construction of "a new answer to make secularism progress."[83] First of all, *Riposte Laïque* advocates "the strict and full application of the Law of 1905," which "is an insurmountable barrier that we need to maintain, to assure the values of Liberty, Equality, and Brotherhood."[84] To achieve this end goal, *Riposte Laïque* calls upon the installation of a "strong government" in the service of the French people, "that will reinstate our republican and secular principles; and in so doing, declare war against Islam."[85] The strategy of secular *Reconquista* is described by *Riposte Laïque* as a measure of "public hygiene [*salubrité publique*]."[86] Cyrano argues that the most important measure to sanitize France is to stop immigration, stating that "without any doubt, we call for a moratorium on immigration."[87] Immigration from Muslim and North African countries should "immediately" be stopped, but also from "all countries."[88] Assimilation, whereby the newly arrived completely adopt French culture and values, should be the new norm; however, Cyrano believes that "in the current context, a peaceful cohabitation between the newly arrived, of which many are Muslim, and the people of France is impossible."[89]

Cyrano also refers to media pundit Michel Onfrey's writings, suggesting that "France and Europe will fall under Muslim domination within two generations"[90]; and concludes that "the only thing to be done [to] push back this cancer … is to deport all those Muslims in France and in Europe who [would] prefer Sharia to the laws of man,"[91] and call upon European governments to "arrest and deport all those Muslims who refuse to denounce Sharia."[92] As *Riposte Laïque* argues that there are no moderate Muslims, and that Islam is Islamism in disguise, this logically implies the deportation of all Muslims from France. In a pragmatic tone, Cyrano stated that the Muslims would be "better off, and so would we"[93]; "hence," he proclaimed, "with determination but without hate, I no longer want to see the disciples of Allah on our territory."[94]

Along with the moratorium on immigration and deportation, *Riposte Laïque* wants to ban "everything that looks like propaganda."[95] This translates to the banning of "Muslim books which contain calls to murder or violence against women"; and that "preaching in Arabic should be forbidden."[96] *Riposte Laïque* adds that "Sharia should be denounced as the fascism it is, and should be banned in the Free World"[97]; and that "it is necessary to declare that the Koran is incompatible with the values of the Republic."[98]

A third measure is to prohibit any type of financial transaction that might benefit Islam and Muslims.[99] *Riposte Laïque* wants to "stop all sorts of financing of anti-racist organizations and the HALDE [the French anti-discrimination bureau]."[100] A fourth suggested measure is to "declare Muslim food (halal) illegal," especially as it indirectly "finances Islam."[101] A fifth suggested measure is to prohibit any public visibility of Islam. Accordingly, "the streets of our country should be cleansed of Muslims who illegally pray every Friday," and "the construction of minarets should be forbidden," as should "the construction of mosques financed with public funds or foreign money."[102] This would also mean "the prohibition, on our streets, of any display that could be considered as [part of the] uniforms of war, like the headscarf, the *kami* or the *djellaba*"; and the "immediate expulsion for those who wear them."[103]

A sixth measure concerns the cultural and traditional identification with Islam, for example: "it should be prohibited to give a non-Western name to a child born in France," as should observing "Ramadan during working hours."[104] Finally, *Riposte Laïque* wishes for the "immediate suspension all political activities by Islam on our territory"; arguing that: "If we are in a period of war, it would be suicidal to let the dogma of the enemy, with a fifth column at its disposal on our territory, to plan the destruction of our country through the execution of the majority of our compatriots, carried out by 'destabilized individuals with knives' or 'reckless drivers'."[105] *Riposte Laïque* concludes: "this thus signifies the dissolution of all Muslim associations, the shutting down [of] all mosques, the closure of all communitarian butcheries, the end of halal slaughter."[106]

As was discussed earlier, virtually any conduct or identification having the potential to be linked with Islam and Muslims is seen as an assault on France. Moreover, *Riposte Laïque* proposes two measures that would safeguard the French from Islamic propaganda and counter discrimination that it perceives is happening against the French white population. First, *Riposte Laïque* urges the necessity "as soon as possible to teach the French the real history of Islam and its fourteen centuries of warfare against the rest of the world."[107] Second, *Riposte Laïque* "naturally" proposes that the services provided by the welfare state "be reserved for only those French who live up to that name."[108] This measure is a direct import of one of Jean-Marie Le Pen and FN's long-term policy plans, *la preference nationale* [the national preference], by which French citizens would be favored over non-French residents in terms of employment, trade, welfare access, and housing.[109] Marine Le Pen semantically polished the policy by replacing "preference" with "priority," which she wanted as a constitutional principle, as well.[110]

The cleansing of France from Islam is depicted by *Riposte Laïque* in a number of images and caricatures. In one, the publication uses a comic-strip from the Belgian cartoon *Tintin*, where one of the main characters, Dupont, violently kicks a praying Muslim man in the behind.[111] In a drawing; Cassen, Tasin, and Hilout are depicted giving a "word of caution": "No Islam in France, nor in Europe."[112] Cyrano appears to concede that these measures might seem extreme to some, and states sarcastically: "I understand that my pathological and paranoid worries can offend leftist sociologists, adherents of multiculturalism and of cohabitation [*le vivre ensemble*]"[113]; however, "to win this war, it is necessary to eliminate Islam in France."[114] In revolutionary phrasing, he concludes: "*Reconquista* or the death of France, there can be no third way."[115]

If purifying the nation through "islamectomy" and measures of "public hygiene" is seen as vital, *Riposte Laïque* declares that it is also "becoming vital, as soon as possible, to get rid of this harmful clique of Francophobes."[116] The mention of a "Francophobic clique" refers to the political elite and privileged class. As shown earlier, they are held responsible for allowing the Islamic onslaught to happen in the first place. They are also held responsible for the many attacks committed by self-proclaimed jihadi freedom fighters in France; and they are killing France. *Riposte Laïque* is particularly furious about the Hollande administration, which it refers to as "dirty leftards [*socialaud(s)*]" and "murderers."[117] To settle the score with the leftards and the "rotten" justice system, Cyrano agitates: "Dirty leftard, you will pay the price for treason, and so will your friends!"[118] He adds: "The people will have your skin!"[119] Thus,

Cyrano explains, just as after the fall of Nazi Germany, justice will be restored: "Once these indispensable expulsions have been effectuated, I really dream of a Nuremberg [trial]" with the "principal collaborators" and "all these traitors that deliver France to globalization, immigration, and Islam."[120] The harshest sentence in the Nuremberg Trials of 1945 was execution by hanging.

In one cartoon, *Riposte Laïque* depicts the Hollande administration, among them Manuel Valls and Christine Tabira, heading towards their judgment.[121] They are dressed in black and yellow prison suits with ball and chain, reminiscent of how the Dalton Brothers in the comic *Lucky Luke* usually end up, wearing signs saying "traitor"; however, execution by hanging is not the only way to wreak vengeance on the political elite. *Riposte Laïque* agrees with René Marchand, who quotes socialist Georges Clemenceau, prime minister and Minister of War at the end of the First World War, who allegedly declared: "'twelve bullets in the skin for treason [*12 balles dans la peau*]!" To those who said that he exaggerated, he answered: "For the half-traitors, six bullets would be enough."[122] *Riposte Laïque* repeats Clemenceau's call to shoot traitors; and the article is coupled with an image of François Hollande being arrested by the police.[123] Cyrano adds, "as Christine Tasin says, the sort of statements that we repeat are only rhetorical, as there is no war being waged on French territory; because if that were the case, the media would surely have informed us!"[124] This statement has an ironic deniability: *Riposte Laïque* seems well aware that calling for the assassination of the President of the Republic is punishable by law; hence, by referring to these sorts of statements as "historical artifacts" that are only valid "if" war was to be waged in France, the journal is merely painting a fictional scenario. As the overarching mission of *Riposte Laïque* is, however, to prove that an actual war against France *is* being waged, as is stated in the large majority of their publications, they continuously preempt any deniability (as when they ask rhetorically whether to euthanize Jacques Attali, and answer: "Not before judging him!"[125])

So the secular *Reconquista*, as per *Riposte Laïque*, consists of deporting or killing Muslims, banning Islam, and convicting and/or executing the political elite and the privileged class: "Only then will France once again become France."[126]

What would this brave New France look like? In one visionary article, Cyrano contemplates on a future without Islam.[127] The article is a long list of proclamations, starting with the introductory statement "Without Islam …," which is followed by another statement describing how France would be radically different. Cyrano begins the article by "confessing" that "it has been a long time since I wrote an article of this kind, so ... I started working on it with the help of my friends on the editorial board, and here is the result." He suggests that "without Islam" there would be no need for a popular resistance: "*Riposte Laïque* would never have existed"; "we would not have to share Michel Onfray's anguish that France will be under total Muslim domination within fifty years; "without Islam, our children would not be confronted with the terrible choice of becoming resistance fighters or dhimmis." Without Islam, the political situation would have been different, the socialists would never have come to power, and political correctness would be nonexistent: "France would not have had to suffer through Hollande, elected thanks to 93 percent of the Muslims"; "we would not have to see this pathetic spectacle where the collaborating politicians prostitute themselves to receive the votes of Allah's disciples"; and *Riposte Laïque* and their acclaimed allies "would never have been dragged as criminals to court by political and anti-racist commissaries, nor by Muslims who dream of imposing Sharia in France." French history would have been altogether different: "there would not have been a war in Algeria, as France would not have had any reason to intervene in the region in 1830, to put an end to the Barbary States"[128]; thus, "North African countries would not be that bad to live in and they would not send us as many young offenders and criminals."

Without Islam, the French people would no longer be blamed for their mere existence and the country's colonial history; "beloved memories would remain gently melancholic and would not have become burning regrets of nostalgia and resentment." Cyrano believes that "without Islam" the Eurabia theory and the theory of the great replacement would not exist: "Qatar would not be on its way to buying entire parts of France"; "we would not be witnessing the workings of the politics of the great replacement and the resulting changes to the population and civilization"; and "we would no longer have the impression of having changed continents when we enter certain neighborhoods."

Without Islam, the welfare state and the health of the population would be better, as Muslims could no longer "ransack" the system; "there would be fewer beneficiaries of health care"[129]; and "we could concentrate more money on the sick and the retired, without forgetting those useful aids that help improve society." In hospitals, "doctors and nurses would not be insulted nor beaten by retarded bearded men who refuse to have their women treated or helped to give birth."

Cyrano also suggests that, without Islam, "the barbaric death" caused to animals by halal slaughter would not exist in France, meaning that "our children would no longer be in danger of the *E. coli* bacillus when they unknowingly eat halal." French society would, according to Cyrano, see a tremendous change in terms of violence and sexism: "we would no longer witness an increase in homophobic, antisemitic, and sexual assaults that are encouraged by the Koran's sacred texts and by Muhammed's life"; "there would not be thousands of assaults and two hundred rapes a day in France"; "we would no longer have video clips of aggressive, sexist, and racist rappers"; "web-sites would no longer be polluted by hateful and threatening messages, with death threats directed against us"; "Mohammed Merah would not have assassinated three military personnel and Jews, of which some were children"[130]; "thousands of psychopaths would never have gone to Iraq and Syria to learn how to a wage a holy war against us and to kill us upon their return"; "fewer knife stabbings to the neck would be reported in the news"; "police officers would no longer suffer from a daily war that aims to undermine the very structure of the French state"; and "without Islam, there would be more room in our prisons."

Cyrano declares that, without Islam, French men would no longer be restrained from approaching "born-Muslim women" and the women of France would no longer have to fear sexual harassment and violence: "Without Islam, we would not be assaulted on the street by headscarves that insult women's freedoms [*la condition des femmes*], that display their being reserved for Muslims only"; "and in so doing, disqualify those men suspected of not being able to control themselves." Above all, such headscarves are a sexist symbol, "incompatible with our values"; "in France, women and girls need only deal with a type of more or less chivalrous banter, when out and about."

Without Islam, France would allegedly be a magnificent and harmonious country: "there would no longer be a fascist danger in France, and we would enjoy the full charm of a formidable country"; "France would still be the country of freedom of expression"; "critique of religion would not be confused with racism"; and "nobody would contest Christmas trees in public spaces, nor the presence of Jesus' crib in city halls"; "France would be populated only by citizens who are believers, agnostics, or atheists who would know how to put their particularities aside; and to unite around their common traits in the name of a secular, social, and democratic Republic." The people "could savor the sweetness, the delicious carefreeness, and the light frivolity that life often offers." In sum, "when France finally gets rid of Islam, France will once again become a formidable country."

It should come as no surprise that the professed methods of *Riposte Laïque* of cleansing the Republic and its territory from unwanted elements have several interdiscursive and intertextual links with other radical nationalist groups and movements. One of the emblematic strategies for *Bloc Identitaire,* for example, is "remigration." According to *Riposte Laïque*, when *Bloc Identitaire* participates in street-based activism, they "bring their dynamism" by placing "remigration at the heart of their slogans."[131]

One of the identitarian movement's more mediatized actions in terms of remigration is the initiative called "Defend Europe," launched in 2017.[132] The stated goal of the mission was to "prepare a large-scale rescue mission in the Mediterranean, a mission to save Europe from illegal immigration."[133] With the boat *C-Star*, there were French and other European identitarians who set out to stop refugees from using the sea as a rescue route. Time will tell how the identitarians spin the success of the mission; however, at the time of writing, it had faced many difficulties and the longevity of the mission was uncertain.[134] In terms of anti-Muslim activism, in 2012 *Bloc Identitaire* drew the attention of major national and international news outlets, when seventy-three activists occupied the roof of a mosque in Poitiers, the iconic site of the Battle of Poitiers in the year 732, under the slogan: "We are here on the mosque in Poitiers, 1,300 years after the historic battle, to say the same thing as they did then. We will not retreat."[135]

Marine Le Pen and the FN are far more contained in their rhetoric than *Riposte Laïque* and the identitarians; and as stated earlier, their politics of secularism leans more towards the French political mainstream in some specific points. First of all, when Marine Le Pen declared war on radical Islam, she was no different from Manuel Valls, who after the January attacks in 2015, declared: "Yes, France is at war against terrorism, jihadism, and radical Islamism. France is not at war against Islam and the Muslims."[136]

Second, by stressing that Islam is compatible with the Republic, Le Pen states that Islam and Muslims have a place in France. This recalls the long debates by the political mainstream regarding the construction of an Islam of France, instead of an Islam in France, as is discussed elsewhere (see Chapter 1); however, secularism is almost exclusively mentioned in relation to Islam and national identity.[137] In the FN's presidential program for 2017, specific policies regarding secularism come under the section "A Proud France" and the headline "Defend the unity of France and its national identity."[138] Here, secularism is articulated as a tool to "fight against communitarianism." A first step in this fight is to add to the issue that "the Republic does not recognize any sub-national community."[139] What this means in detail is left out of the program; but, given that communitarianism is continuously articulated in relation to Islam and poor working-class suburban areas, the underlying sense of the proposition is to fight against the alleged Islamic enclaves that exist in France.[140]

As Le Pen argued during the presidential campaign, accepting communitarianism is to accept multiculturalism. According to her, "a multicultural society is a multi-conflicted society."[141] In the fight against radical Islamism, Marine Le Pen's suggested policies are similar to those of *Riposte*

Laïque, except that *Riposte Laïque* talks about Islam and Muslims in general. The suggestions found in her program are the "eradication of terrorism and the destruction of Islamist networks."[142] This involves forbidding and dissolving "every organization linked to fundamentalist Islamism," and the "expulsion of every foreigner with a link to Islamist fundamentalism." It also implies the "closure of 'every extremist mosque'" and "the prohibition of every type of public financing of places of worship [*lieux de culte*] and religious activities." In the mosques that would remain, any language other than French would be prohibited.[143] Moreover, Marine Le Pen has been particularly clear on one point. During the campaign, she criticized the Hollande administration's policies of deradicalization,[144] that is, measures to prevent jihadism that seemed too permissive and ineffective, as if it were trying deradicalize terrorists "by caressing them, as if they were hamsters, or by reading them articles from the Declaration of the Rights of Man and Citizen. They are indoctrinated. They are dangerous."[145]

Thus, in the program, Marine Le Pen suggests deportations and preventive detentions of anyone with a link to jihadist organizations, or any foreign organization that is hostile toward France and the French. This would be accomplished by the creation of a special anti-terrorist agency, "with extended interior and exterior surveillance measures," which would answer directly to the prime minister.[146]

Even if *Riposte Laïque* and the FN differ in their announced strategies to enforce secularism (to cleanse the nation from Islam in the case of *Riposte Laïque*, or to fight back against radical or fundamentalist Islam, in the case of the FN), they converge in how their measures build on an essential, depoliticizing logic. The enemy and the ills they have brought on are seen as the result of universal cultural, religious, and ethnic features; where the only measures logically available to deal with these alleged ills are repressive ones.[147] Following this logic, when repression cannot come to terms with the disturbing essential traits of the enemy (essential traits that are bound to a physical body), then eradication of the enemy emerges as the logical next step.

A universalist vocation?

In this chapter I sought to show how *Riposte Laïque* articulates itself and its allies as an organic response, as the national immune system, with the aim of curing and purifying the national body from a disease: the "Islamic pest" and the "Islamic cancer."

In the journal's articulation of a response to the alleged Islamic onslaught, its articulation of alterity and enmity being along the two axes of populist identification, coupled with its own construction of the people of France, comes full circle. *Riposte Laïque* surely portrays itself and its allies as a particularly efficient cure, as all the ills of society could be resolved. The *Riposte Laïque* vision of a France without Islam is a France where the people have been resurrected from their abject state of paralysis; and it is a France where the people can rejoice in national autophilic romanticism; it is a vision where France is the beacon of secularism and universalism. Thus, *Riposte Laïque* is not merely on a mission to restore the nation; it is answering a simultaneous universalist and particularly nationalist calling, of rerouting France and its people onto their historical path. As such, the eclectic and selective reading of history by *Riposte Laïque* turns into a resource for mobilization and action, in the quest to resurrect the people and purify the nation.

Universalist vocations of this sort have been, and still are, embedded with fantasies about alterity and reifications of the imagined glory and greatness of the French Republic. During the Revolution, concepts about national purity, race, and belonging were central to the formation of the French Republic.[148] Various forms of exclusionary techniques were employed; where, for example, foreigners had to wear physical markers displaying their place of birth, and were prohibited from politically representing the French people.[149] Universal rights and citizenship were not equally distributed; as Sophie Wahnich explains: "it was in the name and defense of the Enlightenment that populations suspected of not being able to be culturalized into its ideals were excluded."[150]

Enlightenment values were also used as a core foundation in the French colonial endeavors. The *mission civilisatrice* (civilizing mission) was a doctrine by which France took on the self-proclaimed burden of civilizing the colonies. The colonial inhabitants were to be given the universal gift of reason and civilization.[151] For example, Elisa Camiscioli showed "how race and reproduction were critical to the construction of French national identity, and how gender intervened in fabricating racial hierarchies, which cast white Europeans alone as assimilable."[152]

During the twentieth century, universalist discourses were employed to sort out the "other," either as a potentially redeemable body worthy of integration through the grace of universal values, or as a body deemed incapable of being culturalized into the universal, and thus French, national body.[153] This universalist self-understanding has led many French public spokespeople to assert that racist politics in France are anomalies in the teleological fulfillment and embodiment of universalism in the Republic.[154] Although this is changing somewhat, the great taboos of French history (the colonial past, the Dreyfus Affair, and the Vichy Regime) have no real place in French history; however, to quote Camiscioli, racialization and gendering of national borders have been "familiar features of the Republican landscape, not aberrant ideologies which could only garner popular, institutional, and state support under Nazi occupation and Pétain's dictatorship."[155] For example, the anti-Jewish discourse in France during the late twentieth and beginning of the twenty-first centuries "could not have taken root as a political current, were it not for the constant hammering of Jews as a 'problem' in all the press," as Gérard Noiriel points out.[156]

In today's France, Noiriel's statement has bearing on the constant hammering of the Muslim "problem" in all the major news channels in France. As Abdellali Hajjat and Marwan Mohammed point out, "the number of anti-Muslim statements in France are far beyond counting; [they are] made by journalists, politicians, academics, public intellectuals, etc."[157] This is not to suggest that anti-Jewish or anti-Muslim discourse are the same, or monolithic discourses; they change over time and vary in relation to the various contexts in which they emerge and are employed.[158] What I suggest is that this universalist logic is intrinsically interwoven with the discourse on alterity. This is manifested in the concept of the French ideal citizen as being abstract, a citizen whose particularistic traits are confined to the private sphere, or simply erased. As Camiscioli points out, "the embodied person cannot function as the abstract individual of Republican universalism, because that person is infused with her or his particularist identity (whether gender, race, class, religion, or ethnicity) and is, therefore, informed by the distinctive experiences said to emanate from these subject-positions."[159]

Today, the dominant discourses on secularism articulate secularism as being a type of double-sided emblem: on the one hand, as the path to Enlightenment for the embodied uncivilized other; on the other hand, as a reification of the abstract and universal grandeur of its enunciators. In this sense, the dominant discourses on secularism should be understood as being sites for the production of the very alterity that it seeks to integrate.[160] Through the policy of national preference and priority, FN has turned this logic, by which the acclaimed universality of republican laws and rights are selectively distributed, into a foundation of the FN party's program. As Marine Le Pen explained in an interview in the weekly journal *La Croix*, in 2017:

> "The universality of these rights concerns the French. Basically, the principle means that they should not be treated differently based on their sex, origin, convictions, or sexual orientation. But there is nothing that prohibits the

creation of different situations ... if one is not a citizen. I cannot see that it would
be illegal nor immoral to prioritize the French in their own country."[161]

As discussed, *Riposte Laïque* takes this logic to an extreme, by turning the national
preference into a foundational part of the publication's proposed measures for
public hygiene. To *Riposte Laïque*, the ideal type of a French citizen is described
as patriotic, Gallic, white, and secular; any other type of citizen and non-citizen
should be eradicated from the Republican territory, to safeguard the prosperity of
the nation and the demographic continuity of the French people. The proposed
measures for this range from democratic measures, such as opinion-forming and
voting, to state-organized military invention, extra-legal war tribunes, and an armed
non-democratic resistance. Considering the intertextual and inter-discursive links
with French neo-fascism of the 1960s and 1970s, and the contemporary forms of
radical and revolutionary nationalism, this gives rise to the question of whether or
not the proposals given by *Riposte Laïque* should be considered fascist.

The answer to that question is surely dependent on what is considered fascist
or fascism. This is not the place to recount the long scholarly debate on what
fascism is, or could be, but I will start from Robert Paxton's definition of fascism
as a "form of political behavior" marked by a bundle of "mobilizing passions."[162]
These passions are:

(a) "a sense of overwhelming crisis beyond the reach of any traditional
solutions";
(b) "the primacy of the group, toward which one has duties superior to every
right, whether individual or universal, and the subordination of the individual to it";
(c) "the belief that one's group is a victim, a sentiment that justifies any action,
without legal or moral limits, against its enemies, both internal and external";
(d) "dread of the group's decline under the corrosive effects of individualistic
liberalism, class conflict, and alien influences";
(e) "the need for closer integration of a purer community, by consent if possible, or by exclusionary violence if necessary";
(f) "the need for authority by natural chiefs (always male), culminating in a
national chieftain who alone is capable of incarnating the group's historical
destiny";
(g) "the superiority of the leader's instincts over abstract and universal reason";
(h) "the beauty of violence and the efficacy of will, when they are devoted to
the group's success";

(i) "the right of the chosen people to dominate others, without restraint from any kind of human or divine law, right being decided by the sole criterion of the group's prowess within a Darwinian struggle."[163]

The diagnosis by *Riposte Laïque* of society and solutions for public hygiene do fit Paxton's list of mobilizing passions, that is, the sense of a crisis that demands a response beyond what the democratic order allows; the victimization of the people as the justification for measures to eradicate the people's enemies; the stressed importance to strengthen national identity and the right of the people to dominate other groups; and lastly, the framing of the people's struggle along assumed universal ethnic, cultural, and religious boundaries.

Love and hate should also be added to the list of mobilizing passions; however, the acclaimed republican, democratic, and socialist legacy leads *Riposte Laïque* to stress the importance of public sovereignty, universal reason, and the importance of having representative electives, and not one superior leader. The statements on redemptive violence are articulated by *Riposte Laïque* in terms of unwanted necessity; and, when taken to the extreme, execution should be the result of judicial processes. Thus, by referencing Paxton, central features in the populist discourses by *Riposte Laïque* on secularism and nationhood can be classified as fascist; but some core elements are missing in order to classify them as outright fascist.

A similar conclusion emerges from Roger Griffin's generic definition of fascism as "palingenetic ultra-nationalism," which builds on "the myth that the organically conceived nation is to be cleansed of decadence and comprehensively renewed."[164] According to Griffin, fascism is, accordingly, "an ideologically driven attempt by a movement or regime to create a new type of post-liberal national community that will be the vehicle for the comprehensive transformation of political, social and aesthetic culture; with the effect of creating an alternative modernity."[165] What is missing from the *Riposte Laïque* populist discourses on secularism and nationhood is the will to replace the current republican and liberal democratic national community. As Griffin argues, here referring to "the radical right," the most emblematic development during the latter half of the twentieth century "occurred outside the parameters of fascism."[166] Instead of fascism, Griffin suggests that the contemporary radical right (parties and movements that I refer to as being radical nationalist) is marked by "ethnocratic liberalism."[167]

While ethnocratic liberalism might draw on fascist discourse, as is the case with *Riposte Laïque*, it "is not technically a form of fascism, even a disguised form of it, for it [this ethnocratic liberalism] lacks the core palingenetic vision of a 'new order' [that would] totally replace the liberal system. Rather [instead], it enthusiastically embraces the liberal system, [yet] considers only one ethnic group as [being] full members of civil society."[168] The vision of society held by *Riposte Laïque* can, henceforth, be seen as an ethnocratic form of a popular republican and liberal democracy, underpinned by a strong sense of national romanticism.

A rough but instructive way to conceptualize the dividing line between *Riposte Laïque* and dominant articulations of secularism, including official policies at FN, is by the analytical categories *anthropophagy* and *anthropoemy*. As Sigmund Bauman states, these are central strategies in how the modern nation-states deal with strangers. The anthropophagic strategy, which relates to dominant articulations to secularism, means "annihilating the strangers by devouring them and then metabolically transforming into a tissue indistinguishable from one's own"; that is, "the strategy of assimilation: making the different similar; [a] smothering of cultural or linguistic distinctions; [a] forbidding [of] all traditions and loyalties except those meant to feed the conformity to the new and all-embracing order; [the] promoting and enforcing [of] one and only one measure of conformity."[169]

The other strategy, anthropoemic, relates to *Riposte Laïque*'s articulations of Islam and Muslims, means "vomiting the strangers, banishing them from the limits of the orderly world and barring them from all communication with those inside"; that is, "the strategy of exclusion: confining the strangers within the visible walls of the ghettos or behind the invisible, yet no less tangible, prohibitions of commensality, connubium and commercium; 'cleansing' [by] expelling the strangers beyond the frontiers of the managed and manageable territory; or, when neither of the two measures was feasible, destroying the strangers physically."[170]

Time will tell how *Riposte Laïque* develops its strategies for societal and political change; however, these types of anthropoemically ethnocratic liberal and republican discourse need to be taken seriously. Liberalism and republicanism are not immune to exclusivist articulations of nationhood. To quote Arjun Appadurai: "No modern nation, however benign its political system and however eloquent its public voices may be about the virtues of tolerance, multiculturalism, and inclusion, is free of the idea that its national sovereignty is built on some sort of ethnic genius."[171] As I've argued throughout this book, while the discourse on secularism and nationhood at *Riposte Laïque* is indeed radical, in comparison with the dominant mainstream articulations of this discourse, they are not of a different species. Rather, they simply take the dominant discourse to a logical extreme.

Echoes from the Past

An Outlook on Europe

In this book, I sought to account for how the web-based journal *Riposte Laïque* and its associated activist network, the RR, diagnose the state of contemporary French society and politics, and the ills that are plaguing France and its people. Moreover, I showed how and by which means their authors and leaders seek to cure France of these ills. I have analyzed the *Riposte Laïque* diagnosis and countermeasures used as discourse, and have focused on how the journal articulates populist discourse on both secularism and nationhood.

I have approached populism as a mode of identification that is structured along one horizontal and one vertical axis of articulation of the category of 'true French people.' The underlying logic of these articulations is one that reduces the current social, political, economic, and geopolitical struggles into a battle between two essential groups: the true people and its enemies. The enemies of the people are turned into a projection surface for the ills identified by the publication *Riposte Laïque*. Thus, along the horizontal axis of populist identification, *Riposte Laïque* articulates a preeminently universal civilizational, cultural, religious, ethnic, and political alterity: the enemy being Islam and its Muslims.

While Muslims are articulated as the quintessential external enemy, the categories of immigrant and being clandestine are widely attributed to non-French and non-European citizens, even though these people may be fourth- or fifth-generation French. They are continuously racialized through articulations that tie their somatic features to alleged cultural and religious universal identities, and they are seen to pose an existential threat to the French nation and its people. According to *Riposte Laïque*, they have declared war against France and seek to colonize the nation through the use of veils, mosques, halal food, street prayers, and by manipulating French political leaders and gullible journalists, academics, and activists. Also, *Riposte Laïque* reproduced the Eurabia thesis, stating that

Muslims together with the Gulf States are joined in a mission to turn Europe into "Arabia."

The declared essential identity of the external enemy is juxtaposed with essentialized concepts about the people's identity. *Riposte Laïque* rearticulates and reframes the dominant articulations of the current social and political identification categories; and it seeks to legitimize and hegemonize their meanings through the reclassification and restructuring of history, by employing pseudo-scholarly lingua and commonsense rhetoric. While *Riposte Laïque* claims to be anti-racist, the analyzed material seems imbued with an abundance of racial markers. Moreover, the identification of their "true people" racializes whiteness, through the many allusions to pure French Gallic ancestry, the French nation, European civilization, and Christianity. *Riposte Laïque* professes that it is the true bearer of feminism, while it uncritically absorbs and reproduces anti-feminist thoughts and a biological essentialization of gender. The heterosexual nuclear family is articulated in *Riposte Laïque* as being the organic base of the nation, by which the cultivation of the people's Gallic ancestry (hence, pure blood) can be reassured. The publication's writers also cherish the inherent characteristics of the people, in an autophilic manner: In the logic of *Riposte Laïque*, the acts of eating ham, drinking wine, buying a baguette, celebrating Christmas, and singing the national anthem are by no means mundane, normalized, and neutralized traditions; these are turned into fetishized, active expressions and practices of true nationhood.

Through the vertical axis of populist identification, *Riposte Laïque* articulates which enemies are internal to the national body. The political elite, the privileged class, feminists, and the LGBTQ lobby are articulated as reasons why Islam and Muslims came to be a threat to the people in the first place. The political elite and the privileged class are articulated as being detached and corrupt: they have handed France over on a plate to the Eurabic conspiracy. In addition, they are impotent and have led France and the French people into a state of abjection, leaving the door open for the Islamic onslaught and the spread of immigrant violence and anti-white racism.

Feminists and LGBTQ activists are articulated as being complicit in devirilizing the French nation and French men. As such, gender equality and LGBTQ rights are simultaneously articulated as being quintessential identities of the French nation and one of the core features that distinguish the French from Muslims; and they are seen as a moral, cultural, and biological threat to the continuity of the French nation.

In the end, to *Riposte Laïque* it is the socialists, and more specifically the Jewish statesman Jacques Attali, guided by capitalist self-interest and political megalomania, that orchestrate France's abjection. Attali's goal is seen as being to replace the white French population with Muslim migrants, to ensure cheap labor and to secure a stable electoral base for the socialists; since, as *Riposte Laïque* suggests, virtually all Muslims in France vote socialist. Moreover, Attali supposedly wants France to dissolve into a federal Europe and a regime of global governance, thus enabling the decommissioning of the French altogether. So exoteric anti-Muslim discourse merges with esoteric anti-Jewish discourse.

To *Riposte Laïque*, the stakes are high and a resurrection of the people from its abject state to resist the war against the French people is of utmost importance; otherwise France will be turned into an Oriental Frankistan within a couple of decades. The people's retributive resistance is articulated as being secular; and the suggested means range from civil activism to ballot-casting, with the goal of: replacing the political elite, imposing an all-out ban on Islam in France, and the institutionalization of a policy of national preference, or positive discrimination, in favor of the true French people. Also, *Riposte Laïque* advocates non-democratic action, such as: taking up arms, imposing extra-legal tribunals and capital punishment, as well as, in a worst-case scenario, employing the military to execute Muslims.

Riposte Laïque envisions and preaches a monocultural and ethnocratic form of republican and liberal democracy that is guided by a romantic, culturally and ethnically homogeneous nationalist discourse that is founded on popular majority rule. Secularism is articulated as the glue that holds the nation together and as the emblematic shibboleth distinguishing the true French people from the external others, as well as from the internal others. Thus, secularism becomes the emblem for the resurrection of the people's true inner identity and of their mobilized resistance.

As argued, the populist discourses on secularism and nationhood in *Riposte Laïque* converge intertextually and through interdiscursivity with other radical nationalist movements and with the FN in France, as well as with mainstream and dominant articulations of these discourses; however, the emphasis by *Riposte Laïque* on anthropoemic strategy being coupled with alterity (such as by cleansing and expulsion) does differ from the anthropophagic strategies of the political mainstream and the FN (i.e., smothering alterity through assimilation). In this regard, the populist discourses on secularism and nationhood used by *Riposte Laïque* are surely radically entextualized, but not epistemically different. This is also why I argue that it is important to understand radical movements like

Riposte Laïque and *Résistance Républicaine*, in order to assess the logical extremes of their discursive foundations and the 'logics' that today dominate political and societal debates on nationhood and alterity in Europe. In this sense, *Riposte Laïque* is as much a window into the debates on alterity, nationhood, and secularism, and their continuities and discontinuities from the post-fascist movements in France, as France is a window into Europe.

According to *Riposte Laïque*, "the wind is shifting" in Europe and a growing consciousness of the need to de-islamize Europe is spreading.[1] The success of radical nationalist parties throughout Europe in the 2015 election to the European Parliament is taken as evidence of this awakening; and looking further afield, many populist radical nationalist voices seek icons to carry the voice of the people among billionaires and career politicians, and *Riposte Laïque* is no different.[2]

In the lead-up to the American presidential election in 2016, *Riposte Laïque* admired, and its writers were inspired by, the Republican candidate Donald Trump and his promise to put "America first," to purge the political elite from Washington by "draining the swamp," to put an end to the supposed mass immigration by "building the wall" against Mexico, and to stop Muslim immigration.[3] As *Riposte Laïque* states, if the "formidable" Republican candidate "succeeds and wins in the USA, then everything is possible [in France] for Marine Le Pen in 2017."[4] After Trump's electoral success, *Riposte Laïque* announced an *apéro* with champagne and sausages, to celebrate the victory.[5] As Brubaker points out, today's radical nationalists have globalized their struggle into a "Pan-European and trans-Atlantic populist conjuncture."[6] In the words of Roger Griffin, "the struggle for the rebirth of their nation or homeland is but one theater of an international race war."[7]

The European allies acknowledged by *Riposte Laïque* range from anti-Islamic and radical nationalist movements, to intellectuals and political parties. The most noteworthy anti-Muslim and counter-jihadi voices include the English Defence League and one of its founders, Tommy Robinson, who stated that "every single Muslim" is responsible for the attacks in London on July 7, 2005[8]; the Stop Islamization of Europe network and its leader Anders Gravers; the German PEGIDA, who organize mass demonstrations calling for an end to immigration, islamization, and the genderization of Germany and Europe[9]; the German political party *Alternative für Deutschland*, which has incorporated parts of PEGIDA into its party, and received 13 percent of the votes in the German federal election in 2017, thus winning 92 of the 703 seats in the *Bundestag*[10]; Thilo Sarrazin, the German statesman and best-selling author known for his anti-Muslim and anti-immigration statements; Geert Wilders of the Dutch (Holland) PVV, who has compared the Quran to Hitler's *Mein Kampf*[11]; the Belgian *Parti+*, founded by Pierre Renversez, whose party program suggests halting immigration, severely restraining Islamic practices, and the intention to "put the Belgians first"[12]; the Italian anti-immigration and anti-Muslim activist Armando Manocchia, who is known for his many rants on Muslims and immigration; the Swiss politician Jean-Luc Addor (UDC/VC), who in 2014 celebrated the murder of a Muslim man in a Swiss mosque by calling on Twitter for "another one [*on en redemande*]!"[13]; and Oskar Freysinger, the much esteemed Swiss politician who is behind the Swiss anti-minaret campaign. According to *Riposte Laïque*, these actors inform the European people about the reality of the supposed large-scale Islamic onslaught in Europe, and work to organize "the resistance against the Islamization of our countries in [each of] their respective countries."[14]

The allies of *Riposte Laïque* are, however, not restricted to Europe: in the USA, the publication supports and draws upon the American Jihad Watch website and its director Robert Spencer, as well as the American Freedom Defense Initiative founded by Spencer along with Pamela Geller.[15]

While these actors, groups, and parties are far from a homogeneous group, their populist discourse on alterity and nationhood converges in how Muslims, Islam, and immigration are articulated as a threat, not only to their respective nations, but also to the claimed superior identity in common with European or Western civilization. In an eclectic, anachronistic, and depoliticized melting pot, categories like gender-equality, democracy, anti-racism, and Christianity are articulated retrospectively as essentializing indentificatory emblems around which fantasies of ethnically- and culturally homogenous nation-states and of a common European civilization are negotiated, construed, and contrasted to imagined national 'others'.[16] The slippage between the esoteric and exoteric articulations of racism/anti-racism, ethnocratic/pluralist democracy, and Christianity/secularism indicates that the embracing of these putative progressive markers should be read with caution.[17] They are challenged and rearticulated to fit an integralist and populist, radical nationalist, romantic fantasy of an imagined organic past.

To *Riposte Laïque*, the fight against the imagined Islamization of Europe surely rests on the credo "the enemy of my enemy is my friend." For example, the publication does not hesitate to cherish authoritarian and illiberal political individuals and parties; like the Hungarian PM Viktor Orban and his party *Fidesz-Magyar Polgári Szövetség*, who call Syrian refugees "Muslim invaders."[18]

In this vein, the publication argues that the Russian news channel *Sputnik* is a beacon for the freedom of the press, regardless of its strong connection with the Russian government and the many accounts of misinformation it has accumulated in order to meddle in foreign affairs, like the false claim that the German Chancellor Angela Merkel had happily taken selfies with an IS jihadi fighter.[19]

New formal and informal alliances are being forged in radical nationalist milieus. Through media-savvy strategies, political tactics, street-based activism, and calumnious articulations of the order of things, populist radical nationalist discourse is gaining ground in Europe. Time will tell whether or not we are witnessing the emergence of a new European neo-fascist era, and whether groups and movements like *Riposte Laïque* have a role in the realization of such an era; however, for now it is crucial to assess the mobilizing force of the historical echoes from the crusades, the *Reconquista*, colonialism, genocide, Nazism, and fascism that resonate in the discourse that is utilized by *Riposte Laïque* and their French and European peers, as they appear to reverberate within mainstream discourse.[20]

The challenges posed to the contemporary European liberal-republican democratic order should not be underestimated, nor should the responses to these challenges by the self-proclaimed guardians of this order. These types of discourse, dressed in the gown of universalism and truth, may, to quote Griffin, "prove even more insidious than modernized forms of the interwar fascist right in their liberticide effects because they are so easily absorbed into the bloodstream itself."[21]

While history does not repeat itself, due to the contingency of materiality and ideation, it still does echo from the past.

Notes

Introduction

1 *Jugement du* May 3, 2017, *17e chambre correctionelle, n° du parquet 16204000172, Tribunal de grande instance*, Paris, May 5, 2017, p. 1.

2 *Union des étudiants juifs de France* (UEJF), *J'accuse-AIPJ, La ligue de droite de l'homme* (LDH), SOS Racisme, *Touche pas à mon pote*, and *Mouvement contre le racism et pour l'amitié entre les peoples* (MRAP).

3 At the first instance, the 17th chamber failed in their attempt to prove that Cassen was the editor in chief of the journal, as the formal editor (*Riposte Laïque* is based in Switzerland since 2012) and the president of *Riposte Laïque* (in Switzerland) was the Swiss national Alain Jean-Mairet. While Jean-Mairet was initially convicted and asked to pay a fine of 5,000 euros, Cassen was aquitted; however, the 17th chamber overturned their own decision and convicted Cassen on October 5, 2017. See *Jugement du Octobre 1, 2017, 17e chambre correctionelle, n° du parquet 17010000380, Tribunal de grande instance*, Paris, October 5, 2017, p. 7.

4 Ludwig Gallet, "Primaire à droite: *Riposte Laïque*, l'encombrant soutien de Franais Fillon," *L'Express*, November 25, 2016. Available online: https://www.lexpress. fr/actualite/politique/elections/primaire-a-droite-riposte-laique-l-encombrant-soutien-de-francois-fillon_1854040.html (accessed January 26, 2018).

5 On the post-1968 "new-reactionary" intelligentsia, see Pascal Durand and Sarah Sindaco, eds., *Le discours "néo-réactionnaire"* (Paris: CNRS Éditions, 2015).

6 On the challenges facing France, see Roger Célestin, Eliane DalMolin, Todd W. Reeser, and Giuseppina Mecchia, the "Editors' Introduction: '*L'Idée de la France*' [The Idea of France]", *Contemporary French and Francophone Studies* 17, no. 2 (2013): 119–122. On social cleavages in France, see Anne Brunner and Luis Maurin, *Rapport sur les inégalités en France, édition 2017* (Paris: Observatoire des inégalités, 2017); Didier Fassin, *Les nouvelles frontières de la société francaise* (Paris: La Découverte, 2010).

7 In order of appearance: Joan W. Scott, *The Politics of the Veil* (Princeton, NJ: Princeton University Press, 2007); John Bowen, *Why the French Don't Like Headscarves. Islam, the State, and Public Space* (Princeton, NJ: Princeton University Press, 2007); Cécile Laborde, *Critical Republicanism. The Hijab Controversy and Political Philosophy* (Oxford and New York: Oxford University Press, 2008); Jennifer Selby, *Questioning French Secularism. Gender Politics and Islam in a*

French Suburb (New York: Palgrave Macmillan, 2012); Mayanthi L. Fernando, *The Republic Unsettled. Muslim French and the Contradictions of Secularism* (Durham and London: Duke University Press, 2014); Amelie Barras, "Contemporary Laïcité: Setting the terms of a new social contract? The slow exclusion of women wearing headscarves," *Totalitarian Movements and Political Religions* 11, no. 2 (2010): 229–248. I would also add my own analysis on French parliamentarian debates: Per-Erik Nilsson, *Unveiling the French Republic* (Leiden: Brill, 2017).

8 See, for example, Dimitri Almeida, "Exclusionary secularism: The Front national and the reinvention of laïcité," *Modern & Contemporary France* 25, no. 3 (2017): 249–263; Per-Erik Nilsson, "Secular Retaliation: A case study of integralist populism, anti-Muslim discourse, and (il)liberal discourse on secularism in contemporary France," *Politics, Religion & Ideology* 16, no. 1 (2015): 87–106.

9 In order of the year of publication: Robert Paxton, *Vichy France: Old Guard and New Order, 1940–1944* (New York: Columbia University Press, [1972] 2001); Michel Winock, *Nationalism, Antisemitism, and Fascism in France* (Stanford, CA: Stanford University Press, [1982] 2000); Zeev Sternhell, *Neither Right Nor Left: Fascist Ideology in France* (Princeton, NJ: Princeton University Press, [1983] 1986); Jonathan Marcus, *The National Front and French Politics: The Resistable Rise of Jean-Marie Le Pen* (Hampshire and London: Macmillan, 1995); Kevin Passmore, *From Liberalism to Fascism: The Right in a French Province* (Cambridge: Cambridge University Press, 1997); Peter Davies, *The Extreme Right in France, 1789 to the Present: From de Maistre to Le Pen* (London and New York: Routledge, 2002); Jens Rydgren, *The Populist Challenge: Political Protest and Ethno-Nationalist Mobilization in France* (Oxford and New York: Berghahn Books, 2003); J. G. Shields, *The Extreme Right in France: From Pétain to Le Pen* (London and New York: Routledge, 2007); Gabriel Goodliffe, *The Resurgence of the Radical Right in France: From Boulangisme to the Front National* (Cambridge and New York: Cambridge University Press, 2012); Daniel Stockemer, *Continuity and Change Under Jean-Marie Le Pen and Marine Le Pen* (Cham: Springer International Publishing, 2017).

10 Hans-Georg Betz, *Radical Right-Wing Populism in Western Europe* (Hampshire and London: Macmillan, 1994); Cas Mudde, *Radical Right Parties in Europe* (Cambridge: Cambridge University Press, 2007); Jean-Yves Camus and Nicolas Lebourg, *Far-Right Politics in Europe* (Cambridge: Belknap, [2015] 2017); Jan-Werner Müller, *What Is Populism?* (Philadelphia: University of Pennsylvania Press, 2016).

11 Ruth Wodak, Majid KhosraviNik, and Brigitte Mral, eds., *Right-Wing Populism in Europe: Politics and Discourse* (London and New York: Bloomsbury, 2013); Andrea Mammone, Emmanuel Godin, and Brian Jenkins, *Varieties of Right-Wing Extremism in Europe* (Oxon and New York: Routledge, 2013); Maik Fielitz and Laura Lotte Laloire, eds., *Trouble on the Far-Right: Contemporary Right-Wing Strategies and Practices in Europe* (Biefeld: transcript Verlag, 2016); Cas Mudde, ed.,

The Populist Radical Right: A Reader (London and New York: Routledge, 2017); Jens Rydgren, *The Oxford Handbook of the Radical Right* (Oxford and New York: Oxford University Press, 2018).

12 See Olivier Roy, *Saving the People: How Populists Hijack Religion* (C. Hurst & Co. Publishers Ltd, 2016).

13 See Chris Allen, *Islamophobia* (Oxon and New York: Routledge, 2010); Raymond Taras, *Xenophobia and Islamophobia in Europe* (Edinburgh: Edinburgh University Press, 2012); David Tyrer, *The Politics of Islamophobia: Race, Power, and Fantasy* (London: Pluto Books, 2013); Arun Kundnani, *The Muslims Are Coming! Islamophobia, Extremism, and the Domestic War on Terror* (London and New York: Verso, 2014); Todd Green, *The Fear of Islam: An Introduction to Islamophobia in the West* (Minneapolis, MN: Fortress Press, 2015); Ferruh Yilmaz, *How the Workers Became Muslims: Immigration, Culture, and Hegemonic Transformations in Europe* (Ann Arbor, MI: The University of Michigan Press, 2016); Irene Zempi and Imran Awan, *Islamophobia: Lived Experiences of Online and Offline Victimisation* (Policy Press, 2017); Liz Fekete, *Europe's Fault Lines: Racism and the Rise of the Right* (London: Verso, 2018).

14 Project number: 2013-07371.

15 Susan A. Philips, *Wallbangin'. Graffiti and Gangs in L.A.* (Chicago and London: University of Chicago Press, 1999), p. 95.

16 Jean Baubérot makes a similar argument in *Les sept laïcités françaises: Le modèle français de laïcité n'existe pas* (Paris: Maison de droit de l'Homme, 2015).

17 Cyrano, "Qui sommes nous? Pourquoi un nouveau media?", *Riposte Laïque*, August 30, 2007. Available online: http://ripostelaique.com/Qui-sommes-nous-Pourquoi-un/ (accessed February 1, 2018).

Chapter 1

1 Full list of organizers: *Résistance Républicaine; Actions Sita; Free World Academy; Institut Européen de Socialisation et d'Education; L'Elan Nouveau des Citoyens; Bloc Identitaire; Comité Lépante; Ligue du Droit des Femmes; Riposte Laïque; Vérité, valeurs et démocratie; Novopress; L'Ordre républicain; Liberty vox; Rebelles. info; Le Gaulois; Puteaux-libre; Union gaulliste; Drzz.info; SDF; L'Observatoire de l'islamisation; Parti de l'Innocence; Ligue de Défense française; Cared; le Cercle Aristote; le Blog des gaullistes populaires.*

2 See Nigel Copsey, "'Fascism ... but with an open mind': Reflections on the contemporary far right in (Western) Europe," *Fascism* 2 (2013): 1–17, p. 16.

3 Egil Asprem, "The birth of counterjihadist terrorism: Reflections on some nonspoken dimensions," *The Pomegranate* 13, no. 1 (2011): 17–32, p. 19.

4 Cyrano, "Des assises exceptionnelles, des intervenants formidables, un public en or ..." *Riposte Laïque*, December 19, 2010. Available online: http://ripostelaique. com/18-decembre-Un-nouvel-acte-de/ (accessed January 21, 2018).

5 See Abel Mestre and Caroline Monnot, "Les 'Assises sur l'islamisation': pas d'interdiction, mais ..." *Le Monde Blogs: Droite(s) Extrême(s)*, December 16, 2010. Available online: http://droites-extremes.blog.lemonde.fr/2010/12/16/les-assises-sur-lislamisation-pas-dinterdiction-mais (accessed January 21, 2018).

6 See Pierre Birnbaum, *La République et le cochon* (Paris: Le Seuil, 2013).

7 See Laurent Binet, "'Touche pas à mon pain au chocolat!' The theme of food in current French political discourses," *Modern & Contemporary France* 24, no. 3 (2016): 239–252.

8 See Joachim Véliocas, *Ces maires qui courtisent l'islamisme* (Paris: Tatamis, 2010).

9 Cyrano, "Assises sur l'islamisation: gros succès, 600,000 visiteurs en 2 jours, rendez-vous début 2011," *Riposte Laïque*, December 21, 2010. Available online: http://ripostelaique.com/Assises-sur-l-islamisation-Plus/ (accessed January 21, 2018).

10 Cyrano, "Défendre Fanny Truchelet, Ayaan Hirsi Ali et Geert Wilders, une triple coherence," *Riposte Laïque*, April 8, 2008. Available online: http://ripostelaique. com/Defendre-Fanny-Truchelut-Ayaan/ (accessed February 1, 2018).

11 Interview with Pierre Cassen and Christine Tasin, Aix-en-Provence, October 19, 2015.

12 Ibid.

13 Ibid.

14 Ibid.

15 See Dominique Albertini and David Couchet, *La fachiosphère: comment l'extrême droite remporte la bataille du net* (Paris: Flammarion, 2016).

16 Interview with Pierre Cassen and Christine Tasin, Aix-en-Provence, October 19, 2015.

17 See, for example, Cyrano: "En Iran, Police des moeurs! En France, la police de la pensée!" *Riposte Laïque*, December 5, 2011. Available online: http://ripostelaique. com/en-iran-police-des-moeurs-en-france-police-de-la-pensee/ (accessed February 1, 2018). This citation was translated into French by the British author Evelyn Beatrice Hall, who, under the pseudonym S. G. Tallentyre, published *The Life of Voltaire* in 1903, in which she uses this phrase to summarize Voltaire's thoughts.

18 Cyrano, "Défendre celles et ceux que les islamistes traînent devant les tribunaux," *Riposte Laïque*, September 8, 2007. Available online: http://ripostelaique.com/ Defendre-celles-et-ceux-que-les/ (accessed February 1, 2018).

19 Cyrano, "Geert Wilders à 17 % Une sacrée leçon pour le monde politique français," *Riposte Laïque*, June 8, 2009. Available online: http://ripostelaique.com/Geert-Wilders-a-17-Une-sacree/ (accessed February 1, 2018).

20 Numbers collected on December 3, 2017.

21 Cyrano, "Résistance Républicaine, c'est parti!" *Riposte Laïque*, June 7, 2010. Available online: http://ripostelaique.com/Resistance-Republicaine-c-est/ (accessed February 1, 2018).

22 See Catherine Coroller, "Bouffeuse d'islam," *Libération*, March 2, 2011. Available online: http://www.liberation.fr/societe/2011/03/02/bouffeuse-d-islam_718571 (accessed February 1, 2018).

23 Ibid.

24 An *apéro* is a French practice of getting together after work to have wine and charcuterie.

25 See Cyrano, "Résistance Républicaine."

26 John D. McCarthy and Mayer N. Zald, "Resource mobilization and social movements: A partial theory," *American Journal of Sociology* 82, no. 6 (1977): 1212–1241, pp. 1217–1218.

27 Ibid. Also see Michel Wieviorka, "After new social movements," *Social Movement Studies: Journal of Social, Cultural and Political Protest* 4, no. 1 (2005): 1–19.

28 On these issues in France, see Laurence Bell, "Interpreting collective action: Methodology and ideology in the analysis of social movements in France," *Modern & Contemporary France* 9, no. 2 (2001): 183–196; Sarah Waters, "New social movements in France: Une nouvelle vague citoyenne?" *Modern & Contemporary France* 6, no. 4 (1998): 493–504.

29 For an excellent summary see Jamie Bartlett, Jonathan Birdwell, and Mark Littler, *The New Face of Digital Populism* (London: Demos, 2011). See also: Simon Weaver, "A rhetorical discourse analysis of online anti-Muslim and anti-Semitic jokes," *Ethnic and Racial Studies* 36, no. 3 (2013): 483–499.

30 See Ruth Wodak and Majid KhosraviNik, "Dynamics of Discourse and Politics in Right-wing Populism in Europe and Beyond: An Introduction," in *Right-Wing Populism in Europe. Politics and Discourse*, Ruth Wodak, Majid KhosraviNik, and Brigitte Mral, eds. (London, New Delhi, New York, and Sydney: Bloomsbury, 2013), p. xvii.

31 Vincent Campbell discusses citizen journalism from this point of view, although he does not discuss populist movements, Campbell's definition of citizen journalism is applicable to *Riposte Laïque*: "citizen journalism can be broadly described as having: a number of attributes which make it distinct from professional journalism, including unpaid work, absence of professional training, and often unedited publication of content, and may feature plain language, distinct story selection and news judgment, especially hyper-local issues, free accessibility, and interactivity." See Vincent Campbell, "Citizen Journalism and Active Citizenship," in *Contemporary Protest and the Legacy of Dissent*, Stuart Price and Ruth Sanz Sabido, eds. (London and New York: Rowman and Littlefield, 2015).

32 Michael Hameleers and Desirée Schmuck, "It's us against them: A comparative experiment on the effects of populist messages communicated via social media,"

Information, Communication & Society 20, no. 9 (2017): 1425–1444, p. 1425. Also see Benjamin Krämer, "Populist online practices: The function of the Internet in right-wing populism," *Information, Communication & Society* 20, no. 9 (2017): 1293–1309; Sebastian Stier, Lisa Posch, Arnim Bleier, and Markus Strohmaierm, "When populists become popular: Comparing Facebook use by the right-wing movement Pegida and German political parties," *Information, Communication & Society* 20, no. 9 (2017): 1365–1388.

33 John Postill, "Digital Politics and Political Engagement," in *Digital Anthropology*, Heather A. Horst and Daniel Miller, eds. (London and New York: Berg, 2012), p. 176.

34 For more details about these channels, see Albertini and Couchet, *La fashosphère*.

35 On this issue, see Manuela Caiani and Claudius Wagemann, "Online networks of the Italian and German Extreme Right," *Information, Communication & Society* 12, no. 1 (2009): 66–109, p. 67.

36 On the normalization of nationalist discourse, see Lene Austad, "Introduction," in *Nationalism and the Body Politic: Psychoanalysis and the Rise of Ethnocentrism and Xenophobia*, Lena Austad, ed. (London: Karnac, 2014).

37 Paolo Gerbaudo, *Tweets and Streets. Social Media and Contemporary Activism* (London: Pluto Press, 2012), p. 5.

38 Ibid., p. 14.

39 Cyrano, "Pour gagner cette guerre, il faudra éradiquer l'islam en France," *Riposte Laïque*, September 29, 2014. Available online: http://ripostelaique.com/pour-gagner-cette-guerre-il-faudra-eradiquer-lislam-en-france/ (accessed February 1, 2018).

40 For a similar approach, see Timothy Fitzgerald, *Discourse on Civility and Barbarity* (Oxford and New York: Oxford University Press, 2008).

41 I agree with Emile Chabal that any understanding of the contemporary configurations of secularism has more to gain from assessing the changes in French politics and society in the 1970s and the 1980s, than in the Third Republic or the Revolution. See Emile Chabal, "From the banlieue to the burkini: The many lives of French republicanism," *Modern & Contemporary France* 25, no. 1 (2017): 68–74, p. 69. For more detailed analysis of these affairs, see Alain Gabon, "La République et ses voiles intégraux," *Contemporary French and Francophone Studies* 18, no. 2 (2014): 133–141.

42 The "Muslim Problem" refers to the many ways republican spokespeople have framed Islam and Muslims in France as problems; problems in terms of gender equality, integration, security, etc. See Julien Beaugé and Abdellali Hajjat, "Élites françaises et construction du 'problème musulman.' Le cas du Haut Conseil à l'intégration (1989/2012)," *Sociologie* 5, no. 1 (2014): 31–59.

43 "La laïcité c'est par où? La laïcité dans l'entreprise, à l'école, dans le monde …" *Charlie Hebdo* (hors-série), September–October 2013.

44 For a more detailed account of this reasoning, see Nilsson, *Unveiling*. For a discussion on Hegelian teleological thought's relation to liberal myths of liberation, see Joan W. Scott, *The Fantasy of Feminist History* (Durham and London: Duke University Press, 2011), p. 91ff.

45 These observations are based on my own participation in the demonstrations. For similar observations, see Henri Tincq, "Liberté, égalité, fraternité, laïcité. Mais quelle laïcité?" *Slate*, January 13, 2015. Available online: http://www.slate.fr/story/96767/liberte-egalite-fraternite-laicite (accessed February 1, 2018); "Contre le terrorisme, la plus grande manifestation jamais recensée en France", *Le Monde*, January 11, 2015. Available online: http://www.lemonde.fr/societe/article/2015/01/11/la-france-dans-la-rue-pour-defendre-la-liberte_4553845_3224.html (accessed February 1, 2018).

46 In Marie-Estelle Pech, "Éducation: les 10 principales mesures sur la laïcité," *Le Figaro,* January 22, 2015. Available online: http://www.lefigaro.fr/actualite-france/2015/01/22/01016-20150122ARTFIG00193-education-les-10-principales-mesures-sur-la-laicite.php (accessed January 21, 2018); "320.000 enseignants formés à la laïcité dans les mois à venir," *Le Figaro*, January 30, 2015. Available online: http://www.lefigaro.fr/actualite-france/2015/01/30/01016-20150130ARTFIG00138-320000-enseignants-formes-a-la-laicite-dans-les-mois-a-venir.php (accessed January 21, 2018).

47 Ministère de l'Éducation Nationale de l'Enseignement Supérieur et de la Recherche, *Grande mobilisation de l'École pour les valeurs de la République* (Paris: La Règplique Française). Available online: http://www.education.gouv.fr/cid85644/onze-mesures-pour-un-grande-mobilisation-de-l-ecole-pour-les-valeurs-de-la-republique.html (accessed January 21, 2018).

48 See Claude Halmos, "Contre les kalachnikovs: l'école," in *Nous sommes Charlie*, Collectif (Paris: Livre de poche, 2015), pp. 76–77.

49 Commission de réflexion sur l'application du principe de laïcité dans la République, *Rapport au Président de la République*, 2003, p. 10. Available online: http://www.ladocumentationfrancaise.fr/var/storage/rapports-publics/034000725.pdf (accessed January 21, 2018).

50 Jacques Chirac, *Discours prononcé par M. Jacques Chirac, Président de la République, relatif au respect du principe de laïcité dans la République*, Palais de l'Elysée, December 17, 2003.

51 *Journal télévisé de 20h* (2007), [a TV program] TF1, March 15, 2000.

52 In order of appearance: Christophe Miqueu and Pascal Gros, *Comprendre la laïcité* (Paris: Max Milo Éditions, 2017); Régis Debray and Didier Leschi, *La laïcité au quotidien: Guide pratique* (Paris: Éditions Gallimard, 2016); Jean Baubérot and Le Cercle Des Enseignant.E.S Laïques, *Petit manuel pour une laïcité apaisée: À l'usage des profs, des élèves, et de leurs parents* (Paris: La découverte, 2016).

53 Henri Pena-Ruiz, *Dictionnaire amoureux de la Laïcité* (Paris: Plon, 2014), p. 16.

54 Charles de Gaulle, *Mémoires de Guerre Vol I* (Paris: Plon, 1954), p. 1.

55 "La laïcité", *Charlie Hebdo*.

56 For historical analysis of the Law of 1905, see Jean Baubérot, *Laïcité 1905–2005, entre passion et raison* (Paris: Editions Seuil, 2005); Patrick Weil, ed., *Politiques de la laïcité au XXe siècle* (Paris: PUF, 2007). For an analysis of the law and its relation to gender equality, see Florence Rochefort, ed., *Le pouvoir du genre. Laïcités et religions 1905–2005* (Toulouse: PUM, 2007).

57 André Gerin, Rapport d'information n°2262. Fait en application de l'article 145 du Règlement au nom de la mission d'information sur la pratique du port du voile intégral sur le territoire national, Assemblée Nationale, Paris, January 27, 2010, p. 88. Available online: http://www.assemblee-nationale.fr/13/rap-info/i2262.asp (accessed January 21, 2018).

58 For further discussion on this issue, see Stéphanie Hennette Vauchez and Vincent Valentin, *L'Affaire Baby Loup ou la Nouvelle Laïcité* (Issy-les-Moulineaux: Lextenso éditions, 2014).

59 The Law of 2010 does not take into account secularism as a foundational principle, since the Constitutional Council and the Council of State made clear that prohibiting religious garments would be unconstitutional; however, the whole debate around this law framed the legislative process as being a question regarding secularism. See "Study of possible legal grounds for banning the full veil. Report adopted by the Plenary General Assembly of the Conseil d'Etat," Conseil d'État, March 25, 2010, Paris. Available online: http://www.conseil-etat.fr/Decisions-Avis-Publications/Etudes-Publications/Rapports-Etudes/Etude-relative-aux-possibilites-juridiques-d-interdiction-du-port-du-voile-integral (accessed January 21, 2018).

60 Gerin, Rapport [report], p. 88.

61 See John Bowen, *Can Islam Be French: Pluralism and Pragmatism in a Secular State* (Princeton: Princeton University Press, 2009).

62 "Valls plaide pour une formation 'obligatoire' des imams en France," *Le Nouvel Observateur*, March 3, 2015. Available online: https://tempsreel.nouvelobs.com/attentats-charlie-hebdo-et-maintenant/20150303.OBS3743/valls-plaide-pour-une-formation-obligatoire-des-imams-en-france.html (accessed January 21, 2018).

63 Ibid.

64 On institutional neutrality and secularism, see Raphaël Liogier, *Une Laïcité "légitime." La France et ses religions d'état* (Paris: Médicis Entrelas, 2006).

65 "La laïcité", *Charlie Hebdo*, p. 2.

66 It should be noted that this is not the representative for the whole of the *Charlie Hebdo* issue, in which a long interview with the journalist and secularist activist Caroline Fourest declares that, today, fundamentalist Catholicism presents the greatest threat to secularism. See Gérard Biard, "Entretien avec Caroline Fourest" in "La laïcité," *Charlie Hebdo*, pp. 9–11.

67 Jean-Louis Debré, Rapport fait au nom de la Commission d'information sur la question du port des signes religieux à l'école. Auditions (Vol. 1275, tome II, 2ème partie), Assemblée Nationale, Paris, December 4, 2003, p. 11. Available online: http://www.assemblee-nationale.fr/12/rap-info/i1275-T2.asp (accessed January 21, 2018).

68 Assemblée Nationale, Session ordinaire de 2003–2004. 151e séance. Compte rendu intégral. 2e séance du mercredi février 4, 2004. *Journal officiel de la République française* 16, no. 2 (2004): 1394–1425, p. 1403.

69 Assemblée Nationale, Mission information sur la pratique du port de la burqa et du niqab sur le territoire national [Information about the practice of wearing a burqa and a *niqab* within the national territory]. Séance de 17h. Compte rendu n°3, July 15, 2009, p. 2. Available online: http://www.assemblee-nationale.fr/13/pdf/cr-miburqa/08-09/c0809003.pdf (accessed January 21, 2018).

70 On the French state and feminism and secularism, see Fernando, *The Republic Unsettled;* Anna Kemp, "Marianne d'aujourd'hui? The figure of the beurette in contemporary French feminist discourses," *Modern & Contemporary France* 17, no. 1 (2009): 19–33; Jennifer A. Selby, "Un/veiling women's bodies: Secularism and sexuality in full-face veil prohibitions in France and Québec," *Studies in Religion/ Sciences Religieuses* 43, no. 3 (2014): 439–466.

71 Nicolas Sarkozy, Discours du Président de la République, 12 Juillet. Remise collective de décorations Palais de l'Élysée. *Palais de l'Élysée*, Paris, July 12, 2007. For my analysis of citizenship and secularism, see Per-Erik Nilsson, "'Who is Madame M?' Staking out the borders of secular France", *Religion as a Category of Government and Sovereignty*, Timothy Fitzgerald, Trevor Stack, and Naomi Goldenberg, eds. (Leiden: Brill, 2015).

72 *Primaire de droite*, [TV program] TF1/Public Sénat, October 16, 2016.

73 During the Vichy Regime, Jacques Chevalier, Minister for Public Instruction, went against the Law of 1905 by reinstating the Catholic Church's influence in public schools; however, this was short-lived. See Kay Chadwick, "Education in secular France: (re)defining *laïcité*," *Modern & Contemporary France* 5, no. 1 (1997): 47–59.

74 "La laïcité", *Charlie Hebdo*, p. 13.

75 Jean Baubérot, *La laïcité falsifiée* (Paris: Cahiers Libres, 2012) [e-book], Loc 3.

76 Dominique Albertini, "Marine Le Pen et sa relecture de l'occupation' devant le tribunal," *La Libération*, October 19, 2015. Available online: http://www.liberation. fr/france/2015/10/19/marine-le-pen-et-sa-relecture-de-l-occupation-devant-le-tribunal_1407378 (accessed January 21, 2018).

77 "Islam et Occupation: Marine Le Pen provoque un tollé," *Le Figaro*, December 11, 2010. Available online: http://www.lefigaro.fr/politique/2010/12/11/01002-20101211ARTFIG00475-islam-et-occupation-la-provocation-de-marine-le-pen. php (accessed January 21, 2018).

78 Ibid.

79 Dominique Albertini, " 'Prières de rue et 'occupation': Marine Le Pen relaxée,"
    La Libération, December 15, 2015. Available online: http://www.liberation.fr/
    france/2015/12/15/prieres-de-rue-et-occupation-marine-le-pen-relaxee_1420902
    (accessed January 21, 2018).

80 Marine Le Pen, Discours de Marine Le Pen, Présidente du Front National, lors du
    Congrès de Tours des 15 et janvier 16, 2011, Front National, January 16, 2011.
    Available online: http://www.frontnational.com/videos/congres-du-fn-a-tours-
    discours-d'investiture-de-marine-le-pen/ (accessed January 21, 2018).

81 Ibid.

82 Ibid.

83 Marine Le Pen was, for example, behind a noteworthy election poster that depicted
    a young *maghrebine* giving a thumbs down, accompanied by the text: "Nationality,
    assimilation, social ladder, secularism–the Left and the Right have destroyed it all."
    See: "Une jeune Maghrébine sur une affiche de Le Pen," *Le Nouvel Observateur*,
    December 12, 2012. Available online: http://tempsreel.nouvelobs.com/politique/
    elections-2007/20061211.OBS2440/une-jeune-maghrebine-sur-une-affiche-de-le-
    pen.html (accessed January 21, 2018).

84 Cécile Alduy and Stéphane Wahnich, *Marine Le Pen prise aux mots: Décryptage du
    nouveau discours frontiste* (Paris: Seuil, 2015), p. 156ff.

85 For a lengthy and detailed discussion about GRECE and the *Nouvelle Droite*
    [the New Right], see Roger Griffin, "Plus ça change! The Fascist Pedigree of
    the Nouvelle Droite," in *The Development of the Radical Right in France. From
    Boulanger to Le Pen*, Edward J. Arnold, ed. (London and New York: Palgrave
    Macmillan, 2000).

86 See Antonio Santucci, *Antonio Gramsci* (New York: Monthly Review Press, 2010),
    p. 156.

87 Alduy and Wahnich, *Marine Le Pen*, p. 159.

88 Emile Chabal, *A Divided Republic: Nation, State and Citizenship in Contemporary
    France* (Cambridge: Cambridge University Press, 2015), p. 263.

89 Pierre Tévanian, "A Conservative Revolution within Secularism," *Les mots sont
    importants* [The words are important], March 15, 2014. Available online: http://
    lmsi.net/A-Conservative-Revolution-within (accessed January 1, 2015).

90 Barras comments on the anti-racist organization *Collectif contre l'islamophobie en
    France* [Collective against Islamophobia in France], but her remark is applicable to
    a broad range of critics of secularism. See Amélie Barras, "Secularism in France,"
    in *The Oxford Handbook of Secularism*, Phil Zuckerman and John R. Shook, eds.
    (Oxford: Oxford University Press, 2017), p. 149.

91 The foundational work on discourse theory is Ernesto Laclau and Chantal Mouffe's
    Hegemony and Socialist Strategy (London: Verso, 1985).

92 Jacob Torfing, "Discourse Theory: Achievements, Arguments, and Challenges," in *Discourse Theory in European Politics Identity: Policy and Governance*, David Howarth and Jacob Torfing, eds. (Hampshire and New York: Palgrave Macmillan, 2005), p. 13.

93 Ibid.

94 Articulatory practices are various forms of statements through speech, imagery, or actions that ascribe a certain meaning to social categories. See David Howarth and Yannis Stavrakakis, "Introducing Discourse Theory and Political Analysis," in *Discourse Theory and Political Analysis*, David Howarth, Aletta J. Noval, and Yannis Stavrakakis, eds. (Manchester and New York: Manchester University Press, 2000).

95 On discourse and discourse formation, see ibid.

96 Torfing, "Discourse," p. 18.

97 Ibid.

98 This relates to and draws on Michel Foucault's work on truth formations. See Michel Foucault, *Sécurité, territoire, population. Cours au Collège de France, 1977–1978* (Paris: Seuil-Gallimard, 2004), p. 5.

99 *A vous de juger*, [TV program "It is up to you to judge"] France 2, December 9, 2010.

100 Jean-Luc Mélenchon, *Qu'ils s'en aillent tous!* [May they all go!] (Paris: Flammarion, 2010), pp. 11–12.

101 On these issues, see Yannis Stavrakakis and Anton Jäger, "Accomplishments and limitations of the 'new' mainstream in contemporary populism studies," *European Journal of Social Theory* [online first] (2017): 1–19.

102 Ibid.

103 Michel Foucault, *L'Archéologie du savoir* [The archaeology of knowing] (Paris: Gallimard, 1969).

104 Ernesto Laclau, *On Populist Reason* (London: Verso, 1994), p. 117. Also see Francisco Panizza, "Introduction," in *Populism and the Mirror of Democracy*, Francisco Panizza, ed. (London: Verso, 2005).

105 See Margaret Canovan, *The People* (Cambridge: Polity Press, 2005); Ernesto Laclau, "Why constructing a people is the main task of radical politics," *Critical Inquiry* 32 (2006): 646–680. When referring to "the people" as a category, it is in singular contrast to the general usage of people in plural.

106 Constitutive outside, see Laclau, *On Populist Reason*.

107 Asprem, "The birth," p. 19.

108 See Stavrakakis and Jäger, "Accomplishments."

109 See Rogers Brubaker, "Why populism?" *Theory and Society* 46, no. 5 (2017): 357–385.

110 There are other similar ways of structuring the analysis of populism; see, for example, Benjamin Moffit's take on populism as a political style that features an

appeal to "the people" versus "the elite," "bad manners" and the performance of crisis, breakdown, or threat in *The Global Rise of Populism: Performance, Political Style, and Representation* (Stanford: Stanford University Press, 2016), p. 45.

111 On banal nationalism, see Michael Billig, *Banal Nationalism* (London: Sage, 2014).

112 For a recent discussion on far-right and extreme-right labels, see Sarah Harrison and Michael Bruter. *Mapping Extreme Right Ideology: An Empirical Geography of the European Extreme Right* (New York: Palgrave Macmillan, 2011).

113 Benjamin Teitelbaum, *Lions of the North. Sounds of the New Nordic Radical Nationalism* (Oxford: Oxford University Press, 2017), p. 8.

114 Rogers Brubaker, *Nationalism Reframed: Nationhood and the National Question in the New Europe* (Cambridge and New York: Cambridge University Press, 1996), p. 18.

115 Rogers Brubaker, "Between nationalism and civilizationism: The European populist moment in comparative perspective," *Ethnic and Racial Studies* 40, no. 8 (2017): 1191–1226, p. 1211.

116 Barras, "Secularism in France," p. 232.

117 Ibid.

Chapter 2

1 Other participants were: SIEL (*Souveraineté, Indépendance et Libertés*), *Génération patriotes*, Anne Zelensky, co-founder of the *Ligue du Droit des Femmes*, *Parti de l'Innocence*, *Ligue du Midi*, *La Droite Libre*, *Ligue Francilienne*, *Union des Français juifs*, UJP, *Non au Remplacement de Peuple et de Civilisation*, Free World Academy, RPF, *La Ligue savoyarde*, CARED (*Comité d'Action pour le Respect de l'Etat de Droit*), *Front de Défense de la France* (FDF), *Minurne Résistance*, *Puteaux Libre*, *Français de France*, *Agenda patriote*, *La Blonde de Youtube*, *Blog Hernani*, Mireille Vallette, and Laurence Nguyen.

2 Cyrano, "La 'laïcité ferme et tolérante' de Marianne est-elle la bonne réponse à la 'laïcité positive' de Sarkozy?" *Riposte Laïque*, February 27, 2008. Available online: http://ripostelaique.com/La-laicite-ferme-et-tolerante-de/ (accessed February 5, 2018).

3 Cyrano, "Les vrais esprits libres ne devraient pas craindre le discours d'Ayaan Hirsi Ali," *Riposte Laïque*, February 21, 2008. Available online: http://ripostelaique. com/Les-vrais-esprits-libres-ne/ (accessed February 5, 2018). "Secular" (laic(s)/ laïque(s)) here refers to a person who is being identified or who identifies with secularism.

4 Ibid.

5 Cyrano, "Feminisme et laïcité: des alliés naturels," *Riposte Laïque*, October 21, 2007. Available online: http://ripostelaique.com/Feminisme-et-laicite-des-allies/ (accessed February 5, 2018).

6 Cyrano, "Osons demeurer des esprits libres, envers et contre tous," *Riposte Laïque*, December 1, 2007. Available online: http://ripostelaique.com/Osons-demeurer-des-esprits-libres/ (accessed February 5, 2018).

7 See Claude Martin, "The PACS and marriage and cohabitation in France," *International Journal of Law, Policy and the Family* 14, no 3 (2001): 135–158.

8 Cyrano, "Feminisme et laïcité."

9 See Catherine Gouëset, "Comment la droite parlait du PACS il y a dix ans," *L'Express*, October 13, 2009. Available online: https://www.lexpress.fr/actualite/societe/comment-la-droite-parlait-du-pacs-il-y-a-dix-ans_794199.html (accessed December 10, 2017).

10 Cyrano, "Osons demeurer."

11 Cyrano, "Une pétition qui pose des questions incontournables à toute la société française," *Riposte Laïque*, August 24, 2009. Available online: http://ripostelaique.com/Une-petition-qui-pose-des/ (accessed February 5, 2018).

12 Ibid.

13 Cyrano, "Delanoë trahit la France laïque pour l'islam et son ramadan moyen-âgeux," *Riposte Laïque*, August 22, 2011. Available online: http://ripostelaique.com/delanoe-trahit-la-france-laique-pour-lislam-et-son-ramadan-moyen-ageux/ (accessed February 5, 2018).

14 Ibid.

15 Cyrano, "Pourquoi *Riposte Laïque* dérange-t-il autant?" *Riposte Laïque*, November 14, 2011. Available online: http://ripostelaique.com/pourquoi-riposte-laique-derange-t-il-autant/ (accessed February 5, 2018).

16 Ibid. The Two France(s) names a division of France between the pro-clerical and counter-clerical forces in the country.

17 Cyrano, "Deux nouveaux autocollants pour illustrer la résistance à l'agression islamiste," *Riposte Laïque*, May 3, 2010. Available online: http://ripostelaique.com/Deux-nouveaux-autocollants-pour/ (accessed February 5, 2018).

18 Cyrano, "La France en a plus qu'assez qu'on lui crache au visage!" *Riposte Laïque*, October 21, 2008. Available online: http://ripostelaique.com/La-France-en-a-plus-qu-assez-qu-on/ (February 5, 2018).

19 Ibid.

20 Ibid.

21 Ibid.

22 Cyrano, "Copé-Mariani ou la couardise de l'UMP," *Riposte Laïque*, May 12, 2014. Available online: http://ripostelaique.com/cope-mariani-ou-la-couardise-de-lump/ (accessed February 5, 2018).

23 Cyrano, "Par quel miracle une jeune femme de 25 ans peut-elle encore aimer la France?" *Riposte Laïque*, October 18, 2010. Available online: http://ripostelaique. com/Par-quelle-miracle-une-jeune-femme/ (accessed February 5, 2018).

24 Ibid.

25 Ibid.

26 Cyrano, "La France est en état de guerre civile, c'est un fait …," *Riposte Laïque*, April 20, 2010. Available online: http://ripostelaique.com/La-France-est-en-etat-de-guerre/ (accessed February 5, 2018).

27 Cyrano, "L'armée dernier rempart de notre démocratie face aux barbares?" *Riposte Laïque*, August 26, 2013. Available online: http://ripostelaique.com/larmee-dernier-rempart-de-notre-democratie-face-aux-barbares/ (accessed February 5, 2018).

28 The real name of the author is Georges Bensoussans.

29 See Jacques Chirac, "Allocution de M. Jacques CHIRAC, Président de la République, à Valenciennes," *l'Elysée*, October 21, 2003. Available online: http://www.jacqueschirac-asso.fr/archives-elysee.fr/elysee/elysee.fr/francais/interventions/discours_et_declarations/2003/octobre/allocution_du_president_de_la_republique_a_valenciennes.1406.html (accessed February 5, 2018). See Alain Finkelkraut, "C'est parce que j'ai déstabilisé l'édifice idéologique de la gauche avec mon livre que j'ai fait l'objet de tant de hargne," *Atlantico*, November 24, 2013. Available online: http://www.atlantico.fr/decryptage/finkielkraut-c-est-parce-que-j-ai-destabilise-edifice-ideologique-gauche-avec-livre-que-j-ai-fait-objet-tant-hargne-907138.html (accessed February 5, 2018).

30 See Alain Finkelkraut, *L'identité malheureuse* (Paris: Stock), p. 123.

31 Laurent Obertone, *La France orange mécanique* (Paris: Ring, 2013), p. 192.

32 Fabienne Cosnay, "La France orange mécanique, ce livre polémique," *Europe 1*, March 8, 2013. Available online: http://www.europe1.fr/politique/la-france-orange-mecanique-ce-livre-polemique-1440885 (December 11, 2017).

33 See AFP, "Robert Ménard entendu par la police sur le 'fichage' des écoliers de Béziers," *Le Monde*, March 5, 2015. Available online: http://www.lemonde.fr/politique/article/2015/05/05/quand-robert-menard-fiche-les-enfants-des-ecoles-de-beziers_4627511_823448.html (accessed December 11, 2017).

34 Cosnay, "La France orange mécanique."

35 Cyrano, "Je me demande si je ne vais pas soutenir la Halde …," *Riposte Laïque*, May 26, 2009. Available online: http://ripostelaique.com/Je-me-demande-si-je-ne-vais-pas/ (accessed February 5, 2018).

36 Cyrano, "L'armée dernier rampart."

37 Cyrano, "Ils livrent la République laïque à l'islam! Rassemblons-nous pour sauver la France," *Riposte Laïque*, November 1, 2010. Available online: http://ripostelaique. com/Ils-livrent-la-Republique-laique-a/ (accessed February 5, 2018).

38 Raufer is a pseudonym for Christian de Bongain. See Mathieu Rigouste, *L'enneni intérieure: La généalogie coloniale et militaire de l'ordre sécuritaire dans la France*

contemporaine (Paris: La Découverte, 2009); Pierre Ancery and Clément Guillet, "Qu'est-ce qu'un criminologue," *Slate*, June 28, 2012. Available online: http://www. slate.fr/story/58037/criminologue-merah-magnotta-definition (accessed December 13, 2017).

39 Cyrano, "Le peuple de France doit se préparer à un nouveau 1789," *Riposte Laïque*, June 26, 2010. Available online: http://ripostelaique.com/Le-peuple-de-France-doit-se/ (accessed February 5, 2018).

40 Ibid.

41 Cyrano, "Après Grenoble, cela peut-il continuer ainsi?" *Riposte Laïque*, July 19, 2010. Available online: http://ripostelaique.com/Apres-Grenoble-cela-peut-il/ (accessed February 5, 2018).

42 Cyrano, "Ce que sera la France de Normal 1er en 2017 … s'il va au bout de son mandat," *Riposte Laïque*, October 1, 2012. Available online: http://ripostelaique. com/ce-que-sera-la-france-de-normal-1er-en-2017-sil-va-au-bout-de-son-mandat/ (accessed February 5, 2018). "Frankistan" is an adaptation of the neology "Londonistan," a term initially used in French counter-terrorist discourse to designate London as a hot-bed for Islamist terrorism.

43 See Imam Amrani, "The French hip-hop star fighting the far-right," *The Guardian*, June 10, 2016. Available online: https://www.theguardian.com/music/2016/jun/10/ kalash-nekfeu-and-the-french-rappers-fighting-racism (accessed December 13, 2017).

44 Cyrano, "Burqa, République, insécurité, Zemmour, immigration, laïcité 2010, avenir de RL: une vidéo pour débattre," *Riposte Laïque*, April 14, 2010. Available online: http://ripostelaique.com/Burqa-Republique-insecurite/ (accessed February 5, 2018).

45 Cyrano, "Bobos antiracistes bien-pensants, lisez bien les propos d'Houria Bouteldja …," *Riposte Laïque*, May 17, 2010. Available online: http://ripostelaique. com/Bobos-antiracistes-bien-pensants/ (accessed February 5, 2018).

46 Cyrano, "Ils livrent la République."

47 Cyrano, "La France est en état de guerre civile."

48 Laurent Mouloud, "Affaire Sniper. Le mauvais cible de Sarkozy," *L'Humanité*, November 11, 2003. Available online: http://www.humanite.fr/node/486757 (accessed January 27, 2015).

49 Caroline Vigoureux, "Copé et 'l'empiétement sémantique' sur le FN," *Le Journal du Dimanche*, September 26, 2012. Available online: http://www.lejdd.fr/ Politique/Actualite/Racisme-anti-blanc-Cope-reprend-une-expression-du-FN-interview-560852 (accessed December 11, 2017).

50 Valérie Igounet, "Non au racisme anti-français," *France Info*, November 7, 2016. Available online: https://blog.francetvinfo.fr/derriere-le-front/2016/11/07/non-au-racisme-anti-francais.html (accessed December 11, 2017).

51 Nicolas Bégasse, "Marine Le Pen veut une loi contre le racism anti-blanc," *20 Minutes*, March 30, 2012. Available online: http://www.20minutes.fr/

politique/943669-20120530-marine-pen-veut-loi-contre-racisme-anti-blanc (accessed December 11, 2017).

52　See "UMP: Copé, les pains au chocolat et le Ramadan," *Le Parisien*, October 26, 2012. Available online: http://www.leparisien.fr/politique/ump-cope-les-pains-au-chocolat-et-le-ramadan-06-10-2012-2209731.php (accessed February 5, 2018).

53　Jean-François Copé, *Manifeste pour une droite décomplexé* (Paris: Fayard, 2012).

54　Pierre Tremblay, "À Caen, François Fillon dénonce pour la première fois le 'racisme anti-Français," *Huffington Post*, March 17, 2017. Available online: http://www.huffingtonpost.fr/2017/03/16/a-caen-francois-fillon-denonce-pour-la-premiere-fois-le-racism_a_21898525/ (accessed December 13, 2017).

55　Assemblée Nationale. 2010b. Session extraordinaire de 2009–2010. Séances du mercredi 7 juillet 2010 Compte rendu intégral. *Journal officiel de la République française* 70, p. 5394.

56　Stéphane Kovacs, "Trois mois ferme pour du racisme anti-blanc," *Le Figaro*, April 1, 2016. Available online: http://www.lefigaro.fr/actualite-france/2016/04/01/01016-20160401ARTFIG00315-trois-mois-ferme-pour-du-racisme-anti-blanc.php (accessed December 13, 2017).

57　Cyrano, "L'enjeu du procès de Geert Wilders: la libre critique de l'islam," *Riposte Laïque*, January 22, 2010. Available online: http://ripostelaique.com/L-enjeu-du-proces-de-Geert-Wilders/ (accessed February 5, 2018).

58　Cyrano, "Tout recul, à Lille ou à Ankara, de l'offensive islamiste est un progrès pour l'humanité," *Riposte Laïque*, June 10, 2008. Available online: http://ripostelaique.com/Tout-recul-a-Lille-ou-a-Ankara-de/ (accessed February 5, 2018). It is unclear whether Attatürk ever said what RL suggests. See Jacques Benoist-Méchin, *Mustapha Kémal ou la mort d'un empire* (Paris: Albin Michel, 1954), p. 323.

59　Cyrano, "BHL se ridiculise en voulant agresser Riposte Laïque," *Riposte Laïque*, December 27, 2010. Available online: http://ripostelaique.com/BHL-se-ridiculise-en-voulant/ (accessed February 5, 2018).

60　Cyrano, "Pourquoi Riposte Laïque dérange-t-il."

61　Cyrano, "L'actualité donne raison à Pierre et Pascal: que font-ils devant un tribunal?" *Riposte Laïque*, March 25, 2013. Available online: http://ripostelaique.com/lactualite-donne-raison-a-pierre-et-pascal-que-font-ils-devant-un-tribunal/ (accessed February 5, 2018).

62　Cyrano, "Pour gagner cette guerre." Translation of the Quran in M. A. S. Abdel Haleem, *The Qur'an* (Oxford and New York: Oxford University Press, 2004).

63　Ibid.

64　Ibid.

65　Cyrano, "Grâce à Mélenchon, il n'est plus tabou de parler de la remigration musulmanne," *Riposte Laïque*, December 22, 2014. Available online: https://ripostelaique.com/grace-a-melenchon-le-possible-retour-de-millions-de-musulmans-ne-sera-plus-un-sujet-tabou.html (accessed February 5, 2018).

66   Cyrano, "Jihad à Paris, Fourest agressée: Oriana Fallaci avait raison …" *Riposte Laïque*, September 17, 2012. Available online: http://ripostelaique.com/jihad-a-paris-fourest-agressee-oriana-fallaci-avait-raison/ (accessed February 5, 2018).

67   Cyrano, "Il nous faut un Pat Condell en France!" *Riposte Laïque*, February 16, 2009. Available online: http://ripostelaique.com/Il-nous-faut-un-Pat-Condell-en/ (accessed February 5, 2018).

68   Ibid.

69   Cyrano, "L'alternative à l'UMPS ne peut quêtre islamophobe," *Riposte Laïque*, November 26, 2012. Available online: http://ripostelaique.com/lalternative-a-lumps-ne-peut-quetre-islamophobe/ (accessed February 5, 2018).

70   Cyrano, "2018: Année".

71   Cyrano, "Après le discours anti-laïque de Sarkozy, nous sommes tous au pied du mur," *Riposte Laïque*, January 2, 2008. Available online: http://ripostelaique.com/Apres-le-discours-anti-laique-de/ (accessed February 5, 2018).

72   Cyrano, "Résistance européenne pour désislamiser nos pays," *Riposte Laïque*, January 19, 2015. Available online: http://ripostelaique.com/resistance-europeenne-pour-desislamiser-nos-pays/ (accessed February 5, 2018).

73   Cyrano, "Nation, République, laïcité, voile intégral, prières dans la rue, identité nationale, votation suisse … La cohérence de RL," *Riposte Laïque*, December 14, 2009. Available online: http://ripostelaique.com/Nation-Republique-laicite-voile/ (accessed February 5, 2018).

74   Cyrano, "Entre la France et l'islam, l'heure est venue de choisir son camp," *Riposte Laïque*, July 21, 2014. Available online: http://ripostelaique.com/entre-la-france-et-lislam-lheure-est-venue-de-choisir-son-camp/ (accessed February 5, 2018).

75   Ibid.

76   Cyrano, "Les islamistes sortent du bois et annoncent la couleur: une France musulmane, soumise à la charia," *Riposte Laïque*, September 20, 2010. Available online: http://ripostelaique.com/Les-islamistes-sortent-du-bois-et/ (accessed February 5, 2018).

77   Cyrano, "Peut-on s'être battu pour sauver Ingrid Betancourt, et abandonner Mohamed Sifaoui?" *Riposte Laïque*, July 4, 2008. Available online: http://ripostelaique.com/Peut-on-s-etre-battu-pour-sauver/ (accessed February 5, 2018).

78   Cyrano, "Geert Wilders à 17 %".

79   Cyrano, "Islamophobie: Ils rêvent d'une loi contre des livres comme Reconquista ou Mort de l'Europe," *Riposte Laïque*, February 25, 2015. Available online: http://ripostelaique.com/islamophobie-ils-revent-dune-loi-contre-des-livres-comme-reconquista-ou-mort-de-leurope/ (accessed February 5, 2018).

80   Cyrano, "Nous confirmons que l'islam est incompatible avec la République laïque!" *Riposte Laïque*, March 28, 2011. Available online: http://ripostelaique.com/nous-confirmons-que-lislam-est-incompatible-avec-la-republique-laique/ (February 5, 2018).

81 Ibid.

82 Cyrano, "Les autocollants de RL victimes provisoires de la pression islamiste," *Riposte Laïque*, May 10, 2010. Available online: http://ripostelaique.com/Les-autocollants-de-RL-victimes/ (accessed February 5, 2018).

83 See Raphael Liogier, *Le mythe de l'islamsation: Essai sur une obsession collective* (Paris: Points, 2016).

84 Cyrano, "En 2011, nombre de patriotes vont entrer en résistance contre l'islamisation de la France," *Riposte Laïque*, January 10, 2010. Available online: http://ripostelaique.com/En-2011-nombre-de-patriotes-vont/ (accessed February 5, 2018).

85 Cyrano, "Caroline, pourquoi mentir aussi grossièrement pour salir RL?" *Riposte Laïque*, March 1, 2010. Available online: http://ripostelaique.com/Caroline-pourquoi-mentir-aussi/ (February 5, 2018).

86 Cyrano, "Un islamo-collabo à la place d'une islamo-collabo, et Sarkozy- Fillon veulent en finir avec 1905!" *Riposte Laïque*, February 28, 2011. Available online: http://ripostelaique.com/sarkozy-remplace-une-islamo-collabo-ump-par-un-islamo-collabo-ump/ (accessed February 5, 2018).

87 Cyrano, "Les socialistes sont-ils des idiots utiles ou des traitres?" *Riposte Laïque*, July 30, 2012. Available online: http://ripostelaique.com/les-socialistes-sont-ils-des-idiots-utiles-de-lislam-ou-des-traitres-a-la-france-laique/ (accessed February 5, 2018).

88 Cyrano, "Caroline, pourquoi."

89 Cyrano, "Entre la France et l'islam."

90 Cyrano, "Pour un débat franc et loyal avec Henri Pena Ruiz, qui nous reproche de nous focaliser sur l'islam," *Riposte Laïque*, April 20, 2009. Available online: http://ripostelaique.com/Pour-un-debat-franc-et-loyal-avec/ (accessed February 5, 2018).

91 Cyrano, "Socialaud assassin, le peuple aura ta peau," *Riposte Laïque*, September 13, 2015. Available online: http://ripostelaique.com/socialaud-assassin-le-peuple-aura-ta-peau.html (accessed February 5, 2018).

92 Cyrano, "Comparer l'islamophobie à l'antisémitisme des années 30 est une obscénité," *Riposte Laïque*, October 26, 2009. Available online: http://ripostelaique.com/Comparer-l-antisemitisme-des/ (accessed February 5, 2018).

93 For a discussion about the CDHRI and Islamic Human Rights, see Anver M. Emon, Mark S. Ellis, and Benjamin Glahn, eds., *Islamic Law and International Human Rights Law: Searching for Common Ground?* (Oxford: Oxford University Press, 2012), p. 107ff.

94 On the Eurabia thesis, see Matt Carr, "You are now entering Eurabia," *Race & Class* 48, no. 1 (2006): 1–22; Göran Larsson, "The fear of small numbers: Eurabia literature and censuses on religious belonging," *Journal of Muslims in Europe* 1 (2012): 142–165.

95   See Bat Ye'Or, *Eurabia: The Euro-Arab Axis* (Teaneck, NJ: Fairleigh Dickinson, 2005). Some of the most influential figures are Orianna Fallaci, Thilo Sarrazin, Niall Ferguson, Melanie Philips, David Horowitz, Christopher Caldwell, Mark Spencer, and Bruce Bawer. One of its most fervent spokespersons, Mark Steyn, concludes that "much of what we loosely call the Western world will not survive this century, and much of it will effectively disappear in our lifetimes, including many, if not most Western European countries." See Steyn in Nasar Meer, "Racialization and religion: Race, culture and difference in the study of antisemitism and Islamophobia," *Ethnic and Racial Studies* 36, no. 3 (2013): 385–398, p. 393.

96   Tunku Varadarajan, "Prophet of Decline," *The Wall Street Journal*, June 23, 2005. Available online: https://www.wsj.com/articles/SB111948571453267105 (accessed December 12, 2017).

97   Cyrano, "Après Barnier, Moscovici ose nous dire que l'Europe a besoin de la Turquie!" *Riposte Laïque*, June 2, 2009. Available online: http://ripostelaique.com/ Apres-Barnier-Moscovici-ose-nous/ (accessed February 5, 2018).

98   Cyrano, "Les socialistes sont-ils des idiots."

99   See Renaud Camus, *Le grand remplacement* (Plieux: Chez l'auteur, 2012).

100 Cyrano, "Ils veulent en finir avec la laïcité pour mieux imposer leur modèle de société," *Riposte Laïque*, September 9, 2008. Available online: http://ripostelaique. com/Ils-veulent-en-finir-avec-la/ (February 5, 2018).

101 Ibid.

102 Cyrano, "Les islamistes sortent du bois."

103 Cyrano, "Une première marche contre le fascisme islamiste qui en appelle d'autres …," *Riposte Laïque*, November 12, 2012. Available online: http://ripostelaique.com/une-premiere-marche-contre-le-fascisme-islamiste-qui-en-appelle-dautres/ (accessed February 5, 2018).

104 Cyrano,"La guerre impitoyable de la gôche Hollande-Valls-Attali contre les Gaulois," *Riposte Laïque*, October 20, 2014. Available online: http://ripostelaique. com/la-guerre-impitoyable-de-la-goche-hollande-valls-attali-contre-les-gaulois/ (accessed February 5, 2018).

105 Cyrano, "Si la France n'éradique pas l'islam, elle deviendra musulmane," *Riposte Laïque*, April 21, 2014. Available online: http://ripostelaique.com/si-la-france-neradique-pas-lislam-elle-deviendra-musulmane/ (accessed February 5, 2018).

106 Cyrano, "Pourra-t-on vaincre l'offensive islamiste par les seuls moyens démocratiques?" *Riposte Laïque*, October 11, 2010. Available online: http:// ripostelaique.com/Pourra-t-on-vaincre-l-offensive (accessed February 5, 2018).

107 Ibid.

108 Cyrano, "Si La France n'éradique pas."

109 See, for example, Michel Onfray, *Rendre la raison populaire* (Paris: Éditions Autrement, 2013).

110   For a discussion about Onfrey's statements, see Clément Dousset, "Michel Onfray, nouveau soldat contre l'islam et les musulmans," *Mediapart*, November 19, 2013. Available online: https://blogs.mediapart.fr/clement-dousset/blog/191113/michel-onfray-nouveau-soldat-contre-lislam-et-les-musulmans (accessed December 13, 2017).

111   Cyrano, "Bien sûr qu'il y a bien trop de musulmans en France !" *Riposte Laïque*, May 11, 2015. Available online: http://ripostelaique.com/bien-sur-quil-y-a-bien-trop-de-musulmans-en-france.html (accessed February 5, 2018).

112   Cyrano, "Le voile islamique insulte la liberté de tous," *Riposte Laïque*, March 8, 2010. Available online: http://ripostelaique.com/Le-voile-islamique-insulte-la/ (accessed February 5, 2018).

113   See, for example, Ruth Wodak and John E. Richardson, eds., *Analysing Fascist Discourse. European Fascism in Talk and Text* (London and New York: Routledge, 2015), p. 173.

114   AFP, "'Invasion migratoire' et 'Monseigneur Ebola: Jean-Marie Le Pen en campagne," *Nouvel Observateur*, May 21, 2014. Available online: https://tempsreel.nouvelobs.com/politique/elections-europeennes-2014/20140521.OBS7880/invasion-migratoire-et-monseigneur-ebola-jean-marie-le-pen-en-campagne.html (accessed December 13, 2017).

115   On Marion Marechale Le Pen, see Marc De Boni, "Marion Maréchale-Le Pen valide la théorie du 'grand remplacement'," *Le Figaro*, February 4, 2015. Available online: http://www.lefigaro.fr/politique/le-scan/citations/2015/02/03/25002-20150203ARTFIG00176-marion-marechal-le-pen-valide-la-theorie-du-grand-remplacement.php (accessed December 13, 2017).

116   Ivan Valério, "Pour Marine Le Pen, la théorie du 'grand remplacement' relève du 'complotisme'," *Le Figaro*, November 2, 2014. Available online: http://www.lefigaro.fr/politique/le-scan/citations/2014/11/02/25002-20141102ARTFIG00145-pour-marine-le-pen-la-theorie-du-grand-remplacement-releve-du-complotisme.php (accessed December 13, 2017).

117   Elise Le Guevel, "Le double discours de Marine Le Pen sur la théorie du 'grand remplacement'," *France Info*, January 15, 2016. Available online: https://www.francetvinfo.fr/replay-magazine/france-2/envoye-special/video-envoye-special-le-double-discours-de-marine-le-pen-sur-la-theorie-du-grand-remplacement_1270287.html (accessed December 13, 2017).

118   Cyrano, "Une première vidéo qui montre la tension du débat Cassen-Ramadan," *Riposte Laïque*, October 7, 2013. Available online: http://ripostelaique.com/une-premiere-video-qui-montre-la-tension-du-debat-cassen-ramadan/ (accessed February 5, 2018).

119   Ibid.

120   Cyrano, "Le livre qui va faire causer: Musulmans, vous nous mentez, d'Hubert Lemaire," *Riposte Laïque*, December 1, 2014. Available online: http://ripostelaique.

com/le-livre-qui-va-faire-causer-musulmans-vous-nous-mentez-dhubert-lemaire/ (accessed February 5, 2018).

121 Cyrano, "Ras le bol de voir Tariq Ramadan fanfaronner sur les plateaux de télévision!" *Riposte Laïque*, September 28, 2009. Available online: http:// ripostelaique.com/Ras-le-bol-de-voir-Tariq-Ramadan/ (accessed February 5, 2018). This is a pseudo-scientific and theological articulation of the fear of the Islamic "sleeper cell" common in post 9/11 popular culture. See, for example, Jack Shaheen, *Guilty: Hollywood's Verdict on Arabs after 9/11* (Northampton: Olive Branch Press, 2008). *Taqiyya* is an Islamic concept that denotes a tactic to hide one's Muslim identity to avoid persecution, as during the *Reconquista* and the Inquisition.

122 Cyrano, "Le 10 Novembre, tous à Paris contre le fascisme Islamiste," *Riposte Laïque*, September 24, 2012, Available online: http://ripostelaique.com/le-10-novembre-tous-a-paris-contre-le-fascisme-Islamiste.html (accessed January 17, 2018).

123 During the #metoo campaigns (which in France also included #balancetonporc), Ramadan has been accused of sexual harassment and rape. At the time of writing he is under arrest, which, according to RL, proves that Muslims in general are misogynistiic rapists. On the Ramadan story, see Stéphane Joahny, "L'enquête qui accuse Tariq Ramadan," *Le journal du Dimanche*, February 3, 2018. Available online: http://www.lejdd.fr/societe/faits-divers/lenquete-qui-accuse-tariq-ramadan-3564416 (accessed February 5, 2018).

124 Cyrano, "Ras le bol."

125 Cyrano, "Après l'arrestation de futurs Merah, Valls peut-il interdire la manifestation du 10 novembre?" *Riposte Laïque*, October 8, 2012. Available online: http://ripostelaique.com/apres-larrestation-de-futurs-merah-valls-peut-il-interdire-la-manifestation-du-10-novembre/ (accessed February 5, 2018).

126 Cyrano, "Ras le bol."

127 Cyrano, "Sarkozy emmène Boubakeur dans ses valises algériennes, et stigmatise l' 'islamophobie'!" *Riposte Laïque*, December 8, 2007. Available online: http:// ripostelaique.com/Sarkozy-emmene-Boubakeur-dans-ses/ (accessed February 5, 2018).

128 Cyrano, "Tout recul."

129 Cyrano, "Le maire de Trappes et son avocat menacent Riposte Laïque des foudres de la Justice," *Riposte Laïque*, January 4, 2010. Available online: http://ripostelaique. com/Le-maire-de-Trappes-et-son-avocat/ (accessed February 5, 2018).

130 Cyrano, "Voiles et mosquées, armes du jihad contre la France avec la complicité d'élus de la République," *Riposte Laïque*, March 30, 2009. Available online: http:// ripostelaique.com/Voiles-et-mosquees-armes-du-jihad/ (accessed February 5, 2018).

131 Cyrano, "Après Barnier."

132 For a thorough discussion about mosques in France, see Bowen (*Can Islam ...*, p. 31ff.)

133 Enora Ollivier and Manon Rescan, "Radicalisation: 'Le rôle des mosquées est très effacé dans les nouvelles formes du djihadisme'," *Le Monde*, November 26, 2015. Available online: http://www.lemonde.fr/attaques-a-paris/article/2015/11/26/radicalisation-le-role-des-mosquees-est-tres-efface-dans-les-nouvelles-formes-du-djihadisme_4818497_4809495.html (accessed December 13, 2017).

134 AFP, "Quatre mosquées soupçonnées de radicalisation fermées en région parisienne," *Libération*, November 2, 2016. Available online: http://www.liberation.fr/france/2016/11/02/quatre-mosquees-soupconnees-de-radicalisation-fermees-en-region-parisienne_1525834 (accessed December 13, 2017).

135 Cyrano, "Jour de colère: préserver l'unité des patriotes pour virer Hollande," *Riposte Laïque*, January 20, 2014. Available online: http://ripostelaique.com/jour-de-colere-preserver-lunite-des-patriotes-pour-virer-hollande/ (accessed February 5, 2018).

136 Cyrano, "Pourra-t-on vaincre."

137 Cyrano, "Refuser l'islamisation de 'Ma France'," *Riposte Laïque*, March 15, 2010. Available online: http://ripostelaique.com/Refuser-l-islamisation-de-Ma/ (accessed February 5, 2018).

138 Cyrano, "La légitime révolte du peuple de France devant les multiples agressions que subit son pays," *Riposte Laïque*, August 17, 2010. Available online: http://ripostelaique.com/Une-accumulation-de-faits-qui-ne/ (accessed February 5, 2018).

139 Cyrano, "Halal, ramadan, émeutes: trois armes islamistes pour conquérir la France laïque," *Riposte Laïque*, August 9, 2010. Available online: http://ripostelaique.com/Halal-ramadan-emeutes-trois-armes/ (accessed February 5, 2018).

140 Ibid.

141 Guillaume D. Johnson, Kevin D. Thomas, and Sonya A. Grier, "When the burger becomes halal: a critical discourse analysis of privilege and marketplace inclusion," *Consumption Markets & Culture*, online first (2017).

142 Socca is a local pancake made of chick-pea flour.

143 AFP, "Le ministère de l'agriculture dément les propos de Le Pen sur la viande halal," *Le Monde*, February 18, 2012. Available online: http://www.lemonde.fr/election-presidentielle-2012/article/2012/02/18/selon-le-pen-toute-la-viande-distribuee-en-ile-de-france-est-halal_1645353_1471069.html (accessed February 5, 2018).

144 Caroline Politi, "Menu sans porc à la cantine: la fausse polémique de Marine Le Pen," *L'Express*, April 7, 2014. Available online: https://www.lexpress.fr/actualite/societe/menu-sans-porc-a-la-cantine-la-fausse-polemique-de-marine-le-pen_1506856.html (accessed February 5, 2018).

145 Binet, "'Touche pas.'"

146 Cyrano, "Lettre ouverte à Caroline Fourest et à tous ceux qui nous reprochent de soutenir Fanny," *Riposte Laïque*, October 11, 2007. Available online: http://ripostelaique.com/Lettre-ouverte-a-Caroline-Fourest/ (accessed February 5, 2018).

147 Ibid.

148 Cyrano, "Un débat télévisé sur le voile qui confirme les divergences entre laïques," *Riposte Laïque*, December 15, 2007. Available online: http://ripostelaique.com/Un-debat-televise-sur-le-voile-qui/ (accessed February 5, 2018).

149 Cyrano, "Halte à la burqa et au voile, symboles de la soumission des femmes et de l'offensive islamiste," *Riposte Laïque*, August 20, 2009. Available online: http://ripostelaique.com/Halte-a-la-burqa-et-au-voile/ (accessed February 5, 2018).

150 Cyrano, "Deux nouveaux autocollants."

151 Cyrano, "Socialaud assassin."

152 Rosemary Ellen Guiley, *The Encyclopedia of Demons and Demonology* (New York: Facts on File, 2009), pp. 28–29.

153 Assemblée Nationale, Session extraordinaire de 2009–2010, p. 5408.

154 See Scott, *The Politics*.

155 See Nilsson, *Unveiling*.

156 Cyrano, "Besancenot akbar!" *Riposte Laïque*, February 5, 2010. Available online: http://ripostelaique.com/Besancenot-akbar/ (accessed February 5, 2018).

157 Cyrano, "Geert Wilders à 17 %."

158 Carr, "You are now", p. 9.

159 See, for example, José Pedro Zúquete, "The European extreme-right and Islam: New directions?" *Journal of Political Ideologies* 13, no. 3 (2008): 321–344.

160 Edward Said, *Orientalism* (New York: Vintage Books, 1979), p. 1.

161 Bayoumi mentions Ayaan Hirsi Ali, Irshad Manji, and Reza Aslan. See "The God That Failed: The Orientalism of Today's Muslim Commentators," in *Islamophobia/Islamophilia. Beyond the Politics of Enemy and Friend*, Andrew Shryock, ed. (Bloomington and Indianapolis: Indiana University Press, 2010), p. 80.

162 The point here is not to measure the historical validity of these claims, e.g., Muslims have been living in today's Europe since the eighth century. For further discussion see François Soyer, "Faith, culture and fear: Comparing Islamophobia in early modern Spain and twenty-first-century Europe," *Ethnic and Racial Studies* 36, no. 3 (2013): 399–416.

163 For a similar discussion of this type of learned anti-Muslim discourse, see Vincent Geisser, *La nouvelle islamophobie* (Paris: La Découverte, 2003).

164 "[T]he expression solely of the '*far* right,' loony extremists, individual or collective, such as the various forms of 'national front' or neo-Nazi groups waxing and waning across the continent to the tune of foreign presence and perceived local problems. Exceptional racism reinforces the status quo of exonerated, guiltless institutional forms and responsible individuals more silently and invisibly structuring European societies at large." David T. Goldberg, *The Threat of*

Race: Reflections of Racial Neoliberalism (Malden, Oxford, and Carlton: Wiley-Blackwell, 2009), p. 181.

165   David T. Goldberg, *The Racial State* (Malden and Oxford: Blackwell Publishers, 2002), p. 4.

166   Ibid.

167   See Mathew Carr, *Blood and Faith: The Purging of Muslim Spain, 1492–1614* (London: Hurst, 2017), pp. 40–41.

168   See George M. Fredrickson, *Racism: A Short History* (Princeton, NJ and Oxford: Princeton University Press, 2002), p 32.

169   Soyer, "Faith, culture and fear."

170   See Meer, "Racialization and religion," p. 387. Also see Nabil Matar, "Britons and Muslims in the early modern period: From prejudice to (a theory of) toleration," *Patterns of Prejudice* 43, no. 3–4 (2009): 213–231.

171   Alana Lentin, "Post-race, post politics: The paradoxical rise of culture after multiculturalism," *Ethnic and Racial Studies* 37, no. 8 (2014): 1268–1285.

172   Max Silverman, *Deconstructing the Nation* (London and New York: Routledge, 1992), p. 24.

173   Matthew Hughey, *White Bound: Nationalists, Antiracists, and the Shared Meanings of Race* (Stanford, CA: Stanford University Press, 2012), p. 15.

174   Jacqueline Hogan, *Gender, Race, and National Identity* (London and New York: Routledge, 2009), p. 8.

175   Anne McClintock, *Imperial Leather* (London and New York: Routledge, 1995), p. 150.

176   Ibid., p. 22.

177   Ibid.

178   Scott, *The Politics*, p. 55.

179   See Nira Yuval-Davis and Floya Anthias, eds., *Racialized Boundaries. Race, Nation, Gender, Colour and Class and the Anti-Racist Struggle* (London and New York: Routledge, 1992).

Chapter 3

1   See "Présidentielle: au sein du gouvernement, qui soutient Hamon, qui soutient Macron?" *Le Monde*, March 23, 2017. Available online: http://www.lemonde.fr/election-presidentielle-2017/article/2017/03/23/presidentielle-au-sein-du-gouvernement-qui-soutient-hamon-qui-soutient-macron_5099784_4854003.html (accessed December 15, 2017).

2   In earlier statements, Macron has also talked about colonization in terms of occupation and torture, while simultaneously bringing out its supposed positive effects, the latter being common political lingua in France. See AFP, "En Algérie,

Macron qualifie la colonisation de « crime contre l'humanité », tollé à droite," *Le Monde*, February 16, 2017. Available online: http://www.lemonde.fr/election-presidentielle-2017/article/2017/02/15/macron-qualifie-la-colonisation-de-crime-contre-l-humanite-tolle-a-droite-et-au-front-national_5080331_4854003.html (accessed February 7, 2018).

3 *Débat présidentiel*, TF 1 [TV show], March 20, 2017.

4 Ibid.

5 "Emmanuel Macron: 'J'ai prouvé que j'avais une capacité de commandement'", *Le journal du Dimanche*, March 19, 2017. Available online: http://www.lejdd.fr/Politique/Emmanuel-Macron-J-ai-prouve-que-j-avais-une-capacite-de-commandement-855152 (December 15, 2017).

6 Ibid.

7 See James McAuley, "French Muslims enraged by passage of Macron's version of Patriot Act," *The Washington Post*, October 3, 2017. Available online: https://www.washingtonpost.com/world/europe/with-french-patriot-act-macron-enrages-french-muslims/2017/10/03/998a0af4-a841-11e7-9a98-07140d2eed02_story.html?utm_term=.c034c0d15491 (accessed December 15, 2017).

8 Riposte Laïque, "Macron: Le candidat des musulmans veut islamiser la France," *YouTube: Riposte Laïque*, May 2, 2017. Available online: https://www.youtube.com/watch?time_continue=17&v=FaAc7W5vWkY (accessed May 3, 1017).

9 Cyrano, "Présidentielle: Cette exception française qui 'emmerde' Cohn-Bendit et les siens," *Riposte Laïque*, April 9, 2012. Available online: http://ripostelaique.com/presidentielle-cette-exception-francaise-qui-emmerde-cohn-bendit-et-les-siens/ (accessed February 5, 2018).

10 Cyrano, "Quick halal: les Français ont tout compris, ce sera l'islam ou la République!" *Riposte Laïque*, February 24, 2010. Available online: http://ripostelaique.com/Quick-halal-les-Francais-ont-tout/ (accessed February 5, 2018).

11 Ibid.

12 Cyrano, "'Peuple de France', une chanson qui résume le combat de *Riposte Laïque*," *Riposte Laïque*, March 31, 2010. Available online: http://ripostelaique.com/Peuple-de-France-une-chanson-qui/ (accessed February 5, 2018).

13 Cyrano, "Quick halal."

14 Cyrano, "Ils livrent la République."

15 Cyrano, "Voiles et mosquées."

16 Cyrano, "Les islamistes sortent du bois."

17 Ibid.

18 Cyrano, "A mort les profs, à mort les flics!" *Riposte Laïque*, May 18, 2009. Available online: http://ripostelaique.com/A-mort-les-profs-a-mort-les-flics/ (accessed February 5, 2018).

19 Cyrano, "Pourquoi veulent-ils nous faire taire?" *Riposte Laïque*, May 11, 2009. Available online: http://ripostelaique.com/Pourquoi-veulent-ils-nous-faire/ (accessed February 5, 2018).

20 Nicolas Sarkozy, "Allocution devant le Conseil consultatif Riyad (Arabie Saoudite)," *Palais de l'Elysée*, January 14, 2008.

21 Cyrano, "Après le discours anti-laïque."

22 Cyrano, "Ils veulent en finir."

23 Michèle Alliot-Marie, "Inauguration de la Maison de la conference des eveques de France. Ministre de l'Intérieur, de l'Outre-Mer et des Collectivités locales," *Église catholique de France*, July 4, 2007. Available online: http://archives.eglise.catholique. fr/catho/actus/dossiers/2007/breteuil/20070507discoursmam.pdf (accessed December 26, 2017). Alliot-Marié has also stated that her "way of practicing religion is not conspicuous," which the act of publicly displaying, "or billposting," as she put it, one's conviction with a headscarf is. See Nilsson, *Unveiling*, p. X.

24 Geoffrey Bonnefoy and AFP, "Marine Le Pen se dit 'extrêmement croyante' mais est 'fâchée' avec l'Eglise," *L'Express*, April 14, 2017. Available online: https://www. lexpress.fr/actualite/politique/elections/marine-le-pen-se-dit-extrememement-croyante-mais-est-fachee-avec-l-eglise_1899055.html (accessed December 26, 2017).

25 Ibid.

26 Ibid.

27 Ibid.

28 Cyrano, "L'humanisme laïque contre le sectarisme haineux, la République contre la charia," *Riposte Laïque*, June 3, 2008. Available online: http://ripostelaique.com/L-humanisme-laique-contre-le/ (accessed February 5, 2018).

29 Gaël Vaillant, "Martine Aubry veut en finir avec la polemique de la piscine reservée aux femmes," *Le Journal du Dimanche*, March 27, 2012. Available online: http:// www.lejdd.fr/Politique/Actualite/Martine-Aubry-veut-en-finir-avec-la-polemique-de-la-piscine-reservee-aux-femmes-497816 (accessed December 26, 2017).

30 Robin, "Lille: Piscines pour femmes musulmanes ou pour femmes obèses?" *Fdsouche*, April 25, 2012. Available online: http://www.fdesouche.com/296712-lille-piscines-pour-femmes-musulmanes-ou-pour-femmes-obeses-video (accessed December 26, 2017).

31 Cyrano, "Martine Aubry, épouse Brochen, se plaint des 'rumeurs': Nous persistons et nous signons!" *Riposte Laïque*, July 11, 2011. Available online: http:// ripostelaique.com/martine-aubry-epouse-brochen-se-plaint-des-rumeurs-nous-persistons-et-nous-signons/ (accessed February 5, 2018).

32 Ibid.

33 Michel Veron, "A Lille, Aubry a-t-elle vraiment réservé des créneaux de piscine à des musulmanes?" *L'Express*, March 20, 2012. Available online: https://www. lexpress.fr/actualite/politique/aubry-a-t-elle-vraiment-reservee-des-creneaux-de-piscine-a-des-musulmanes_1098551.html (accessed December 26, 2017).

34 Cyrano, "Discours de Grenoble: encore du vent, ou la dernière cartouche de Sarkozy?" *Riposte Laïque*, August 2, 2010. Available online: http://ripostelaique. com/Discours-de-Grenoble-encore-du/ (accessed February 5, 2018).

35 Cyrano, "La majorité des Français ne veut ni de l'Europe de l'UMPS, ni de la laïcité positive de Sarkozy," *Riposte Laïque*, March 26, 2008. Available online: http:// ripostelaique.com/La-majorite-des-Francais-ne-veut/ (accessed February 5, 2018).

36 See, for example, Cyrano, "Les fossiles de Génération Mitterrand veulent faire taire les jeunes de Génération Identitaire," *Riposte Laïque*, October 22, 2012. Available online: http://ripostelaique.com/les-fossiles-de-generation-mitterrand-veulent-faire-taire-les-jeunes-de-generation-identitaire/ (accessed February 5, 2018).

37 Cyrano, "Accompagnatrices voilées, Saint-Gratien: la laïcité recule sous la pression de l'islam," *Riposte Laïque*, August 29, 2011. Available online: http://ripostelaique. com/accompagnatrices-voilees-saint-gratien-la-laicite-recule-sous-la-pression-de-lislam/ (accessed February 5, 2018).

38 Cyrano, "Oskar Freysinger a-t-il raison de dire que la France est foutue?" *Riposte Laïque*, December 21, 2009. Available online: http://ripostelaique.com/Oskar-Freysinger-a-t-il-raison-de/ (accessed February 5, 2018).

39 Cyrano, "Le peuple de France doit se preparer."

40 Cyrano, "Voiles et mosquées."

41 Cyrano, "La liberté d'expression menacée de mort par l'islam et ses complices," *Riposte Laïque*, January 27, 2009. Available online: http://ripostelaique.com/La-liberte-d-expression-menacee-de/ (accessed February 5, 2018).

42 Cyrano, "Le président Hollande va-t-il devoir désavouer le socialiste Flamby?" *Riposte Laïque*, May 14, 2012. Available online: http://ripostelaique.com/le-president-hollande-va-t-il-devoir-desavouer-le-socialiste-flamby/ (accessed February 5, 2018).

43 Cyrano, "La France est-elle foutue? Oui, sauf si …," *Riposte Laïque*, May 7, 2012. Available online: http://ripostelaique.com/la-france-est-elle-foutue-oui-sauf-si/ (accessed February 5, 2018).

44 Cyrano, "La collabosphère en mission contre la Résistance européenne," *Riposte Laïque*, December 15, 2014. Available online: http://ripostelaique.com/les-islamocollabos-en-premiere-ligne-contre-les-peuples-europeens/ (accessed February 5, 2018).

45 Ibid.

46 Cyrano, "Belkacem-djihadistes: même islam, même combat!" *Riposte Laïque*, October 27, 2014. Available online: http://ripostelaique.com/belkacem-djihadistes-meme-islam-meme-combat/ (accessed February 5, 2018).

47 Ibid.

48 Ibid.

49 Mireille Greschter, "Guillaume Faye explique la logique islamisatrice de la réforme Belkacem," *Riposte Laïque*, May 13, 2015. Available online: https://ripostelaique.

com/guillaume-faye-explique-la-logique-islamistrice-de-la-reforme-belkacem.html (accessed December 26, 2017).

50 Cyrano, "La Folle de Cayenne et la Parasite incompétente veulent tuer notre civilisation," *Riposte Laïque*, September 1, 2014. Available online: http:// ripostelaique.com/la-folle-de-cayenne-et-la-parasite-incompetente-veulent-tuer-notre-civilisation/ (accessed February 5, 2018).

51 Loi n° 2001–434 du 21 mai 2001 tendant à la reconnaissance de la traite et de l'esclavage en tant que crime contre l'humanité, *JORF*, n°0119, May 23, 2001. Available online: https://www.legifrance.gouv.fr/affichTexte.do?cidTexte=JORFTEX T000000405369&categorieLien=id (accessed December 26, 2017).

52 Cyrano, "Pourquoi ont-ils si peur des référendums?" *Riposte Laïque*, October 14, 2013. Available online: http://ripostelaique.com/pourquoi-ont-ils-si-peur-des-referendums/ (accessed February 7, 2018).

53 Cyrano, "Hénin-Beaumont: quelle claque pour Ayrault et Mélenchon!" *Riposte Laïque*, March 24, 2014. Available online: http://ripostelaique.com/henin-beaumont-quelle-claque-pour-ayrault-et-melenchon/ (accessed February 7, 2018).

54 AFP, "Taubira veut que 'les infractions reconnues dans l'espace public' le soient aussi sur Internet," *Le Monde*, February 22, 2015. Available online: http://www.lemonde. fr/societe/article/2015/02/22/christiane-taubira-veut-renforcer-l-arsenal-juridique-contre-les-derives-d-internet_4581277_3224.html (accessed December 26, 2017).

55 Cyrano, "Le vrai péril fasciste, c'est l'islam, la clique Valls-Hollande et les collabos," *Riposte Laïque*, February 2, 2015. Available online: http://ripostelaique.com/le-vrai-peril-fasciste-cest-hollande-valls-lislam-et-les-collabos/ (accessed February 5, 2018).

56 Ibid.

57 Cyrano, "La dictature des juges Taubira contre la liberté d'expression," *Riposte Laïque*, May 13, 2013. Available online: http://ripostelaique.com/la-dictature-des-juges-taubira-contre-la-liberte-dexpression/ (accessed February 5, 2018).

58 Cyrano, "La société totalitaire que veulent mettre en place Hollande et sa clique," *Riposte Laïque*, July 1, 2013. Available online: http://ripostelaique.com/la-societe-totalitaire-que-veulent-mettre-en-place-hollande-et-sa-clique/ (accessed February 5, 2018).

59 Cyrano, "Spécial 'Traité de Lisbonne," *Riposte Laïque*, January 20, 2008. Available online: http://ripostelaique.com/Special-Traite-de-Lisbonne/ (accessed February 5, 2018).

60 Cyrano, "Ils servent la soupe à la pire extrême droite, et ils se croient de gauche!" *Riposte Laïque*, July 12, 2010. Available online: http://ripostelaique.com/lls-servent-la-soupe-a-la-pire/ (accessed February 5, 2018).

61 Cyrano, "Une gauche qui méprise le peuple n'est plus la gauche," *Riposte Laïque*, October 3, 2011. Available online: http://ripostelaique.com/une-gauche-qui-meprise-le-peuple-nest-plus-la-gauche/ (accessed February 5, 2018).

62 Cyrano, "La société totalitaire."

63 Jean Robin, *La nouvelle extreme-droite* (Paris: Xenia Éditions, 2010).

64 Cyrano, "Pour préparer la Résistance, retrouvons notre liberté de parole!" *Riposte Laïque*, September 21, 2009. Available online: http://ripostelaique.com/Pour-preparer-la-Resistance/ (accessed February 5, 2018).

65 Cyrano, "Eric Zemmour condamné, Pascal Hilout convoqué par la police: où est la véritable extrême droite?" *Riposte Laïque*, February 26, 2011. Available online: http://ripostelaique.com/eric-zemmour-condamne-pascal-hilout-convoque-par-la-police-cela-suffit-halte-au-fascisme-vive-la-liberte-dexpression/ (accessed February 5, 2018).

66 Cyrano, "Apéro géant et scandale Anelka-Ribery: ce que comprennent les Français …," *Riposte Laïque*, June 21, 2010. Available online: http://ripostelaique.com/Apero-geant-et-scandale-Anelka/ (accessed February 5, 2018).

67 Cyrano, "Socialistes vous nous mentez, Musulmans vous nous mentez," *Riposte Laïque*, January 26, 2015. Available online: http://ripostelaique.com/socialistes-vous-nous-mentez-musulmans-vous-nous-mentez/ (accessed February 5, 2018).

68 See Davies, *The Extreme Right*, p. 12ff.

69 Ibid., p. 20.

70 "Maintenant, le Front national cible les élites," *Le Parisien*, October 2, 2015. Available online: http://www.leparisien.fr/politique/maintenant-le-front-national-cible-les-elites-02-10-2015-5147247.php (accessed December 26, 2017).

71 "Quand le FN faisait grand bruit," *Libération*, September 9, 2012. Available online: http://www.liberation.fr/france/2012/09/09/quand-le-fn-faisait-grand-bruit_845032 (accessed December 26, 2017).

72 Jacques Chirac, "Déclaration de M. Jacques Chirac, Président de la République et candidat à l'élection présidentielle 2002, après l'annonce de sa réélection à la Présidence de la République, Paris le 5 mai 2002," *La vie publique*, May 6, 2002. Available online: http://discours.vie-publique.fr/notices/027000128.html (accessed December 26, 2017).

73 Dominique Albertini, " 'Front républicain': Marine Le Pen moque 'l'UMPS décomplexé," *Libération*, November 12, 2015. Available online: http://www.liberation.fr/france/2015/11/12/front-republicain-marine-le-pen-moque-l-umps-decomplexe_1412843 (accessed December 26, 2017).

74 Attended meeting in Marseille, Pullman Hotel, March 18, 2015.

75 "La leçon de Trump selon Marine Le Pen: 'Ce que le peuple veut, le peuple peut,'" *L'Express*, November 9, 2016. Available online: https://www.lexpress.fr/actualite/politique/fn/la-lecon-de-trump-selon-marine-le-pen-ce-que-le-peuple-veut-le-peuple-peut_1849079.html (accessed December 26, 2017).

76 Philippe Vardon, "Avant-propos: La première ligne," in *Génération identitaire: Une declaration de guerre contre les soixante huitards*, Markus Willinger, ed. (London: Arktos Media Ltd., 2014), p. 8.

77 Pascal Ory, "François Fillon, un candidat 'antisystème'… pur produit du serial," *Le Monde*, November 22, 2016. Available online: http://www.lemonde.fr/idees/article/2016/11/22/francois-fillon-un-candidat-antisysteme-pur-produit-du-serail_5035725_3232.html (accessed December 26, 2017).

78 "Appelez-le désormais François 'Le Rebelle' Fillon," *France info*, March 10, 2017. Available online: https://www.francetvinfo.fr/politique/francois-fillon/appelez-le-desormais-francois-le-rebelle-fillon_2090779.html (accessed December 26, 2017).

79 See Jules Pecnard, "Présidentielle: la chute de François Fillon dans les sondages," *L'Express*, February 10, 2017. Available online: https://www.lexpress.fr/actualite/politique/elections/presidentielle-la-chute-de-francois-fillon-dans-les-sondages-en-deux-graphiques_1878117.html (accessed December 26, 2017).

80 See Brubaker, "Between nationalism."

81 Laclau, *On Populist*, p. 118.

82 See Anton Pelinka, "Right-Wing Populism: Concept and Typology," in *Right-Wing Populism in Europe*, Ruth Wodak, Majid KhosraviNik, and Brigitte Mral, eds. (New York and London: Bloomsbury, 2013), p. 8.

83 Cyrano, "Mariage homo, islam: la caste contre le people," *Riposte Laïque*, January 28, 2013. Available online: https://ripostelaique.com/mariage-homo-islam-la-caste-contre-le-peuple.html (accessed February 5, 2018).

84 Cyrano, "Causeur et *Riposte Laïque*: débattre entre Républicains, sans trop se chamailler …," *Riposte Laïque*, November 8, 2010. Available online: http://ripostelaique.com/Causeur-et-Riposte-Laique-debattre/ (accessed February 5, 2018).

85 Ibid.

86 Cyrano, "2008: année de la liberté d'expression," *Riposte Laïque*, January 1, 2008. Available online: http://ripostelaique.com/2008-annee-de-la-liberte-d/ (accessed February 8, 2018).

87 Sociology in France is often used as a broader academic label than in Anglo-Saxon countries; here they refer more to scholars in the social sciences, in general.

88 Cyrano, "Le politiquement correct a besoin de lepéniser ses contradicteurs," *Riposte Laïque*, February 2, 2009. Available online: http://ripostelaique.com/Le-politiquement-correct-lepenise/ (accessed February 5, 2018).

89 Cyrano, "Du terrorisme intellectuel de la bien-pensance aux intimidations physiques contre *Riposte Laïque*," *Riposte Laïque*, April 7, 2010. Available online: http://ripostelaique.com/Du-terrorisme-intellectuel-de-la/ (accessed February 5, 2018).

90 Cyrano, "2008: année."

91 Cyrano, "Sommes-nous d'affreux franchouillards si nous aimons notre pays, la France?" *Riposte Laïque*, November 11, 2008. Available online: http://ripostelaique.com/Sommes-nous-d-affreux/ (accessed February 5, 2018).

92 Cyrano, "Burqa, République, insécurité."

93 Cyrano, "En finir avec la tyrannie post-soixante-huitarde et retrouver la vraie France," *Riposte Laïque*, March 5, 2012. Available online: http://ripostelaique.com/en-finir-avec-la-tyrannie-post-soixante-huitarde-et-retrouver-la-vraie-france/ (accessed February 5, 2018).

94 Cyrano, "Insécurité, islam: honte aux dirigeants de cette 'gôche', qui abandonnent le peuple et la République," *Riposte Laïque*, August 23, 2010. Available online: http://ripostelaique.com/Insecurite-islam-honte-aux/ (accessed February 5, 2018).

95 Ibid.

96 Cyrano, "Todd-Mélenchon-Fourest: vrais rebelles ou chiens de garde?" *Riposte Laïque*, November 21, 2011. Available online: http://ripostelaique.com/todd-melenchon-fourest-vrais-rebelles-ou-chiens-de-garde/ (accessed February 5, 2018).

97 Cyrano, "15 ans après, les chiens de garde nouveaux sont arrivés," *Riposte Laïque*, April 18, 2011. Available online: http://ripostelaique.com/15-ans-apres-les-chiens-de-garde-nouveaux-sont-arrives/ (accessed February 6, 2018).

98 Cyrano, "Le maire de Trappes."

99 Cyrano, "Quick *halal*."

100 Cyrano, "Lozès a osé: l'apéro saucisson-pinard coupable du drame d'Oslo!" *Riposte Laïque*, July 25, 2011. Available online: http://ripostelaique.com/lozes-a-ose-lapero-saucisson-pinard-coupable-du-drame-doslo/ (accessed February 6, 2018).

101 Ibid.

102 Cyrano, "Le politiquement correct."

103 Cyrano, "La prochaine étape des socialauds: contraindre les Français à loger les migrants," *Riposte Laïque*, September 6, 2015. Available online: http://ripostelaique.com/la-prochaine-etape-des-socialauds-contraindre-les-francais-a-loger-les-migrants.html (accessed February 6, 2018).

104 Cyrano, "Au secours, Voltaire, ils sont devenus fous!" *Riposte Laïque*, December 8, 2012. Available online: http://ripostelaique.com/Au-secours-Voltaire-ils-sont/ (accessed February 6, 2018).

105 Cyrano, "L'ordre nouveau des islamogauchistes au service du fascisme vert," *Riposte Laïque*, September 6, 2010. Available online: http://ripostelaique.com/L-ordre-nouveau-des/ (accessed February 6, 2018).

106 Cyrano, "En Iran, police."

107 Cyrano, "Une pétition qui marche, un journal qui fait causer," *Riposte Laïque*, November 5, 2011. Available online: http://ripostelaique.com/Une-petition-qui-marche-un-journal/ (accessed February 6, 2018).

108 Cyrano, "Pourquoi veulent-ils nous faire."

109 Ibid.

110 Cyrano, "Burqa, République, insécurité."

111 Cyrano, "Défendre la pensée juste et ne pas subir le politiquement correct," *Riposte Laïque*, July 26, 2010. Available online: http://ripostelaique.com/Defendre-la-pensee-juste-et-ne-pas/ (accessed February 6, 2018).

112 Cyrano, "Pour préparer la Résistance."

113 Cyrano, "La LDH veut se faire Riposte Laïque devant les tribunaux!" *Riposte Laïque*, January 24, 2011. Available online: http://ripostelaique.com/La-LDH-veut-se-faire-Riposte/ (accessed February 6, 2018).

114 Cyrano, "Pourquoi veulent-ils nous faire."

115 Ibid.

116 Cyrano. "Sommes-nous d'affreux franchouillards." HALDE has been criticized by the Court of Auditors for its rising costs. See Cécilia Gabizon, "La Cour des comptes revoit sa copie sur la HALDE," *L'Express*, December 13, 2010. Available online: http://www.lefigaro.fr/conjoncture/2010/12/13/04016-20101213ARTFIG00622-la-cour-des-comptes-revoit-sa-copie-sur-la-halde.php (accessed December 26, 2017).

117 Cyrano, "Qui sont vraiment les 'nouveaux fachos'?" *Riposte Laïque*, January 17, 2011. Available online: http://ripostelaique.com/Qui-sont-vraiment-les-nouveaux/ (accessed February 8, 2018).

118 Clémence Bauduin, "Marine Le Pen se déchaîne contre les médias lors d'un meeting à Bordeaux," *RTL*, April 2, 2017. Available online: http://www.rtl.fr/actu/politique/marine-le-pen-se-dechaine-contre-les-medias-lors-d-un-meeting-a-bordeaux-7787920817 (accessed December 26, 2017).

119 V. R., "Vidéo. Des journalistes de *Quotidien* violemment expulsés lors d'une visite de Marine Le Pen," *Sud Ouest*, February 1, 2017. Available online: http://www.sudouest.fr/2017/02/01/video-des-journalistes-de-quotidien-violemment-expulses-lors-d-une-visite-de-marine-le-pen-3158730-5208.php (accessed December 26, 2017).

120 AFP, "Plusieurs journalistes agressés lors du défilé du Front national," *Le Monde*, May 1, 2015. Available online: http://www.lemonde.fr/politique/article/2015/05/01/plusieurs-journalistes-agresses-lors-du-defile-du-front-national_4626214_823448.html#D5dL4SQ2ZTqM3DRT.99 (accessed December 26, 2017).

121 See Marcus, *The National Front*.

122 Marine Le Pen, @MLP_Officiel, Twitter, November 19, 2014. Available online: https://twitter.com/mlp_officiel/status/535332620218171392 (accessed December 26, 2017).

123 Emmanuel Galiero, "Marine Le Pen se voit comme une «exception» de la présidentielle," *Le Figaro*, September 3, 2016. Available online: http://www.lefigaro.fr/politique/2016/09/03/01002-20160903ARTFIG00078-marine-le-pen-se-voit-comme-une-exception-de-la-presidentielle.php (accessed December 26, 2017).

124 AFP, "Maréchal-Le Pen (FN): Cukierman 'broyé par le politiquement correct'," *L'Express*, February 24, 2015. Available online: https://www.lexpress.fr/actualites/1/politique/marechal-le-pen-fn-cukierman-broye-par-le-politiquement-correct_1654816.html (accessed December 26, 2017).

125 Ibid.

126 Ibid.

127 Ibid.

128 France info, "Marine Le Pen appelle ses partisans à utiliser les réseaux sociaux pour court-circuiter les medias," *France Télévisions*, May 1, 2016. Available online: https://www.francetvinfo.fr/politique/front-national/video-marine-le-pen-appelle-ses-partisans-a-utiliser-les-reseaux-sociaux-pour-court-circuiter-les-medias_1431019.html (accessed December 26, 2017).

129 Ibid.

130 One of the most discussed policies has been to problematize gender roles in public schools with the program *ABCD de l'égalité* [ABCD of Equality].

131 During a conference in Nancy in November 2013, Cassen held a speech titled "Homo-Marriage and Islamization, Two Attacks Against Our Civilizations."

   See Cyrano, "Cirque Taubira: ils tirent leurs dernières cartouches mais ils vont dégager!" *Riposte Laïque*, November 18, 2013. Available online: http://ripostelaique.com/cirque-taubira-ils-tirent-leurs-dernieres-cartouches-mais-ils-vont-degager/ (accessed February 8, 2018).

132 Cyrano, "Ce que sera la France."

133 Cyrano, "Le 25 mai, châtiez dans les urnes les fossoyeurs de la France," *Riposte Laïque*, May 19, 2014. Available online: http://ripostelaique.com/le-25-mai-chatiez-dans-les-urnes-les-fossoyeurs-de-la-france/ (accessed February 6, 2018).

134 Ibid.

135 Cyrano, "Mariage homo: le bal des faux-culs socialistes," *Riposte Laïque*, January 7, 2013. Available online: http://ripostelaique.com/mariage-homo-les-faux-culs-socialistes/ (accessed February 6, 2018).

136 Ibid.

137 Ibid.

138 Cyrano, "La Folle de Cayenne."

139 Ibid.

140 Cyrano, "La France est-elle foutue?"

141 Cyrano, "Valls livre délibérément la France aux jihadistes," *Riposte Laïque*, August 6, 2012. Available online: http://ripostelaique.com/valls-livre-deliberement-la-france-aux-jihadistes/ (accessed February 6, 2018).

142 Cyrano, "Dal-Bordeaux, antiracistes,Trappes: une même guerre contre la France," *Riposte Laïque*, July 22, 2013. Available online: http://ripostelaique.com/dal-bordeaux-antiracistes-bregignytrappes-une-meme-guerre-menee-contre-la-france/ (accessed February 7, 2018).

143   Cyrano, "Larmes de Cazeneuve: qu'est-ce qu'ils doivent se marrer les égorgeurs!" *Riposte Laïque*, July 6, 2015. Available online: http://ripostelaique.com/larmes-de-cazeneuve-quest-ce-quils-doivent-se-marrer-les-egorgeurs.html (accessed February 7, 2018).

144   Cyrano, "Valls livre délibérément."

145   See Alduy and Wahnich, *Marine Le Pen*, p. 63.

146   Marine Le Pen, *À contre flots* (Paris: Éditions Jacques Granchier, 2006), p. 188.

147   Ibid.

148   Ibid, p. 189.

149   Xavier Frison, "Marine Le Pen se pose en gardienne des droits des femmes … mais ne veut pas s'en mêler," *Marianne*, October 16, 2016. Available online: https://www.marianne.net/politique/marine-le-pen-se-pose-en-gardienne-des-droits-des-femmes-mais-ne-veut-pas-s-en-meler (accessed December 27, 2017).

150   "Au nom du people: 144 engagements présidentielles: Marine 2017," *Front National*, 2017, point 9. Available online: http://www.frontnational.com/pdf/144-engagements.pdf (accessed December 27, 2017).

151   Victor Dhollande-Monnier, "Avec la 'crise migratoire,' Marine le Pen craint 'le début de la fin du droit des femmes,'" *Europe 1*, January 12, 2016. Available online: http://lelab.europe1.fr/avec-la-crise-migratoire-marine-le-pen-craint-le-debut-de-la-fin-du-droit-des-femmes-2649923 (accessed December 27, 2017).

152   "Programme politique," *Front National*, 2015, p. 37.

153   Frison, "Marine Le Pen."

154   Ibid.

155   *Front National*, "Au nom," point 9.

156   Dhollande-Monnier, "Avec la."

157   Hadrien Mathoux, "Droits de LGBT: Marine Le Pen prépare discrètement la grande régression," *Marianne*, April 28, 2017. Available online: https://www.marianne.net/politique/droits-des-lgbt-marine-le-pen-prepare-discretement-la-grande-regression (accessed December 27, 2017).

158   See Francesca Scrinzi, "A 'New' National Front? Gender, Religion, Secularism, and the French Populist Radical Right," in *Gender and Far Right Politics in Europe*, Michaela Köttig, Renate Bitzan, and Andrea Pető, eds. (Cham: Palgrave Macmillan, 2017).

159   Thibaut Pézerat, "Le directeur des jeunes du FN favorable à une interdiction de la 'propagande gay' comme en Russie," *Europe 1*, January 8, 2014. Available online: http://lelab.europe1.fr/le-president-des-jeunes-du-fn-favorable-a-une-loi-similaire-a-l-interdiction-de-la-propagande-gay-en-russie-12386 (accessed December 27, 2017).

160   Ibid.

161   Dimitri Almeida, "Decadence and indifference in the ideology of the Front National," *French Cultural Studies* 25, no. 2 (2014): 221–232, p. 225.

162 See the annual report of SOS Homophobie, "Rapport sur l'homophobie 2017: Lutte contre la lesbophobie, la gayophobie, la biphobie et la transphobie," 2017. Available online: https://www.sos-homophobie.org/sites/default/files/rapport_annuel_2017.pdf (accessed December 27, 2017).

163 Maxime Bourdeau, "Gérald Darmanin et ses tweets anti-mariage gay passent mal quand Macron veut que 'chacun puisse aimer librement,'" *Huffington Post*, March 17, 2017. Available online: http://www.huffingtonpost.fr/2017/05/17/gerald-darmanin-et-ses-tweets-anti-mariage-pour-tous-passent-mal_a_22096235/ (accessed December 27, 2017).

164 Ibid.

165 "C Politique: L'essayiste Pascal Bruckner associe LGBT et pédophilie," *Huffington Post*, October 22, 2017. Available online: http://www.huffingtonpost.fr/2017/10/22/c-politique-lessayiste-pascal-bruckner-associe-lgbt-et-pedophile_a_23252007/ (accessed December 27, 2017).

166 AFP, "Canular homophobe dans TPMP: amende de 3 millions d'euros contre Hanouna et C8," *Le Parisien*, July 27, 2017. Available online: http://www.leparisien.fr/culture-loisirs/tv/canular-homophobe-dans-tpmp-amende-de-3-millions-d-euros-contre-c8-et-cyril-hanouna-26-07-2017-7158105.php (accessed December 27, 2017).

167 Cyrano, "Après les JO du voile, place à la qatarisation du football ... et de la politique francaise," *Riposte Laïque*, August 13, 2012. Available online: http://ripostelaique.com/apres-les-jo-du-voile-place-a-la-qatarisation-du-football-et-de-la-politique-francaise/ (accessed February 7, 2018).

168 Ibid.

169 Cyrano, "Oskar Freysinger a-t-il raison."

170 Cyrano, "Présidentielles: Le PS demande aux électeurs du FN et de l'UMP de choisir son candidat!" *Riposte Laïque*, May 30, 2011. Available online: http://ripostelaique.com/presidentielles-le-ps-demande-aux-electeurs-du-fn-et-de-lump-de-choisir-son-candidat/ (accessed February 7, 2018).

171 Cyrano, "Au bout de 2 mois l'imposteur Normal 1er est déjà nu!" *Riposte Laïque*, July 16, 2012. Available online: http://ripostelaique.com/au-bout-de-2-mois-limposteur-normal-1er-est-deja-nu/ (accessed February 7, 2018).

172 Cyrano, "La société totalitaire."

173 Cyrano, "Le vrai programme de François Hollande c'est Jacques Attali," *Riposte Laïque*, February 27, 2012. Available online: http://ripostelaique.com/le-vrai-programme-de-francois-hollande-cest-jacques-attali/ (accessed February 7, 2018).

174 Cyrano, "Médias et justice complices de Hollande et du changement de civilisation," *Riposte Laïque*, May 6, 2013. Available online: http://ripostelaique.com/medias-et-justice-complices-de-hollande-et-du-changement-de-civilisation/ (accessed February 7, 2018).

175 Ibid.

176 Cyrano, "Le seul intérêt de ces élections régionales …," *Riposte Laïque*, March 12,
     2010. Available online: http://ripostelaique.com/Le-seul-interet-de-ces-elections/
     (accessed February 7, 2018).

177 Cyrano, "Non content de tuer la France, Attali rêve d'en finir avec les Français,"
     Riposte Laïque, February 11, 2013. Available online: http://ripostelaique.com/
     non-content-de-tuer-la-france-attali-reve-den-finir-avec-les-francais/ (accessed
     February 7, 2018).

178 Attali is articulated in a very similar manner as George Soros, who has been targeted
     by radical nationalist voices in the UK, the USA, and Hungary, among other
     countries. See Adam Lusher, "George Soros: The billionaire investor who became
     the favourite target of conspiracy theories and antisemitic hatred," *The Independent*,
     February 8, 2018. Available online: http://www.independent.co.uk/news/uk/politics/
     geore-soros-brexit-antisemitism-jew-conspiracy-theories-telegraph-story-plot-
     hungary-broke-bank-of-a8201651.html (accessed February 14, 2018).

179 Cyrano, "Le vrai visage de Manuel Valls: un dangereux menteur mondialiste,"
     Riposte Laïque, April 28, 2014. Available online: http://ripostelaique.com/le-vrai-
     visage-de-manuel-valls-un-dangereux-menteur-mondialiste/ (accessed February
     7, 2018).

180 Emmanuel Ratier, *Le vrai visage de Manuel Valls* (Paris: Éditions Facta, 2014), p. 57.

181 Ibid.

182 See, for example, Yves Lejeune, "Le vrai visage de Manuel Valls. Entretien
     avec Emmanuel Ratier," *Novopresse*, April 28, 2014. Available online: https://
     fr.novopress.info/164634/vrai-visage-manuel-valls-entretien-emmanuel-ratier/
     (accessed December 27, 2017).

183 Dumas has become infamous for his support of comedian Dieudonné's anti-
     Semitic sketches. See Raphaëlle Bacqués, "Roland Dumas, l'amoraliste," *Le
     Monde*, January 12, 2012. Available online: http://www.lemonde.fr/politique/
     article/2011/01/12/roland-dumas-l-amoraliste_1464572_823448.html (accessed
     December 27, 2017).

184 "Jean-Marie Le Pen repris par ses vieux demons," *Le Parisien*, June 8, 2014.
     Available online: http://www.leparisien.fr/espace-premium/actu/jean-marie-le-
     pen-repris-par-ses-vieux-demons-08-06-2014-3905737.php (accessed December
     27, 2017).

185 "JM Le Pen: le 'detail de l'Histoire," *L'heure de vérité* [TV-program], Antenne 2,
     January 27, 1988. Available online: http://www.ina.fr/video/I00005274 (accessed
     February 8, 2018).

186 AFP, "Jean-Marie Le Pen exclut du Front National," *Le Monde*, August 20, 2015.
     Available online: http://www.lemonde.fr/politique/article/2015/08/20/jean-marie-
     le-pen-se-defend-face-au-bureau-executif-du-fn_4731727_823448.html (accessed
     February 8, 2018).

187 Olivier Faye, "Marine Le Pen choque en déclarant que 'la France n'est pas responsable' de la rafle du Vél' d'Hiv," *Le Monde*, April 10, 2017. Available online: http://www.lemonde.fr/election-presidentielle-2017/article/2017/04/10/marine-le-pen-choque-en-declarant-que-la-france-n-est-pas-responsable-de-la-rafle-du-vel-d-hiv_5108622_4854003.html#I2cPIAMcE92xJm12.99 (accessed February 9, 2018).

188 Ibid.

189 On the intersection of anti-Muslim and anti-Jewish discourse, see Gil Anidjar, "Antisemitism and Its Critics," in *Antisemitism and Islamophobia in Europe. A Shared Story?* James Renton and Ben Gidley, eds. (London: Palgrave Macmillan, 2017).

190 Alduy and Wahnich, *Marine Le Pen*, p. 31.

191 See, for example, Sylvain Crépon, *La nouvelle extrême droite. Enquête sur les jeunes militants du Front National* (Paris: L'Harmattan, 2006); Nonna Mayer, *Ces français qui votent Le Pen* (Paris: Flammarion, 2002).

192 See Brigitte Beauzamy, "Continuities of Fascist Discourses, Discontinuities of Extreme-Right Political Actors? Overt and Covert Antisemitism in the Contemporary French Radical Right," in *Analysing Fascist Discourse. European Fascism in Talk and Text*, Ruth Wodak and John E. Richardson, eds. (London and New York: Routledge, 2015), p. 173.

193 Laclau, *On Populist Reason*, p. 97.

194 Davies, *The Extreme Right*, p. 18.

195 Stavrakakis and Jäger, "Accomplishments and limitations," p. 13.

196 Dino Franco Felluga, *Critical Theory: The Key Concepts* (London and New York: Routledge, 2015), p. 3. See also Julia Kristeva, *Powers of Horror: An Essay on Abjection* (New York: Columbia University Press, 1982).

Chapter 4

1 *Riposte Laïque*, "Peuple de France," *YouTube: Riposte Laïque*, November 9, 2010. Available online: https://www.youtube.com/watch?v=9hJBtGhgkJc (accessed February 8, 2018).

2 Cyrano, "Mariage homo, islam."

3 Ibid.

4 Cyrano, "Pourquoi suis-je français?" *Riposte Laïque*, November 23, 2009. Available online: http://ripostelaique.com/POURQUOI-SUIS-JE-FRANCAIS/ (accessed February 8, 2018).

5 Cyrano, "Insécurité, islam."

6 Cyrano, "Pourquoi suis-je français?"

7 Ibid.

8 Ibid.

9   Cyrano, "Identité(s) nationale(s): la parole au(x) peuple(s)!" *Riposte Laïque*,
    November 9, 2009. Available online: http://ripostelaique.com/Identite-s-nationale-
    s-la-parole/ (accessed February 8, 2018).

10 Ibid.

11 Ibid.

12 The historical records of the alleged Battle of Poitiers and its consequences contest
    this interpretation. Moreover, Charles Martel has been used as a mythic reference
    throughout French history, to legitimize anachronistic readings of history. For a
    thorough analysis, see William Blanc and Christophe Naudin, *Charles Martel et la
    bataille de Poitiers: De l'histoire au mythe identitaire* (Paris: Libertalia, 2015).

13 See Christine Tasin, "Je ne suis pas Charlie, je suis Charles Martel," *Résistance
    Républicaine*, January 9, 2015. Available online: http://resistancerepublicaine.
    eu/2015/01/09/je-ne-suis-pas-charlie-je-suis-charles-martel/ (accessed January 12,
    2018).

14 Cyrano, "Identité(s) nationale(s)."

15 Ibid.

16 Cyrano, "Pourquoi suis-je français?"

17 Ibid.

18 Cyrano, "Poitiers: Rencontres Charles Martel et Congrès des socialo-collabos,"
    Riposte Laïque, June 1, 2015. Available online: https://ripostelaique.com/poitiers-
    rencontres-charles-martel-et-congres-des-socialo-collabos.html (accessed February
    8, 2018).

19 Cyrano, "En 2011, nombre de patriotes."

20 Cyrano, "Sommes-nous d'affreux franchouillards."

21 Cyrano, "Insécurité, Islam."

22 Cyrano, "Le 8 mars est arrive," *Riposte Laïque*, March 5, 2008. Available online:
    http://ripostelaique.com/Le-8-mars-nouveau-est-arrive/ (accessed February 8, 2018).

23 See, for example, Pierre Cassen and Christine Tasin, *La faute du Bobo Jocelyn*
    (Mérginac: Éditions Riposte Laïque, 2011), pp. 156–157.

24 Cyrano, "Mariage homo, islam." The names refer to the former socialist mayor of
    Paris, Bertrand Delanoë, and the journalist Caroline Fourest, and their alleged
    respective partners at the time of publication.

25 Cyrano, "Le vrai clivage se situe entre ceux qui aiment la France, et ceux qui veulent
    qu'elle disparaisse," *Riposte Laïque*, February 12, 2010. Available online: http://
    ripostelaique.com/Le-vrai-clivage-se-situe-entre/ (accessed February 8, 2018).

26 Cyrano, "Nous aimons la beauté démocratique," *Riposte Laïque*, November 2, 2009.
    Available online: http://ripostelaique.com/Nous-aimons-la-beaute-democratique/
    (accessed February 8, 2018).

27 Cyrano, "L'apéro géant saucisson pinard objet de toute la vindicte médiatique …,"
    Riposte Laïque, June 14, 2010. Available online: http://ripostelaique.com/L-apero-
    geant-saucisson-pinard/ (accessed February 8, 2018).

28 Cyrano, "Coupables de trop aimer la France," *Riposte Laïque*, September 13, 2010. Available online: http://ripostelaique.com/Coupables-de-trop-aimer-la-France/ (accessed February 8, 2018).

29 Ibid.

30 Cyrano, "Une troisième année qui a été décisive pour *Riposte Laïque*," *Riposte Laïque*, July 5, 2010. Available online: http://ripostelaique.com/Une-troisieme-annee-qui-a-ete/ (accessed February 8, 2018).

31 Cyrano, "Les sales méthodes de Marianne pour salir notre initiative du 18 juin," *Riposte Laïque*, June 19, 2011. Available online: http://ripostelaique.com/les-sales-methodes-de-marianne-pour-salir-notre-initiative-du-18-juin/ (accessed February 8, 2018).

32 "Marine Le Pen réussit son pari: 'Ce n'est qu'un début'," *Le Parisien*, April 21, 2012. Available online: http://www.leparisien.fr/election-presidentielle-2012/candidats/marine-le-pen-fait-le-meilleur-sccre-du-fn-a-une-presidentiel le-21-04-2012-1965686.php (accessed January 11, 2018).

33 Marine Le Pen, "CP 002580 Nanterre," *Front National*, June 19, 2015. Available online: http://www.frontnational.com/pdf/statuts2.pdf (accessed January 11, 2018).

34 Nicolas Bay, "Le cri d'amour de la patrie!" *Front National*, December 18, 2015. Available online: http://www.frontnational.com/2015/12/2015-le-cri-damour-de-la-patrie (accessed January 11, 2018).

35 Cyrano, "Burqa, immigration, Hénin-Beaumont: trois défaites du politiquement correct," *Riposte Laïque*, June 29, 2009. Available online: http://ripostelaique.com/Burqa-immigration-Henin-Beaumont/ (accessed February 8, 2018).

36 Cyrano, "Mariage homo, islam." While the public image of Islam and Muslims in France is rather negative, the number (74 percent) that reject Islam is unsubstantiated. Forty-two percent answered yes to the question, "do you think that the Muslim community poses a threat to the identity of our country?" See Ifop, "L'image de l'islam en France," *Le Figaro*, 2012, p. 5. Available online: http://www.lefigaro.fr/assets/pdf/sondage-ipsos-islam-france.pdf (accessed January 11, 2018).

37 Cyrano, "Islamistes et socialistes unis dans la destruction de la France," *Riposte Laïque*, April 27, 2015. Available online: http://ripostelaique.com/islamistes-et-socialistes-unis-dans-la-destruction-de-la-france.html (accessed February 8, 2018).

38 Cyrano, "Le maire de Trappes."

39 Cyrano, "Le baiser de la mort des gauchistes et des bobos aux républicains compassionnels," *Riposte Laïque*, May 27, 2008. Available online: http://ripostelaique.com/Les-republicains-doivent-attaquer/ (accessed February 8, 2018).

40 Cyrano, "Fanny et Monia, deux femmes courageuses," *Riposte Laïque*, September 21, 2007. Available online: http://ripostelaique.com/Fanny-et-Monia-deux-femmes/ (accessed February 8, 2018).

41 Ibid.

42 Cyrano, "La Folle de Cayenne."

43 Cyrano, "Assez d'impuissance face aux voyous racistes et aux fascistes islamistes!" *Riposte Laïque*, April 26, 2010. Available online: http://ripostelaique.com/Assez-d-impuissance-face-aux/ (accessed February 8, 2018).

44 Ibid.

45 Cyrano, "Une pétition qui pose des questions."

46 Cyrano, "Le courage des vraies résistantes," *Riposte Laïque*, October 27, 2007. Available online: http://ripostelaique.com/Le-courage-des-vraies-resistantes/ (accessed February 8, 2018).

47 Ibid.

48 Ibid.

49 Cyrano, "Comparer l'islamophobie à l'antisémitisme."

50 Cyrano, "Après Grenoble."

51 Ibid.

52 For an introduction to the sociology of metropolitan uprisings, see Michel Kokoreff, *Sociologie des émeutes* (Paris: Payot, 2008).

53 Cyrano, "A mort les profs."

54 Ibid.

55 Ibid.

56 Cyrano, "Le système peut dire merci à ceux qui ont cassé, depuis 40 ans, toute autorité républicaine," *Riposte Laïque*, November 4, 2008. Available online: http://ripostelaique.com/Le-systeme-peut-dire-merci-a-ceux/ (accessed February 8, 2018).

57 Cyrano, "Le baiser de la mort."

58 Cyrano, "DSK hors circuit, il va falloir en trouver un autre pour faire le sale boulot des mondialistes," *Riposte Laïque*, May 16, 2011. Available online: http://ripostelaique.com/dsk-hors-circuit-il-va-falloir-en-trouver-un-autre-pour-faire-le-sale-boulot-des-mondialistes/ (accessed February 8, 2018).

59 Cyrano, "Et s'ils se rappelaient qu'ils sont élus pour protéger le peuple de France?" *Riposte Laïque*, March 21, 2011. Available online: http://ripostelaique.com/et-sils-se-rappelaient-quils-sont-elus-pour-proteger-le-peuple-de-france/ (accessed February 9, 2018).

60 Cyrano, "Jour de colère."

61 Cyrano, "Insécurité, islam."

62 Cyrano, "La liberté d'expression menacée."

63 Cyrano, "Nous ne voulons pas être seulement l'honneur de la gauche, nous souhaitons susciter le réveil du peuple français," *Riposte Laïque*, June 15, 2009. Available online: http://ripostelaique.com/Nous-ne-voulons-pas-etre-seulement/ (accessed February 8, 2018).

64 Ibid.

65 Cyrano, "Apéro géant et scandale."

66 Ibid.

67 Cyrano, "La liberté d'expression menacée."

68 Ibid.

69 Cyrano, "Nation, République, laïcité."

70 Ibid.

71 Ibid.

72 Cyrano, "Pas de voile pour Marianne: le livre dont la France avait besoin," *Riposte Laïque*, January 6, 2014. Available online: http://ripostelaique.com/pas-de-voile-pour-marianne-le-livre-dont-la-france-avait-besoin/ (accessed February 8, 2018).

73 Cyrano, "Burqa, République, insécurité."

74 Cyrano, "Assises sur l'islamisation." I have witnessed otherwise firsthand, sitting next to Cassen.

75 Cyrano, "Oseront-ils condamner Pascal et Pierre, après avoir acquitté Bouteldja?" *Riposte Laïque*, January 30, 2012. Available online: http://ripostelaique.com/oseront-ils-condamner-pascal-et-pierre-apres-avoir-acquitte-bouteldja/ (accessed February 8, 2018).

76 Cyrano, "Deux nouveaux autocollants."

77 Cyrano, "Reconquista ou Mort de l'Europe, de René Marchand: LE livre que nous attendions tous," *Riposte Laïque*, February 18, 2013. Available online: http://ripostelaique.com/reconquista-ou-mort-de-leurope-de-rene-marchand-le-livre-que-nous-attendions-tous/ (accessed February 8, 2018).

78 Cyrano, "Du terrorisme intellectuel."

79 Cyrano, "7 Français sur 10 ne veulent plus de Sarkozy-Aubry," *Riposte Laïque*, March 22, 2010. Available online: http://ripostelaique.com/7-Francais-sur-10-ne-veulent-plus/ (accessed February 8, 2018).

80 Cyrano, "La France en a plus qu'assez."

81 Cyrano, "Une pétition qui marche."

82 Cyrano, "Osons demeurer des esprits libres."

83 Cyrano, "La volte-face du maire de Vigneux, grâce à la vigilance d'un lecteur de Riposte Laïque," *Riposte Laïque*, June 24, 2008. Available online: http://ripostelaique.com/La-volte-face-du-maire-de-Vigneux/ (accessed February 8, 2018).

84 Cyrano, "Le nouveau procès, c'est le 3 septembre, tous avec Fanny Truchelut," *Riposte Laïque*, August 26, 2008. Available online: http://ripostelaique.com/Le-nouveau-proces-c-est-le-3/ (accessed February 8, 2018).

85 Cyrano, "Le débat sur le voile ne doit pas s'arrêter à la burqa," *Riposte Laïque*, July 15, 2008. Available online: http://ripostelaique.com/Un-voile-peut-en-cacher-bien-d/ (accessed February 8, 2018).

86 Cyrano, "Deux mois de prison avec sursis, et 4000 euros de dommages et intérêts! Juges, Mrap-LDH et tous ceux qui ont enfoncé Fanny, honte à vous!" *Riposte Laïque*, October 8, 2008. Available online: http://ripostelaique.com/2-mois-de-prison-avec-sursis-et/ (accessed February 8, 2018).

87 See Valérie Igounet, "On est chez nous!" *France TV info*, February 19, 2017. Available online: https://blog.francetvinfo.fr/derriere-le-front/2017/02/19/on-est-chez-nous.html (accessed January 11, 2018).

88 AFP, "FN: le slogan 'On est chez nous,' 'cri du coeur et d'amour,' selon Marine Le Pen," *L'Express*, February 17, 2017. Available online: https://www.lexpress.fr/actualites/1/politique/fn-le-slogan-on-est-chez-nous-cri-du-coeur-et-d-amour-selon-marine-le-pen_1880412.html (accessed January 11, 2018).

89 Cyrano, "Ni l'UMP ni le PS ne pourront arrêter la révolution sociale et identitaire en cours," *Riposte Laïque*, April 25, 2011. Available online: http://ripostelaique.com/ni-l'ump-ni-le-ps-ne-pourront-arreter-la-revolution-sociale-et-identitaire-en-cours/ (accessed February 8, 2018).

90 Cyrano, " Débat laïcité: une conférence de presse, de vraies solutions face à l'islamisation de la France," *Riposte Laïque*, April 5, 2011. Available online: http://ripostelaique.com/debat-laicite-une-conference-de-presse-de-vraies-solutions-face-a-lislamisation-de-la-france/ (accessed February 8, 2018).

91 Cyrano, "Vive les référendums suisses, nous aussi on veut voter …," *Riposte Laïque*, November 29, 2010. Available online: http://ripostelaique.com/Vive-les-referendums-suisses-nous/ (accessed February 8, 2018).

92 Ibid.

93 Cyrano, "Moussaoui, Techno Parade et Limoges: un silence politico-médiatique assourdissant!" *Riposte Laïque*, October 4, 2010. Available online: http://ripostelaique.com/Moussaoui-Techno-Parade-et-Limoges/ (accessed February 8, 2018).

94 Cyrano, "Dal-Bordeaux, antiracistes, Trappes."

95 Cyrano, "Sous la pression de l'islam, l'incroyable acharnement judiciaire contre la liberté d'expression," *Riposte Laïque*, May 10, 2011. Available online: http://ripostelaique.com/sous-la-pression-de-lislam-lincroyable-acharnement-judiciaire-contre-la-liberte-dexpression/ (accessed February 8, 2018).

96 Ibid.

97 "Quatre skinheads renvoyés aux assises pour la mort de Clément Méric, l'intention de tuer pas retenue," *Huffington Post*, March 14, 2017. Available online: http://www.huffingtonpost.fr/2017/03/14/quatre-skinheads-renvoyes-aux-assises-pour-la-mort-de-clement-me_a_21886232/ (accessed January 11, 2018).

98 Cyrano, "Hollande et sa clique répriment les patriotes et bichonnent les islamo-racailles," *Riposte Laïque*, July 29, 2013. Available online: http://ripostelaique.com/hollande-et-sa-clique-repriment-les-patriotes-et-bichonnent-les-islamo-racailles/ (accessed February 8, 2018).

99 Cyrano, "Le 25 mai."

100 Cyrano, " Pour la liberté de diffuser ' Fitna," *Riposte Laïque*, March 12, 2008. Available online: http://ripostelaique.com/Pour-la-liberte-de-diffuser-Fitna/ (accessed February 8, 2018).

101 Ibid.

102 Cyrano, "Burqa, immigration, Hénin-Beaumont."

103 Cyrano, "La colère d'un Français: c'est parti!" *Riposte Laïque*, February 8, 2010. Available online: http://ripostelaique.com/La-colere-d-un-Francais-c-est/ (accessed February 8, 2018).

104 Cyrano, "Défendre la pensée juste."

105 Cyrano, "14 septembre: Comment résister face à un gouvernement collabo?" *Riposte Laïque*, September 9, 2013. Available online: http://ripostelaique.com/14-septembre-comment-resister-face-a-un-gouvernement-collabo/ (accessed February 8, 2018).

106 Ibid.

107 Cyrano, "Fourest-Tubiana veulent tuer Riposte Laïque, parce qu'ils détestent sa liberté d'expression," *Riposte Laïque*, January 31, 2011. Available online: http://ripostelaique.com/Fourest-Tubiana-veulent-tuer/ (accessed February 8, 2018).

108 Ibid.

109 Noémie Rousseau, "À Hayange, nous festoyons comme les Francais," *Libération*, September 6, 2015. Available online: http://www.liberation.fr/societe/2015/09/06/a-hayange-nous-festoyons-comme-les-francais_1376925 (accessed January 12, 2018).

110 Cyrano, "14 septembre."

111 Cyrano, "L'alternative à l'UMPS."

112 Ibid.

113 Ibid.

114 Cyrano, "Les piliers du système perdent les pédales devant la progression de Marine Le Pen," *Riposte Laïque*, March 14, 2011. Available online: http://ripostelaique.com/les-piliers-du-systeme-perdent-les-pedales-devant-la-progression-de-marine-le-pen/ (accessed February 8, 2018).

115 Cyrano, "Ils servent la soupe."

116 Cyrano, "25 mai: Peut-on se dire patriote et se planquer?" *Riposte Laïque*, May 5, 2014. http://ripostelaique.com/25-mai-peut-on-se-dire-patriote-et-se-planquer/ (accessed February 8, 2018).

117 Ibid.

118 Cyrano, "Les islamistes sortent du bois."

119 Cyrano, "Ils servent la soupe."

120 Ibid.

121 Dupont-Aignan was, up until 2007, a member of UMP; but left it for his own party, *Debout la République*, which he founded in 1999.

122 Louis Hausalter, "Immigration: Nicolas Dupont-Aignan s'inquiète d'un 'remplacement de population'," *Libération*, January 18, 2017. Available online: https://www.marianne.net/politique/immigration-nicolas-dupont-aignan-s-inquiete-d-un-remplacement-de-population (accessed January 11, 2018); Dominique Albertini, "Dupont-Aignan, l'étoile du perché," March 29, 2017. Available online: http://www.liberation.fr/france/2016/03/29/dupont-aignan-l-etoile-du-perche_1442657 (accessed January 11, 2018).

123 Nicolas Dupont-Aignan, "Débout la France. Le projet de Nicolas Dupont-Aignan pour l'élection présidentielle 2017," Débout la France, 2017. Available online: http://www.nda-2017.fr/themes/nda/file/projet-nda-20170324.pdf (accessed January 11, 2018). For a summary of his program, see "Nicolas Dupont-Aignan: son programme dans le detail," *Le Journal du Dimanche*, March 17, 2017. Available online: http://www.lejdd.fr/Politique/Nicolas-Dupont-Aignan-son-programme-dans-le-detail-854978 (accessed January 11, 2018).

124 AFP, "Elections européennes: Dupont-Aignan rêve du modèle Ukip," *L'Express*, March 25, 2013. Available online: https://www.lexpress.fr/actualite/politique/elections-europeennes-dupont-aignan-reve-du-modele-ukip_1251767.html (accessed January 11, 2018).

125 Cyrano, "25 mai."

126 Ibid.

127 Cyrano, "Apéro géant et scandale."

128 Laclau, *On Populist Reason*, p. 97.

129 Panizza, "Introduction," p. 5.

130 Austad, "Introduction," p. xviii.

131 Sara Ahmed, *The Cultural Politics of Emotion* (Edinburgh: Edinburgh University Press, 2014), p. 124.

132 Said (1979), pp. 1–2.

133 For thorough discussions on the benefits and shortcomings of Said's Orientalism, see Alexander Lyon Macfie, ed. *Orientalism: A Reader* (Edinburgh: Edinburgh University Press, 2000).

134 Tomaz Mastnak, "Western Hostility toward Muslims: A History of the Present," in *Western Hostility toward Muslims: A History of the Present*, Andrew Shyrock, ed. (Bloomington and Indianapolis: Indiana University Press), p. 33.

135 Cyrano, "Je me demande si je ne vais pas."

Chapter 5

1 AFP, "Le Siel met fin à son alliance avec le Front national," *L'Express*, November 6, 2016. Available online: https://www.lexpress.fr/actualite/politique/le-siel-met-fin-a-son-alliance-avec-le-front-national_1847692.html (accessed January 12, 2018). See also Olivier Faye, "Avec le SIEL, le Front national est en passe de perdre son seul allié," *Le Monde: Droite(s) Extrême(s)*, November 2, 2016. Available online: http://droites-extremes.blog.lemonde.fr/2016/11/02/avec-le-siel-le-front-national-est-en-passe-de-perdre-son-seul-allie/ (accessed January 13, 2018).

2 Karim Ouchikh, "Avec le SIEL, j'apporte mon soutien à Marine Le Pen aux présidentielles et aux candidats de mon parti aux législatives," *SIEL*, February 26, 2017. Available online: http://www.siel-souverainete.fr/actualites/

communiques/803-avec-le-siel-j-apporte-mon-soutien-a-marine-le-pen-aux-presidentielles-et-aux-candidats-de-mon-parti-aux-legislatives.html (accessed January 13, 2018).

3 Ayoub is the founder of the ultra-nationalist and neo-Nazi *Jeunesses nationalistes révolutionnaires* and the *Troisième Voie*, and leader of the neo-Nazi White Wolves Klan.

4 See Nolwenn Le Blevennec, "Sur Twitter, l'antisémite Jérôme Bourbon sort de l'ombre," *Le Nouvel Observateur*, February 24, 2016. Available online: http://tempsreel.nouvelobs.com/rue89/rue89-politique/20160224.RUE2270/sur-twitter-l-antisemite-jerome-bourbon-sort-de-l-ombre.html (accessed January 22, 2018).

5 See Justin Huggler, "Dutch Pegida leader and expelled German deputy hunt migrants on Bulgaria border," *The Telegraph*, July 4, 2016. Available online: http://www.telegraph.co.uk/news/2016/07/04/pegida-pair-hunt-migrants-with-vigilantes-on-bulgaria-border/ (accessed January 22, 2018).

6 Cyrano, "La maison France est en feu: il est urgent de rassembler notre peuple autour de ses idéaux," *Riposte Laïque*, October 25, 2010. Available online: http://ripostelaique.com/La-maison-France-est-en-feu-il-est/ (accessed February 8, 2018).

7 Cyrano, "Après la mission parlementaire, après la votation suisse, plus rien ne devra être comme avant," *Riposte Laïque*, December 7, 2009. Available online: http://ripostelaique.com/Apres-la-mission-parlementaire/ (accessed February 8, 2018).

8 Cyrano, "La 'laïcité ferme et tolérante'."

9 Cyrano, "Que de chemin parcouru … mais que de chemin encore à parcourir!" *Riposte Laïque*, July 6, 2009. Available online: http://ripostelaique.com/Que-de-chemin-parcouru-mais-que-de/ (accessed February 8, 2018).

10 Cyrano, "9 décembre 1905—9 décembre 2008," *Riposte Laïque*, December 15, 2008. Available online: http://ripostelaique.com/9-decembre-1905-9-decembre-2008/ (accessed February 8, 2018).

11 Ibid.

12 Cyrano, "Refuser l'islamisation de 'Ma France'."

13 Cyrano, "Comment protéger la France et les Français contre les fous d'Allah?" *Riposte Laïque*, April 2, 2012. Available online: http://ripostelaique.com/comment-proteger-la-france-et-les-francais-contre-les-fous-dallah/ (accessed February 8, 2018).

14 Cyrano, "La 'laïcité ferme et tolérante'."

15 Cyrano, "Après Barnier."

16 Cyrano, "Barbarie islamiste ou amour de la vie: il faudra choisir, ce sera l'un ou l'autre …" *Riposte Laïque*, November 28, 2011. Available online: http://ripostelaique.com/barbarie-islamiste-ou-amour-de-la-vie-il-faudra-choisir-ce-sera-lun-ou-lautre… (accessed February 8, 2018).

17 Cyrano, "La France subira obligatoirement des attentats-suicides musulmans," *Riposte Laïque*, December 3, 2012. Available online: http://ripostelaique.com/la-france-subira-obligatoirement-des-attentats-suicides-musulmans/ (accessed February 8, 2018).

18 Cyrano, "Reconquista ou Mort de l'Europe."

19 Cyrano. "Peut-on s'être battu pour sauver Ingrid Betancourt."

20 Cyrano, "Leur 4 septembre et le nôtre: deux conceptions inconciliables de la République," *Riposte Laïque*, August 30, 2010. Available online: http://ripostelaique.com/Leur-4-septembre-et-le-notre-deux/ (accessed February 8, 2018).

21 Cyrano, "Faut-il fermer les yeux sur la nature du Hamas pour ne pas désespérer Billancourt?" *Riposte Laïque*, January 5, 2009. Available online: http://ripostelaique.com/Faut-il-fermer-les-yeux-sur-la/ (accessed February 8, 2018).

22 Cyrano, "Déjà 2 ans, et 100 numéros de *Riposte Laïque!*" *Riposte Laïque*, September 7, 2009. Available online: http://ripostelaique.com/Deja-2-ans-et-100-numeros-de/ (accessed February 8, 2018).

23 Cyrano, "Il faut l'unité des patriotes, face au bloc des mondialistes," *Riposte Laïque*, June 27, 2011. Available online: http://ripostelaique.com/il-faut-lunite-des-patriotes-face-au-bloc-des-mondialistes/ (accessed February 8, 2018).

24 Cyrano, "Le 'tout se vaut' et l'anti-occidentalisme primaire préparent la possible victoire de la charia," *Riposte Laïque*, April 27, 2009. Available online: http://ripostelaique.com/Le-tout-se-vaut-et-l-anti/ (accessed February 8, 2018).

25 Cyrano. "Les autocollants de." This quote is nowhere to be found in La Boétie's *Discours sur la servitude volontaire* (Paris: Éditions Mille et une Nuits, 1995). It appears it most likely belongs to Pierre Victurnien Vergniaud (1753–1793), a lawyer and state functionary.

26 Cyrano, "Marine Le Pen en tête au premier tour: racisme ou insurrection démocratique des Français?" *Riposte Laïque*, March 7, 2011. Available online: http://ripostelaique.com/marine-le-pen-en-tete-au-premier-tour-racisme-des-francais-ou-insurrection-democratique/ (accessed February 8, 2018).

27 See Patrick Gaumer, *Dictionnaire mondial de la BD* (Paris: Larousse, 2010).

28 The term "anti-France" was used by authoritarian, and by today's measures, radical, nationalists such as Charles Maurras and Raymond Barres in the early twentieth century, to designate the enemies of the nation.

29 Cyrano, "Je me demande si je ne vais pas."

30 Pierre Carrey, Guillaume Gendron, and Johanna Luyssen, "Glacial," *Libération*, December 5, 2016, pp. 26–29.

31 See *Génération Identitaire*: https://generationidentitaire.org/presentation/ (accessed January 18, 2018).

32 *Bloc Identitaire*, "Communiqué du Bloc identiaire," *Novopress*, January 7, 2015. Available online: https://fr.novopress.info/180677/communique-du-bloc-

identitaire-charlie-hebdo-personne-pourra-pretendre-lutter-contre-djihadisme-remettre-en-cause-limmigration-massive-lislamisation/ (accessed January 18, 2018).

33 Ibid.

34 Marine Le Pen, Déclaration de Marine Le Pen suite aux attentats de Charlie Hebdo, *YouTube: Front National*, January 7, 2015. Available online: https://www.youtube.com/watch?v=RwbS_6GR7U4&bpctr=1516290030 (accessed January 18, 2018).

35 Ibid.

36 Ibid.

37 Ibid.

38 Ségolène De Larquier, "Marine Le Pen en guerre contre l'islam radical [Marine Le Pen is at war with radical Islam]," *Le Point*, January 8, 2015. Available online: http://www.lepoint.fr/politique/marine-le-pen-en-guerre-contre-l-islam-radical-08-01-2015-1894905_20.php (accessed January 18, 2018).

39 Horatius, "Aymeric Chauprade: 'La France est en guerre avec des musulmans,'" *Fdsouche*, January 14, 2015. Available online: http://www.fdsouche.com/553557-aymeric-chauprade-france-en-guerre-musulmans# (accessed January 15, 2015).

40 Ibid.

41 Ibid.

42 Ibid.

43 Marc De Boni and Emmanuel Gallero, "Marine Le Pen désavoue Aymeric Chauprade après ses propos sur les musulmans," *Le Figaro*, January 19, 2015. Available online: http://www.lefigaro.fr/politique/le-scan/couacs/2015/01/19/25005-20150119ARTFIG00131-marine-le-pen-desavoue-aymeric-chauprade-apres-ses-propos-sur-les-musulmans.php (accessed January 19, 2018).

44 Louis Hausalter, "L'islam compatible avec la République," *Marianne*, September 17, 2016. Available online: https://www.marianne.net/politique/lislam-compatible-avec-la-republique-la-phrase-de-marine-le-pen-qui-trouble-les-militants (accessed January 19, 2018).

45 Cyrano, "Le peuple de France doit se préparer." [The people of France need to prepare themselves]

46 Cyrano, "Accompagnatrices voilées." Translation from http://www.columbia.edu/~iw6/docs/dec1793.html (accessed January 14, 2018).

47 Cyrano, "Les manipulations antiracistes de Hollande et sa clique ne marchent plus!" *Riposte Laïque*, December 2, 2013. Available online: http://ripostelaique.com/les-manipulations-antiracistes-de-hollande-et-sa-clique-ne-marchent-plus/ (accessed February 8, 2018).

48 Cyrano, "Sortie du troisième livre de *Riposte Laïque*: 'Résistance républicaine,'" *Riposte Laïque*, April 24, 2010. Available online: http://ripostelaique.com/Sortie-du-troisieme-livre-de/ (accessed February 8, 2018).

49   Cyrano, "Burqa, République, insécurité."

50   Cyrano, "Oskar Freysinger a-t-il raison."

51   Cyrano, "Prières musulmanes: nous ne voulons pas que les rues de Paris ressemblent un jour à celles de Moscou," *Riposte Laïque*, June 13, 2011. Available online: http://ripostelaique.com/prieres-musulmanes-nous-ne-voulons-pas-que-les-rues-de-paris-ressemblent-un-jour-a-celles-de-moscou/ (accessed June 13, 2011).

52   Cyrano, "Blondel sur RFI, Ramadan sur France 24, l'islamophobie sur Beur FM: *Riposte Laïque* sur tous les fronts," *Riposte Laïque*, January 29, 2010. Available online: http://ripostelaique.com/Blondel-sur-RFI-Ramadan-sur-France/ (accessed February 8, 2018).

53   Cyrano, "Le maire de Trappes."

54   Cyrano, "2012: Tous les soirs, à partir de 19 h 50, le Journal des Résistants, avec Christine Tasin," *Riposte Laïque*, December 26, 2011. Available online: http://ripostelaique.com/2012-tous-les-soirs-a-partir-de-19-h-50-le-journal-des-resistants-avec-christine-tasin/ (accessed February 8, 2018).

55   Cyrano, "Le 10 novembre, tous à Paris."

56   Cyrano, "Pour préparer la Résistance."

57   Cyrano, "24 août: Delanoé et ses complices trahissent à nouveau la laïcité," *Riposte Laïque*, August 15, 2011. Available online: http://ripostelaique.com/24-aout-delanoe-et-ses-complices-trahissent-a-nouveau-la-laicite/ (accessed February 8, 2018).

58   20091105.

59   Cyrano, "Moussaoui, Techno Parade et Limoges."

60   Cyrano, "Pour faire voter les étrangers, Hollande-Ayrault devront en passer par le référendum," *Riposte Laïque*, June 18, 2012. Available online: http://ripostelaique.com/pour-faire-voter-les-etrangers-hollande-ayrault-devront-en-passer-par-le-referendum/ (accessed February 8, 2018).

61   Cyrano, "Nous aimons trop la liberté et la France des Lumières pour les abandonner à l'islam des ténèbres," *Riposte Laïque*, August 20, 2012. Available online: http://ripostelaique.com/nous-aimons-trop-la-liberte-et-la-france-des-lumieres-pour-les-abandonner-a-lislam-des-tenebres/ (accessed February 8, 2018).

62   The foundational law regarding freedom of expression in France is the Law of 1881 on the freedom of the press: see Loi du 29 juillet 1881 sur la liberté de la presse, *Legifrance*, January 29, 2017. Available online: https://www.legifrance.gouv.fr/affichTexte.do?cidTexte=LEGITEXT000006070722 (accessed January 22, 2018).

63   AFP, "Marine Le Pen conteste l'étiquette extrême droite accolée au FN," *L'Express*, October 2, 2013. Available online: https://www.lexpress.fr/actualites/1/politique/marine-le-pen-conteste-l-etiquette-extreme-droite-accolee-au-fn_1287384.html (accessed January 15, 2018).

64   Ibid.

65   Cyrano, "Le seul intérêt de ces élections."

66 Cyrano, "Pourra-t-on vaincre."

67 Cyrano, "Sortie du troisième livre."

68 Cyrano, "Hollande et sa clique."

69 Cyrano, "Défendre la pensée juste."

70 Cyrano, "Pour gagner cette guerre." [To win this war.]

71 Ibid.

72 Ibid.

73 Cyrano, "2008: année."

74 Cyrano, "Face à la guerre islamique, que peuvent faire les Français?" [Faced with Islamic war, what can the French do?] *Riposte Laïque*, December 29, 2014. Available online: http://ripostelaique.com/face-a-la-guerre-islamique-que-peuvent-faire-les-francais/ (accessed February 8, 2018). Christine Tasin and René d'Armor discuss the issue further in the book *Les assasins obéissent au Coran* (Paris: Résistance républicaine, 2016), pp. 78–79.

75 Cyrano, "Comment réagira la France au prochain attentat islamique?" *Riposte Laïque*, June 8, 2015. Available online: http://ripostelaique.com/comment-reagira-la-france-au-prochain-attentat-islamique.html (accessed February 8, 2018).

76 Cyrano, "Opération Pédalo et Islamectomie: Comment débarrasser la France de Hollande et de l'islam?" *Riposte Laïque*, August 19, 2013. Available online: http://ripostelaique.com/dans-deux-livres-de-riposte-laique-la-france-reussit-a-se-debarrasser-de-hollande-et-de-lislam/ (accessed February 8, 2018).

77 René Marchand, *Reconquista ou mort de l'Europe. L'enjeu de la guerre islamique. Pour une stratégie de contre-offensive* (Éditions Riposte Laïque), p. 389.

78 Ibid, p. 385 ff.

79 Cyrano, "Ils veulent nous tuer et accélérer la fin de la France." [They want to kill us and accelerate the end of France] *Riposte Laïque*, September 2, 2013. Available online: http://ripostelaique.com/ils-veulent-nous-tuer-et-accelerer-la-fin-de-la-france/ (accessed February 8, 2018).

80 Cyrano, "Pour gagner cette guerre."

81 Cyrano, "Si la France n'éradique pas."

82 Cyrano, "Comment ce régime et ses journaleux préparent notre dissolution," *Riposte Laïque*, July 14, 2014. Available online: http://ripostelaique.com/comment-ce-regime-et-ses-journaleux-preparent-notre-dissolution/ (accessed February 8, 2018).

83 Cyrano, "Nation, République, laïcité."

84 Cyrano, "9 décembre 1905—9 décembre 2008."

85 Cyrano, "Protéger la France de la nuisance d'avocats comme Guez Guez," *Riposte Laïque*, August 18, 2014. Avilable online: http://ripostelaique.com/proteger-la-france-de-la-nuisance-davocats-comme-guez-guez/ (accessed February 8, 2018).

86 Ibid.

87 Cyrano, "Panique chez les intégristes du libre échange, le protectionnisme est de retour!" *Riposte Laïque*, February 9, 2009. Available online: http://ripostelaique. com/Panique-chez-les-integristes-du/ (accessed February 8, 2018).

88 Cyrano, "Face à la guerre islamique."

89 Cyrano, "Est-il vraiment incohérent de dire qu'il faut interdire l'islam en France?" *Riposte Laïque*, May 16, 2015. Available online: http://ripostelaique.com/est-il-vraiment-incoherent-de-dire-quil-faut-interdire-lislam-en-france.html (accessed February 8, 2018).

90 Cyrano, "Grâce à Mélenchon."

91 Ibid.

92 Cyrano, "La faute du bobo Jocelyn: un roman de politique-fiction signé Pierre Cassen et Christine Tasin," *Riposte Laïque*, September 26, 2011. Available online: http://ripostelaique.com/la-faute-du-bobo-jocelyn-un-roman-de-politique-fiction-signe-pierre-cassen-et-christine-tasin/ (accessed February 8, 2018).

93 Cyrano, "Une France sans ramadan, ni supporters algériens ni adorateurs du Hamas …" *Riposte Laïque*, July 28, 2014. Available online: http://ripostelaique. com/une-france-sans-ramadan-ni-supporters-algeriens-ni-adorateurs-du-hamas/ (accessed February 8, 2018).

94 Ibid.

95 Ibid.

96 Cyrano, "La faute du bobo Jocelyn."

97 Ibid.

98 Cyrano, "Face à la guerre islamique."

99 Cyrano, "La faute du bobo Jocelyn."

100 Cyrano, "Pourra-t-on vaincre."

101 Cyrano, "La faute du bobo Jocelyn."

102 Ibid.

103 Cyrano, "Face à la guerre Islamique."

104 Cyrano, "La faute du bobo Jocelyn."

105 Cyrano, "Face à la guerre Islamique."

106 Ibid.

107 Ibid.

108 Ibid.

109 This policy can be understood as a form of positive discrimination for French citizens. See Marcus, *The National Front*, p. 109 ff.; Jim G. Shields, *The Extreme Right in France: From Pétain to Le Pen* (London and New York: Routledge, 2007), pp. 185–186.

110 See Anne-Aël Durand, "Ce que propose Marine Le Pen dans son programme," *Le Monde*, April 23, 2017. Available online: http://www.lemonde.fr/les-

decodeurs/article/2017/04/23/ce-que-propose-marine-le-pen-dans-son-programme_5115963_4355770.html (accessed January 22, 2018).

111   Cyrano, "Protéger la France de la nuisance."

112   Cyrano, "Pour gagner cette guerre."

113   Ibid.

114   Ibid.

115   Cyrano, "Reconquista ou Mort de l'Europe."

116   Cyrano, "Fin de la France: le stupide Ayrault crache le morceau!" *Riposte Laïque*, December 16, 2013. Available online: http://ripostelaique.com/fin-de-la-france-le-stupide-ayrault-crache-le-morceau/ (accessed February 8, 2018).

117   Cyrano, "Socialaud assassin."

118   Cyrano, "Socialauds, vous paierez cher vos trahisons, et vos potes aussi!" *Riposte Laïque*, August 17, 2015. Available online: http://ripostelaique.com/socialauds-paierez-cher-vos-trahisons-vos-potes.html (accessed February 8, 2018).

119   Cyrano, "Socialaud assassin."

120   Cyrano, "Une France sans ramadan."

121   Cyrano, "Il faudra juger Hollande et sa clique pour haute trahison," *Riposte Laïque*, June 17, 2013. Available online: http://ripostelaique.com/il-faudra-juger-hollande-et-sa-clique-pour-haute-trahison (accessed February 8, 2018). Translation of the article title: It will be necessary to judge Hollande and his group for high treason.

122   Cyrano, "Nous sommes gouvernés par les porteurs de valises du FLN et de l'islam," *Riposte Laïque*, March 18, 2013. Available online: http://ripostelaique.com/nous-sommes-gouvernes-par-les-porteurs-de-valises-du-fln-et-de-lislam/ (accessed February 8, 2018). Translation of this title: We are governed by the FLN baggage-carriers and Islam.

123   Cyrano, "La prochaine étape des socialauds."

124   Cyrano, "Nous sommes gouvernés."

125   Cyrano, "Non content de tuer la France."

126   Cyrano, "Protéger la France de la nuisance."

127   Cyrano, "Sans l'islam, la France." Translation of title: Without Islam, [there will be] France.

128   The Barbary States is how Europeans referred to Berber societies and states on the North African Mediterranean coast line from the sixteenth to the nineteenth century.

129   Cyrano refers to the French universal health care insurance as *Couverture maladie universelle* (CMU or universal health coverage) and *Aide medical de l'État* (AME or Medical Aid from the State).

130   Mohammed Merah is the self-proclaimed jihadi who went on a rampage in Montauban and Toulouse in 2012; and who allegedly had ties to the jihadi network called Forsane Alizza.

131 Cyrano, "Immigration-référendum: une manifestation qui fait parler," *Riposte Laïque*, March 10, 2014. Available online: http://ripostelaique.com/immigration-referendum-une-manifestation-qui-fait-deja-parler/ (accessed February 8, 2018). Translation of title: Immigration referendum: a manifestation that makes talk happen.

132 The mission can be followed on Facebook and Twitter: *Génération Identitaire*, "Mission: Defend Europe." https://www.facebook.com/GenerationIdentitaire/videos/vb.203085803133570/1190224071088919/?type=2&theater (accessed January 19, 2018); *Génération Identitaire*, @DefendEuropeID, *Twitter*. Available online: https://twitter.com/defendeuropeid (accessed January 19, 2018). One issue of *Génération Identitaire*'s monthly is specifically about the mission: see "Defend Europe," *Magazine identitaires*, n. 25, November/December, 2017.

133 *Génération identitaire*, "Mission: Defend Europe." Available online: https://www.facebook.com/GenerationIdentitaire/videos/vb.203085803133570/1190224071088919/?type=2&theater (accessed January 19, 2018).

134 Romain Herreros, "C-Star: une ONG pro-réfugiés porte secours au bateau anti-migrants, qui refuse l'aid," *Huffington Post*, August 11, 2017. Available online: http://www.huffingtonpost.fr/2017/08/11/le-bateau-anti-migrants-c-star-secouru-par-une-ong-pro-refugies_a_23074496/ (accessed January 19, 2018).

135 On the issue, see Laurent Mauriac, "Indignation après l'occupation de la mosquée de Poitiers," *Rue 89: Nouvel Observateur*, October 21, 2012. Available online: https://www.nouvelobs.com/rue89/rue89-nos-vies-connectees/20121021.RUE3312/indignation-apres-l-occupation-de-la-mosquee-de-poitiers.html (accessed January 19, 2018).

136 "Manuel Valls: Oui, la France est en guerre contre le terrorisme," *Le Monde*, January 13, 2015. Available online: http://www.lemonde.fr/politique/article/2015/01/13/manuel-valls-oui-la-france-est-en-guerre-contre-le-terrorisme_4555301_823448.html (accessed January 19, 2018). Translation of title: Manuel Valls: Yes, France is at war against terrorism.

137 See, for example, Baubérot, *La laïcité falsifié*.

138 *Front National*, "Marine 2017," p. 15.

139 Ibid.

140 See Marine Le Pen, "Conference de presse: La France au défi terroriste," April 10, 2017. Available online: http://www.frontnational.com/videos/conference-presidentielle-n5-la-france-face-au-defi-terroriste/ (January 19, 2018).

141 Ibid.

142 "Marine 2017," pp. 5–6.

143 Le Pen, "Conference de presse: La France au défi terroriste."

144 On the politics of (de-)radicalization in France, see Farhad Khosrokhavar, *Radicalisation* (Paris: EMSH, 2014).

145 Le Pen, "Conference de presse: La France au défi terroriste."

146 "Marine 2017," p. 6.

147 Compare, for example, with Wendy Brown, who employs the category of culturalization of politics in *Regulating Aversion: Tolerance in the Age of Identity and Empire* (Princeton, NJ and Oxford: Princeton University Press, 2008), p. 34ff.

148 In the *Ancien Régime* [ancient regime or old government], race was a central marker for distinguishing the Frankish nobility from the Gaulist plebs, the former being noble German descendants and the latter being native Gauls. This divide was used by the nobility to legitimize their political status in the monarchy; however, this divide was turned on its head during the Revolution, when the *Tiers État* used this theory to classify the nobility as foreign intruders. See Carole Reynaud Paligot, *La République raciale 1860–1930* (Paris: Presse Universitaires de France, 2009).

149 Sophie Wahnich, *L'impossible citoyen: l'étranger dans le discours de la Révolution française* (Paris: Albin Michel, 2010), p. 10.

150 Ibid., p. XVII.

151 See Silverman, *Deconstructing*.

152 Elisa Camiscioli, *Reproducing the French Race. Immigration, Intimacy, and Embodiment in the Early Twentieth Century* (Durham & London: Duke University Press), p. 2.

153 See Patrick Weil, *Qu'est-ce qu'un Français? Histoire de la nationalité française depuis la Révolution* (Paris: Folio, 2005). Translation of title: What is a Frenchman? History of French nationality after the revolution.

154 On the post-racial society, see David T. Goldberg, *Are We All Post-Racial Yet?* (Cambridge and Malden: Polity Press, 2015).

155 Camiscioli, *Reproducing*, p. 159.

156 Gérard Noiriel, *Immigration, antisémitisme et racisme (XIXe-XXe siècle): Discours publics, humiliations privées* (Paris: Fayard, 2007) p. 232. Title translation: Immigration, antisemitism and racism (nineteenth and twentieth centuries): Public discourse, private humiliation.

157 Abdellali Hajjat and Marwan Mohammed, *Islamophobie* (Paris: La Découverte, 2013, loc. 263. Title translation: Islamophobia.

158 Ibid, loc. 397.

159 Camiscioli, *Reproducing*, p. 10.

160 See Talal Asad, "Trying to Understand French Secularism," in *Political Theologies. Public Religions in a Post-Secular World*, Hent De Vries, ed. (Fordham University Press: New York, 2005); Nilsson, "Madame M."

161 AFP, "Tariq Ramadan écroué dans l'attente de son procès, la communauté musulmane troublée," *La Croix*, February 7, 2018. Available online: https://www.la-croix.com/France/Justice/Marine-Le-Pen-La-priorite-nationale-nest-illegal-immoral-2017-04-13-1200839426 (accessed February 8, 2018).

162 Robert Paxton, *The Anatomy of Fascism* (New York: Alfred A. Knopf, 2004), pp. 218–219.

163 Ibid., p. 219.

164 Roger Griffin, "Introduction: God's counterfeiters? Investigating the triad of fascism, totalitarianism and (political) religion," *Totalitarian Movements and Political Religions* 5, no. 3 (2004): 291–325, p. 299.

165 Ibid.

166 Roger Griffin, "Interregnum or Endgame? The Radical Right in the 'Post-Fascist' Era," in *The Populist Radical Right: A Reader*, Cas Mudde, ed. (London and New York: Routledge, 2017), p. 16.

167 Ibid.

168 Ibid., p. 23.

169 Zygmunt Bauman, *Postmodernity and Its Discontents* (New York: New York University Press, 1997), p. 18.

170 Ibid.

171 Arjun Appadurai, *Fear of Small Numbers* (Durham and London: Duke University Press, 2006), p. 3.

Chapter 6

1 Cyrano, "Le maire de Trappes."

2 Brubaker, "Between nationalism," p. 1192.

3 See, for example, Donald Trump, "Inaugural Address," *The White House*, January 20, 2017. Available online: https://www.whitehouse.gov/briefings-statements/the-inaugural-address/ (accessed January 31, 2018).

4 Cyrano, "Quoi qu'il arrive, merci au formidable Donald Trump!" [Whenever he arrives, thanks to the formidable Donald Trump!] *Riposte Laïque*, November 6, 2016. Available online: http://ripostelaique.com/quoi-quil-arrive-merci-au-formidable-donald-trump.html (accessed February 13, 2018).

5 Cyrano, "Donald Trump élu Président des Etats-Unis: Apéro saucisson-Champagne!" *Riposte Laïque*, November 9, 2016. Available online: http://ripostelaique.com/donald-trump-elu-president-des-etats-unis-apero-saucisson-champagne.html (accessed February 13, 2018).

6 Brubaker, "Between nationalism," p. 1191.

7 Griffin, "Interregnum or endgame," p. 18.

8 Robinson, whose real name is Stephen Yaxley-Lennon, left the EDL in 2013. Since then, he has publicly apologized for his hateful statements against Muslims; however, he has continued his counter-jihadi activism, for example, by participating in the PEGIDA movement. See Jamie Bartlett, "Across Europe with Tommy Robinson: Inside the new wave of anti-immigration protest coming soon to Britain," *The Telegraph*, December 4, 2015. Available online: http://www.telegraph.co.uk/news/uknews/immigration/12031679/Across-Europe-with-Tommy-Robinson-inside-the-new-wave-of-anti-immigration-protest-coming-soon-to-Britain.html (accessed February 13, 2018).

9   Stier et al., "When populists become popular."

10 Cas Mudde, "What the stunning success of AFD means for Germany and Europe," *The Guardian*, September 24, 2017. Available online: https://www.theguardian.com/commentisfree/2017/sep/24/germany-elections-afd-europe-immigration-merkel-radical-right (accessed February 13, 2018).

11 "Surge for Dutch anti-Islam Freedom Party," *BBC News*, June 10, 2010. Available online: http://www.bbc.com/news/10271153 (accessed February 13, 2018).

12 Parti Plus, "Présentation du Parti Plus," *PartiPlus: YouTube*, April 30, 2013. Available online: https://www.youtube.com/watch?v=gbSgFEcrT6k (accessed February 13, 2018).

13 "L'UDC valaisan Jean-Luc Addor condamné pour discrimination raciale," *Radio Télévision Suisse*, August 17, 2017. Available online: https://www.rts.ch/info/regions/valais/8848544-l-udc-valaisan-jean-luc-addor-condamne-pour-discrimination-raciale.html (accessed February 13, 2018).

14 Cyrano, "Résistance européenne pour désislamiser." [European resistance for de-Islamization]

15 On American counter-jihadism, see Wajahat Ali, Eli Clifton, Matthew Duss, Lee Fang, Scott Keyes, and Faiz Shakir, *Fear, Inc. The Roots of the Islamophobia Network in America* (Center for American Progress, 2011).

16 On retrospective identification, see Scott, "Fantasy Echo," p. 287ff.

17 Brubaker, "Between nationalism," p. 1203.

18 Harriet Agerholm, "Refugees are 'Muslim invaders,' not running for their lives, says Hungarian PM Viktor Orban," *The Independent*, January 9, 2018. Available online: http://www.independent.co.uk/news/world/europe/refugees-muslim-invaders-hungary-viktor-orban-racism-islamophobia-eu-a8149251.html (accessed February 13, 2018).

19 Lizzie Dearden, "Nato accuses Sputnik News of distributing misinformation as part of 'Kremlin propaganda machine,'" *The Independent*, February 11, 2017. Available online: http://www.independent.co.uk/news/world/europe/sputnik-news-russian-government-owned-controlled-nato-accuses-kremlin-propaganda-machine-a7574721.html (accessed February 13, 2018).

20 On 'mainstreaming,' see Zúquete, "The European Extreme-right and Islam," p. 323; Aristotle Kallis, "Breaking Taboos and 'Mainstreaming the Extreme': The Debates on Restricting Islamic Symbols in Contemporary Europe," *Right-Wing*, p. 55–70.

21 Griffin, "Interregnum or endgame," p. 16.

References

A

Abdel Haleem, M. A. S. *The Qur'an*. Oxford and New York: Oxford University Press, 2004.

AFP. "Le ministère de l'agriculture dément les propos de Le Pen sur la viande halal." *Le Monde*, February 18, 2012. Available online: http://www.lemonde.fr/election-presidentielle-2012/article/2012/02/18/selon-le-pen-toute-la-viande-distribuee-en-ile-de-france-est-halal_1645353_1471069.html (accessed February 5, 2018).

AFP. "Elections européennes: Dupont-Aignan rêve du modèle Ukip." *L'Express*, March 25, 2013. Available online: https://www.lexpress.fr/actualite/politique/elections-europeennes-dupont-aignan-reve-du-modele-ukip_1251767.html (accessed January 11, 2018).

AFP. "Marine Le Pen conteste l'étiquette extrême droite accolée au FN." *L'Express*, October 2, 2013. Available online: https://www.lexpress.fr/actualites/1/politique/marine-le-pen-conteste-l-etiquette-extreme-droite-accolee-au-fn_1287384.html (accessed January 15, 2018).

AFP. "'Invasion migratoire' et 'Monseigneur Ebola:' Jean-Marie Le Pen en campagne." *Nouvel Observateur*, May 21, 2014. Available online: https://tempsreel.nouvelobs.com/politique/elections-europeennes-2014/20140521.OBS7880/invasion-migratoire-et-monseigneur-ebola-jean-marie-le-pen-en-campagne.html (accessed December 13, 2017).

AFP. "Taubira veut que 'les infractions reconnues dans l'espace public' le soient aussi sur Internet." *Le Monde*, February 22, 2015. Available online: http://www.lemonde.fr/societe/article/2015/02/22/christiane-taubira-veut-renforcer-l-arsenal-juridique-contre-les-derives-d-internet_4581277_3224.html (accessed December 26, 2017).

AFP. "Maréchal-Le Pen (FN): Cukierman 'broyé par le politiquement correct.'" *L'Express*, February 24, 2015. Available online: https://www.lexpress.fr/actualites/1/politique/marechal-le-pen-fn-cukierman-broye-par-le-politiquement-correct_1654816.html (accessed December 26, 2017).

AFP. "Robert Ménard entendu par la police sur le 'fichage' des écoliers de Béziers." *Le Monde*, March 5, 2015. Available online: http://www.lemonde.fr/politique/article/2015/05/05/quand-robert-menard-fiche-les-enfants-des-ecoles-de-beziers_4627511_823448.html (accessed December 11, 2017).

AFP. "Plusieurs journalistes agressés lors du défilé du Front National." *Le Monde*, May 1, 2015. Available online: http://www.lemonde.fr/politique/article/2015/05/01/ plusieurs-journalistes-agresses-lors-du-defile-du-front-national_4626214_823448. html#D5dL4SQ2ZTqM3DRT.99 (accessed December 26, 2017).

AFP. "Jean-Marie Le Pen exclut du Front National." *Le Monde*, August 20, 2015. Available online: http://www.lemonde.fr/politique/article/2015/08/20/jean-marie-le-pen-se-defend-face-au-bureau-executif-du-fn_4731727_823448.html (accessed February 8, 2018).

AFP. "Quatre mosquées soupçonnées de radicalisation fermées en région parisienne." *Libération*, November 2, 2016. Available online: http://www.liberation.fr/ france/2016/11/02/quatre-mosquees-soupconnees-de-radicalisation-fermees-en-region-parisienne_1525834 (accessed December 13, 2017).

AFP. "Le Siel met fin à son alliance avec le Front National." *L'Express*, November 6, 2016. Available online: https://www.lexpress.fr/actualite/politique/le-siel-met-fin-a-son-alliance-avec-le-front-national_1847692.html (accessed January 12, 2018).

AFP. "En Algérie, Macron qualifie la colonisation de « crime contre l'humanité », tollé à droite." *Le Monde*, February 16, 2017. Available online: http://www.lemonde.fr/ election-presidentielle-2017/article/2017/02/15/macron-qualifie-la-colonisation-de-crime-contre-l-humanite-tolle-a-droite-et-au-front-national_5080331_4854003. html (accessed February 7, 2018).

AFP. "FN: le slogan 'On est chez nous,' 'cri du coeur et d'amour,' selon Marine Le Pen." *L'Express*, February 17, 2017. Available online: https://www.lexpress.fr/actualites/1/ politique/fn-le-slogan-on-est-chez-nous-cri-du-coeur-et-d-amour-selon-marine-le-pen_1880412.html (accessed January 11, 2018).

AFP. "Canular homophobe dans TPMP: amende de 3 millions d'euros contre Hanouna et C8." *Le Parisien*, July 27, 2017. Available online: http://www.leparisien.fr/ culture-loisirs/tv/canular-homophobe-dans-tpmp-amende-de-3-millions-d-euros-contre-c8-et-cyril-hanouna-26-07-2017-7158105.php (accessed December 27, 2017).

Agerholm, Harriet. "Refugees are 'Muslim invaders' not running for their lives, says Hungarian PM Viktor Orban." *The Independent*, January 9, 2018. Available online: http://www.independent.co.uk/news/world/europe/refugees-muslim-invaders-hungary-viktor-orban-racism-islamophobia-eu-a8149251.html (accessed February 13, 2018).

Ahmed, Sara. *The Cultural Politics of Emotion*. Edinburgh: Edinburgh University Press, 2014.

Albertini, Dominique. "Marine Le Pen et sa relecture de l''occupation' devant le tribunal." *La Libération*, October 19, 2015. Available online: http://www.liberation. fr/france/2015/10/19/marine-le-pen-et-sa-relecture-de-l-occupation-devant-le-tribunal_1407378 (accessed January 21, 2018).

Albertini, Dominique. "'Front républicain': Marine Le Pen moque 'l'UMPS décomplexé.'" *Libération*, November 12, 2015. Available online: http://www.

liberation.fr/france/2015/11/12/front-republicain-marine-le-pen-moque-l-umps-decomplexe_1412843 (accessed December 26, 2017).

Albertini, Dominique. "Prières de rue et «occupation»: Marine Le Pen relaxée." *La Libération*, December 15, 2015. Available online: http://www.liberation.fr/france/2015/12/15/prieres-de-rue-et-occupation-marine-le-pen-relaxee_1420902 (accessed January 21, 2018).

Albertini, Dominique. "Dupont-Aignan, l'étoile du perché." *La Libération*, March 29, 2017. Available online: http://www.liberation.fr/france/2016/03/29/dupont-aignan-l-etoile-du-perche_1442657 (accessed January 11, 2018).

Alduy, Cécile and S. Wahnich. *Marine Le Pen prise aux mots: Décryptage du nouveau discours frontiste*. Paris: Seuil, 2015.

Ali, Wajahat, E. Clifton, M. Duss, S. Keyes and F. Shakir. *Fear, Inc. The Roots of the Islamophobia Network in America*. Washington: Center for American Progress, 2011.

Allen, Chris. *Islamophobia*. Oxon and New York: Routledge, 2010.

Alliot-Marie, Michèle. "Inauguration de la Maison de la conference des eveques de France. Ministre de l'Intérieur, de l'Outre-Mer et des collectivités locales." *Église Catholique de France*, July 4, 2007. Available online: http://archives.eglise.catholique.fr/catho/actus/dossiers/2007/breteuil/20070507discoursmam.pdf (accessed December 26, 2017).

Almeida, Dimitri. "Decadence and indifferentiation in the ideology of the Front National." *French Cultural Studies*, **25**, no. 2 (2014): 221–232.

Amrani, Imam. "The French hip-hop star fighting the far-right." *The Guardian*, June 10, 2016. Available online: https://www.theguardian.com/music/2016/jun/10/kalash-nekfeu-and-the-french-rappers-fighting-racism (accessed December 13, 2017).

Ancery, Pierre and C. Guillet. "Qu'est-ce qu'un criminologue." *Slate*, June 28, 2012. Available online: http://www.slate.fr/story/58037/criminologue-merah-magnotta-definition (accessed December 13, 2017).

Anidjar, Gil. "Antisemitism and Its Critics." In *Antisemitism and Islamophobia in Europe. A Shared Story?*, edited by James Renton and Ben Gidley, 187–214. London: Palgrave Macmillan, 2017.

Appadurai, Arjun. *Fear of Small Numbers*. Durham and London: Duke University Press, 2006.

Asad, Talal. "Trying to Understand French Secularism." In *Political Theologies. Public Religions in a Post-Secular World*, edited by Hent De Vries, 497–516. New York: Fordham University Press, 2005.

Asprem, Egil. "The birth of counterjihadist terrorism: Reflections on some unspoken dimensions." *The Pomegranate* **13**, no. 1 (2011): 17–32.

Assemblée Nationale. "Session extraordinaire de 2009–2010. Séances du mercredi 7 juillet 2010 Compte rendu intégral." *Journal Officiel de la République Française* **70** (2010): 5392–5433.

Austad, Lene. "Introduction." In *Nationalism and the Body Politics: Psychoanalysis and the Rise of Ethnocentrism and Xenophobia*, edited by Lena Austad, XV–XXVIII. London: Karnac, 2014.

B

Bacqués, Raphaëlle. "Roland Dumas, l'amoraliste." *Le Monde*, January 12, 2012. Available online: http://www.lemonde.fr/politique/article/2011/01/12/roland-dumas-l-amoraliste_1464572_823448.html (accessed December 27, 2017).

Barras, Amelie. "Contemporary *Laïcité*: Setting the terms of a new social contract? The slow exclusion of women wearing headscarves. Totalitarian movements and political secularism in France." In *The Oxford Handbook of Secularism*, edited by Phil Zuckerman and John Shook, 142–154. Oxford: Oxford University Press, 2017.

Bartlett, Jamie. "Across Europe with Tommy Robinson: Inside the new wave of anti-immigration protest coming soon to Britain." *The Telegraph*, December 4, 2015. Available online: http://www.telegraph.co.uk/news/uknews/immigration/12031679/Across-Europe-with-Tommy-Robinson-inside-the-the-new-wave-of-anti-immigration-protest-coming-soon-to-Britain.html (accessed February 13, 2018).

Bartlett, Jamie, J. Birdwell, and M. Littler. *The New Face of Digital Populism*. London: Demos, 2011.

Baubérot, Jean. *Laïcité 1905–2005, entre Passion et Raison*. Paris: Editions Seuil, 2005.

Baubérot, Jean. *La Laïcité Falsifiée*. Paris: Cahiers Libres, 2012 [e-book].

Baubérot, Jean. *Les Sept Laïcités Françaises: Le Modèle Français de Laïcité n'Existe pas*. Paris: Maison de Droit de l'Homme, 2015.

Baubérot, Jean and Le Cercle des Enseignantes Laïques. *Petit Manuel pour une Laïcité Apaisée: À l'Usage des Profs des Élèves et de leurs Parents*. Paris: La Découverte, 2016.

Bauduin, Clémence. "Marine Le Pen se déchaîne contre les médias lors d'un meeting à Bordeaux." *RTL*, April 2, 2017. Available online: http://www.rtl.fr/actu/politique/marine-le-pen-se-dechaine-contre-les-medias-lors-d-un-meeting-a-bordeaux-7787920817 (accessed December 26, 2017).

Bay, Nicolas. "Le cri d'amour de la patrie!" *Front National*, December 18, 2015. http://www.frontnational.com/2015/12/2015-le-cri-damour-de-la-patrie (accessed January 11, 2018).

Bayoumi, Moustafa. "The God That Failed: The Orientalism of Today's Muslim Commentators." In *Islamophobia/Islamophilia. Beyond the Politics of Enemy and Friend*, edited by Andrew Shyrock, 79–83. Bloomington and Indianapolis: Indiana University Press, 2010.

BBC News. "Surge for Dutch anti-Islam Freedom Party." June 10, 2010. Available online: http://www.bbc.com/news/10271153 (accessed February 13, 2018).

Beaugé, Julien and Abdellali Hajjat. "Élites françaises et construction du 'problème musulman.' Le cas du Haut Conseil à l'Intégration (1989/2012)." *Sociologie* 5, no. 1 (2014): 31–59.

Beauzamy, Brigitte. "Continuities of Fascist discourses, Discontinuities of extreme-right political actors? Overt and covert antisemitism in the contemporary French radical right." In *Analysing Fascist Discourse. European Fascism in Talk and Text*, edited by Ruth Wodak and John E. Richardson, 163–180. London and New York: Routledge, 2015.

Bégasse, Nicolas. "Marine Le Pen veut une loi contre le racism anti-blanc." *20 Minutes,* March 30, 2012. Available online: http://www.20minutes.fr/politique/943669-20120530-marine-pen-veut-loi-contre-racisme-anti-blanc (accessed December 11, 2017).

Bell, Laurence. "Interpreting collective action: Methodology and ideology in the analysis of social movements in France." *Modern & Contemporary France* **9**, no. 2 (2001): 183–196.

Benoist-Méchin, Jacques. *Mustapha Kémal ou la Mort d'un Empire.* Paris: Albin Michel, 1954.

Betz, Hans-Georg. *Radical Right-Wing Populism in Western Europe.* London: Macmillan, 1994.

Billig, Michael. *Banal Nationalism.* London: Sage, 2014.

Binet, Laurent. "'Touche pas à mon pain au chocolat!' The theme of food in current French political discourse." *Modern & Contemporary France* **24**, no. 3 (2016): 239–252.

Birnbaum, Pierre. *La République et le Cochon.* Paris: Le Seuil, 2013.

Blanc, William, and C. Naudin. *Charles Martel et la Bataille de Poitiers: De l'Histoire au Mythe Identitaire.* Paris: Libertalia, 2015.

Bloc Identitaire. "Communiqué du Bloc Identiaire." *Novopress,* January 7, 2015. Available online: https://fr.novopress.info/180677/communique-du-bloc-identitaire-charlie-hebdo-personne-pourra-pretendre-lutter-contre-djihadisme-remettre-en-cause-limmigration-massive-lislamisation/ (accessed January 18, 2018).

Brubaker, Rogers. *Nationalism Reframed: Nationhood and the National Question in the New Europe.* Cambridge and New York: Cambridge University Press, 1996.

Brubaker, Rogers. "Why populism?" *Theory and Society* **46**, no. 5 (2017): 357–385.

Brubaker, Rogers. "Between nationalism and civilizationism: The European populist moment in comparative perspective." *Ethnic and Racial Studies* **40**, no. 8 (2017): 1191–1226.

Brunne, Anner and L. Maurin. *Rapport sur les Inégalités en France, Édition 2017.* Paris: Observatoire des Inégalités, 2017.

Bonnefoy, Geoffrey and AFP. "Marine Le Pen se dit 'extrêmement croyante' mais est 'fâchée' avec l'Eglise." *L'Express,* April 14, 2017. Available online: https://www.lexpress.fr/actualite/politique/elections/marine-le-pen-se-dit-extremement-croyante-mais-est-fachee-avec-l-eglise_1899055.html (accessed December 26, 2017).

Bourdeau, Maxime. "Gérald Darmanin et ses tweets anti-mariage gay passent mal quand Macron veut que 'chacun puisse aimer librement." *Huffington Post,* March 17, 2017. Available online: http://www.huffingtonpost.fr/2017/05/17/gerald-darmanin-et-ses-tweets-anti-mariage-pour-tous-passent-mal_a_22096235/(accessed December 27, 2017).

Bowen, John. *Why the French Don't Like Headscarves. Islam, the State, and Public Space.* Princeton: Princeton University Press, 2007.

Bowen, John. *Can Islam be French? Pluralism and Pragmatism in a Secular State.* Princeton: Princeton University Press, 2009.

Brown, Wendy. *Regulating Aversion: Tolerance in the Age of Identity and Empire* (Princeton and Oxford: Princeton University Press, 2008).

C

Caiani, Manuela and C. Wagemann. "Online networks of the Italian and German extreme right." *Information, Communication & Society* **12**, no. 1 (2009): 66–109.

Camiscioli, Elisa. *Reproducing the French Race. Immigration, Intimacy, and Embodiment in the Early Twentieth Century.* Durham and London: Duke University Press.

Campbell, Vincent. "Citizen journalism and active citizenship." In *Contemporary Protest and the Legacy of Dissent*, edited by Stuart Price and Ruth Sanz Sabido, 207–222. London and New York: Rowman and Littlefield, 2015.

Camus, Jean-Yves and N. Lebourg. *Far-Right Politics in Europe.* Cambridge: Belknapp, 2017.

Canovan, Margaret. *The People.* Cambridge: Polity Press, 2005.

Carr, Matthew. "You are now entering Eurabia." *Race & Class* **48**, no. 1 (2006): 1–22.

Carr, Mathew. *Blood and Faith: The Purging of Muslim Spain, 1492–1614.* London: Hurst, 2017.

Carrey, Pierre, G. Gendron, and J. Luyssen. "Glacial." *Libération*, December 5, 2016, pp. 26–29.

Cassen, Pierre and C. Tasin. *La faute du Bobo Jocelyn.* Mérginac: Éditions Riposte Laïque, 2011.

Célestin, Roger, E. DalMolin, T. W. Reeser, and G. Mecchia. "Editors' introduction: 'The idea of France/L'idée de La France'." *Contemporary French and Francophone Studies* **17**, no. 2 (2013): 119–122.

Chabal, Emile. *A Divided Republic: Nation, State and Citizenship in Contemporary France.* Cambridge: Cambridge University Press, 2015.

Chabal, Emile. "From the banlieue to the burkini: The many lives of French republicanism." *Modern & Contemporary France* **25**, no. 1 (2017): 68–74.

Chadwick, Kay. "Education in secular France: (re)defining *laïcité*." *Modern & Contemporary France* **5**, no. 1 (1997): 47–59.

Charlie Hebdo (hors-série). "La laïcité c'est par où? La laïcité dans l'entreprise, à l'école, dans le monde ..." *Charlie Hebdo*, September–October 2013.

Chirac, Jacques. "Déclaration de M. Jacques Chirac, Président de la République et candidat à l'élection présidentielle 2002, après l'annonce de sa réelection à la Présidence de la République, Paris le 5 mai 2002." *La Vie Publique*, May 6, 2002. Available online: http://discours.vie-publique.fr/notices/027000128.html (accessed December 26, 2017).

Chirac, Jacques. "Allocution de M. Jacques Chirac, Président de la République, à Valenciennes." Palais de l'Elysée, October 21, 2003. Available online: http://www.jacqueschirac-asso.fr/archives-elysee.fr/elysee/elysee.fr/francais/interventions/

discours_et_declarations/2003/octobre/allocution_du_president_de_la_republique_a_valenciennes.1406.html (accessed February 5, 2018).

Chirac, Jacques. "Discours prononcé par M. Jacques Chirac, Président de la République, relatif au respect du principe de laïcité dans la République." Palais de l'Elysée, December 17, 2003.

Commission de réflexion sur l'application du principe de laïcité dans la République. *Rapport au Président de la République.* 2003. Available online: http://www.ladocumentationfrancaise.fr/var/storage/rapports-publics/034000725.pdf. (accessed January 21, 2018).

Conseil d'État. "Study of possible legal grounds for banning the full veil. Report adopted by the Plenary General Assembly of the Conseil d'Etat." March 25, 2010, Paris. Available online: http://www.conseil-etat.fr/Decisions-Avis-Publications/Etudes-Publications/Rapports-Etudes/Etude-relative-aux-possibilites-juridiques-d-interdiction-du-port-du-voile-integral. (accessed January 21, 2018).

Copé, Jean-François. *Manifeste pour une Droite Décomplexé.* Paris: Fayard, 2012.

Copsey, Nigel. "'Fascism … but with an open mind: Reflections on the contemporary far right in (Western) Europe." In *Fascism* 2 (2013): 1–17.

Coroller, Catherine. "Bouffeuse d'islam." *Libération*, March 2, 2011. Available online: http://www.liberation.fr/societe/2011/03/02/bouffeuse-d-islam_718571 (accessed February 1, 2018).

Cosnay, Fabienne. "La France Orange Mécanique, ce livre polémique." *Europe 1*, March 8, 2013. Available online: http://www.europe1.fr/politique/la-france-orange-mecanique-ce-livre-polemique-1440885 (accessed December 11, 2017).

Crépon, Sylvain. *La Nouvelle Extrême Droite. Enquête sur les Jeunes Militants du Front National.* Paris: L'Harmattan, 2006.

Cyrano. "Qui sommes nous? Pourquoi un nouveau media?" *Riposte Laïque*, August 30, 2007. Available online: http://ripostelaique.com/Qui-sommes-nous-Pourquoi-un/ (accessed February 1, 2018).

Cyrano. "Défendre celles et ceux que les islamistes traînent devant les tribunaux." *Riposte Laïque*, September 8, 2007. Available online: http://ripostelaique.com/Defendre-celles-et-ceux-que-les/ (accessed February 1, 2018).

Cyrano. "Fanny et Monia, deux femmes courageuses." *Rispote Laïque*, September 21, 2007. Available online: http://ripostelaique.com/Fanny-et-Monia-deux-femmes/ (accessed February 8, 2018).

Cyrano. "Lettre ouverte à Caroline Fourest et à tous ceux qui nous reprochent de soutenir Fanny." *Riposte Laïque*, October 11, 2007. Available online: http://ripostelaique.com/Lettre-ouverte-a-Caroline-Fourest/ (accessed February 5, 2018).

Cyrano. "Feminisme et laicité: des alliés naturels." *Riposte Laïque*, October 21, 2007. Available online: http://ripostelaique.com/Feminisme-et-laicite-des-allies/ (accessed February 5, 2018).

Cyrano. "Le courage des vraies résistantes." *Riposte Laïque*, October 27, 2007. Available online: http://ripostelaique.com/Le-courage-des-vraies-resistantes/ (accessed February 8, 2018).

Cyrano. "Osons demeurer des esprits libres, envers et contre tous." *Riposte Laïque*,
    December 1, 2007. Available online: http://ripostelaique.com/Osons-demeurer-des-
    esprits-libres/ (accessed February 5, 2018).

Cyrano. "Sarkozy emmène Boubakeur dans ses valises algériennes, et stigmatise
    l' 'islamophobie'!" *Riposte Laïque*, December 8, 2007. Available online: http://
    ripostelaique.com/Sarkozy-emmene-Boubakeur-dans-ses/ (accessed February 5,
    2018).

Cyrano. "Un débat télévisé sur le voile qui confirme les divergences entre laïques."
    Riposte Laïque, December 15, 2007. Available online: http://ripostelaique.com/Un-
    debat-televise-sur-le-voile-qui/ (accessed February 5, 2018).

Cyrano. "2008: Année de la liberté d'expression." *Riposte Laïque*, January 1, 2008.
    Available online: http://ripostelaique.com/2008-annee-de-la-liberte-d/ (accessed
    February 8, 2018).

Cyrano. "Après le discours anti-laïque de Sarkozy, nous sommes tous au pied du mur."
    Riposte Laïque, January 2, 2008. Available online: http://ripostelaique.com/Apres-le-
    discours-anti-laique-de/ (accessed February 5, 2018).

Cyrano. "Spécial 'Traité de Lisbonne'." *Riposte Laïque*, January 20, 2008. Available
    online: http://ripostelaique.com/Special-Traite-de-Lisbonne/ (accessed February 5,
    2018).

Cyrano. "Les vrais esprits libres ne devraient pas craindre le discours d'Ayaan Hirsi Ali."
    Riposte Laïque, February 21, 2008. Available online: http://ripostelaique.com/Les-
    vrais-esprits-libres-ne/ (accessed February 5, 2018).

Cyrano. "La 'laïcité ferme et tolérante' de Marianne est-elle la bonne réponse à la
    'laïcité positive' de Sarkozy?" *Riposte Laïque*, February 27, 2008. Available online:
    http://ripostelaique.com/La-laicite-ferme-et-tolerante-de/ (accessed February 5,
    2018).

Cyrano. "Le 8 mars noveau est arrivé." *Riposte Laïque*, March 5, 2008. Available online:
    http://ripostelaique.com/Le-8-mars-nouveau-est-arrive/ (February 8, 2018).

Cyrano. "La majorité des Français ne veut ni de l'Europe de l'UMPS, ni de la laïcité
    positive de Sarkozy." *Riposte Laïque*, March 26, 2008. Available online: http://
    ripostelaique.com/La-majorite-des-Francais-ne-veut/ (accessed February 5, 2018).

Cyrano. "Défendre Fanny Truchelet, Ayan Hirsi Ali et Geert Wilders, une triple
    coherence." *Riposte Laïque*, April 8, 2008. Available online: http://ripostelaique.com/
    Defendre-Fanny-Truchelut-Ayaan/ (accessed February 1, 2018).

Cyrano. "Le baiser de la mort des gauchistes et des bobos aux républicains
    compassionnels." *Riposte Laïque*, May 27, 2008. Available online: http://ripostelaique.
    com/Les-republicains-doivent-attaquer/ (accessed February 8, 2018).

Cyrano. "L'humanisme laïque contre le sectarisme haineux, la République contre la
    charia." *Riposte Laïque*, June 3, 2008. Available online: http://ripostelaique.com/L-
    humanisme-laique-contre-le/ (accessed February 5, 2018).

Cyrano. "Tout recul, à Lille ou à Ankara, de l'offensive islamiste est un progrès pour
    l'humanité." *Riposte Laïque*, June 10, 2008. Available online: http://ripostelaique.
    com/Tout-recul-a-Lille-ou-a-Ankara-de/ (accessed February 5, 2018).

Cyrano. "La volte-face du maire de Vigneux, grâce à la vigilance d'un lecteur de *Riposte Laïque*." *Riposte Laïque*, June 24, 2008. Available online: http://ripostelaique.com/La-volte-face-du-maire-de-Vigneux/ (accessed February 8, 2018).

Cyrano. "Peut-on s'être battu pour sauver Ingrid Betancourt, et abandonner Mohamed Sifaoui?" *Riposte Laïque*, July 4, 2008. Available online: http://ripostelaique.com/Peut-on-s-etre-battu-pour-sauver/ (accessed February 5, 2018).

Cyrano. "Le débat sur le voile ne doit pas s'arrêter à la burqa." *Riposte Laïque*, July 15, 2008. Available online: http://ripostelaique.com/Un-voile-peut-en-cacher/ (accessed February 8, 2018).

Cyrano. "Le nouveau procès, c'est le 3 septembre, tous avec Fanny Truchelut." *Riposte Laïque*, August 26, 2008. Available online: http://ripostelaique.com/Le-nouveau-proces-c-est-le-3/ (accessed February 8, 2018).

Cyrano. "Ils veulent en finir avec la laïcité pour mieux imposer leur modèle de société." *Riposte Laïque*, September 9, 2008. Available online: http://ripostelaique.com/Ils-veulent-en-finir-avec-la/ (accessed February 5, 2018).

Cyrano. "Deux mois de prison avec sursis, et 4000 euros de dommages et intérêts! Juges, Mrap-LDH et tous ceux qui ont enfoncé Fanny, honte à vous!" *Riposte Laïque*, October 8, 2008. Available online: http://ripostelaique.com/2-mois-de-prison-avec-sursis-et/ (accessed February 8, 2018).

Cyrano. "La France en a plus qu'assez qu'on lui crache au visage!" *Riposte Laïque*, October 21, 2008. Available online: http://ripostelaique.com/La-France-en-a-plus-qu-assez-qu-on/ (accessed February 5, 2018).

Cyrano. "Le système peut dire merci à ceux qui ont cassé, depuis 40 ans, toute autorité républicaine." *Riposte Laïque*, November 4, 2008. Available online: http://ripostelaique.com/Le-systeme-peut-dire-merci-a-ceux/ (accessed February 8, 2018).

Cyrano. "Sommes-nous d'affreux franchouillards si nous aimons notre pays, la France?" *Riposte Laïque*, November 11, 2008. Available online: http://ripostelaique.com/Sommes-nous-d-affreux/ (accessed February 5, 2018).

Cyrano. "9 décembre 1905—9 décembre 2008." *Riposte Laïque*, December 15, 2008. Available online: http://ripostelaique.com/9-decembre-1905-9-decembre-2008/(accessed February 8, 2018).

Cyrano. "Faut-il fermer les yeux sur la nature du Hamas pour ne pas désespérer Billancourt?" *Riposte Laïque*, January 5, 2009. Available online: http://ripostelaique.com/Faut-il-fermer-les-yeux-sur-la/ (accessed February 8, 2018).

Cyrano. "La liberté d'expression menacée de mort par l'Islam et ses complices." *Riposte Laïque*, January 27, 2009. Available online: http://ripostelaique.com/La-liberte-d-expression-menacee-de/ (accessed February 5, 2018).

Cyrano. "Le politiquement correct a besoin de lepéniser ses contradicteurs." *Riposte Laïque*, February 2, 2009. Available online: http://ripostelaique.com/Le-politiquement-correct-lepenise/ (accessed February 5, 2018).

Cyrano. "Panique chez les intégristes du libre échange, le protectionnisme est de retour!" *Riposte Laïque*, February 9, 2009. Available online: http://ripostelaique.com/Panique-chez-les-integristes-du/ (accessed February 8, 2018).

Cyrano. "Il nous faut un Pat Condell en France!" *Riposte Laïque*, February 16, 2009. Available online: http://ripostelaique.com/Il-nous-faut-un-Pat-Condell-en/ (accessed February 5, 2018).

Cyrano. "Voiles et mosquées, armes du jihad contre la France avec la complicité d'élus de la République." *Riposte Laïque*, March 30, 2009. Available online: http://ripostelaique.com/Voiles-et-mosquees-armes-du-jihad/ (accessed February 5, 2018).

Cyrano. "Pour un débat franc et loyal avec Henri Peña Ruiz, qui nous reproche de nous focaliser sur l'Islam." *Riposte Laïque*, April 20, 2009. Available online: http://ripostelaique.com/Pour-un-debat-franc-et-loyal-avec/ (accessed February 5, 2018).

Cyrano. "Le 'tout se vaut' et l'anti-occidentalisme primaire préparent la possible victoire de la charia." *Riposte Laïque*, April 27, 2009. Available online: http://ripostelaique.com/Le-tout-se-vaut-et-l-anti/ (accessed February 8, 2018).

Cyrano. "Deux nouveaux autocollants pour illustrer la résistance à l'agression islamiste." *Riposte Laïque*, May 3, 2010. Available online: http://ripostelaique.com/Deux-nouveaux-autocollants-pour/ (accessed February 5, 2018).

Cyrano. "Pourquoi veulent-ils nous faire taire?" *Riposte Laïque*, May 11, 2009. Available online: http://ripostelaique.com/Pourquoi-veulent-ils-nous-faire/ (accessed February 5, 2018).

Cyrano. "A mort les profs, à mort les flics!" *Riposte Laïque*, May 18, 2009. Available online: http://ripostelaique.com/A-mort-les-profs-a-mort-les-flics/ (accessed February 5, 2018).

Cyrano. "Je me demande si je ne vais pas soutenir la Halde …" *Riposte Laïque*, May 26, 2009. Available online: http://ripostelaique.com/Je-me-demande-si-je-ne-vais-pas/ (accessed February 5, 2018).

Cyrano. "Après Barnier, Moscovici ose nous dire que l'Europe a besoin de la Turquie!" *Riposte Laïque*, June 2, 2009. Available online: http://ripostelaique.com/Apres-Barnier-Moscovici-ose-nous/ (accessed February 5, 2018).

Cyrano. "Geert Wilders à 17 %. Une sacrée leçon pour le monde politique français." *Riposte Laïque*, June 8, 2009. Available online: http://ripostelaique.com/Geert-Wilders-a-17-Une-sacree/ (accessed February 1, 2018).

Cyrano. "Nous ne voulons pas être seulement l'honneur de la gauche, nous souhaitons susciter le réveil du peuple français." *Riposte Laïque*, June 15, 2009. Available online: http://ripostelaique.com/Nous-ne-voulons-pas-etre-seulement/ (accessed February 8, 2018).

Cyrano. "Burqa, immigration, Hénin-Beaumont: trois défaites du politiquement correct." *Riposte Laïque*, June 29, 2009. Available online: http://ripostelaique.com/Burqa-immigration-Henin-Beaumont/ (accessed February 8, 2018).

Cyrano. "Que de chemin parcouru … mais que de chemin encore à parcourir!" *Riposte Laïque*, July 6, 2009. Available online: http://ripostelaique.com/Que-de-chemin-parcouru-mais-que-de/ (accessed February 8, 2018).

Cyrano. "24 août: Delanoé et ses complices trahissent à nouveau la laïcité." *Riposte Laïque*, August 15, 2011. Available online: http://ripostelaique.com/24-aout-delanoe-et-ses-complices-trahissent-a-nouveau-la-laicite/ (accessed February 8, 2018).

Cyrano. "Halte à la burqa et au voile, symboles de la soumission des femmes et de l'offensive islamiste." *Riposte Laïque*, August 20, 2009. Available online: http://ripostelaique.com/Halte-a-la-burqa-et-au-voile/ (accessed February 5, 2018).

Cyrano. "Une pétition qui pose des questions incontournables à toute la société française." *Riposte Laïque*, August 24, 2009. Available online: http://ripostelaique.com/Une-petition-qui-pose-des/ (accessed February 5, 2018).

Cyrano. "Déjà 2 ans, et 100 numéros de Riposte Laïque!" *Riposte Laïque*, September 7, 2009. Available online: http://ripostelaique.com/Deja-2-ans-et-100-numeros-de/ (accessed February 8, 2018).

Cyrano. "Pour préparer la Résistance, retrouvons notre liberté de parole!" *Riposte Laïque*, September 21, 2009. Available online: http://ripostelaique.com/Pour-preparer-la-Resistance/ (accessed February 5, 2018).

Cyrano. "Ras le bol de voir Tariq Ramadan fanfaronner sur les plateaux de télévision!" *Riposte Laïque*, September 28, 2009. Available online: http://ripostelaique.com/Ras-le-bol-de-voir-Tariq-Ramadan/ (accessed February 5, 2018).

Cyrano. "Comparer l'islamophobie à l'antisémitisme des années 30 est une obscénité." *Riposte Laïque*, October 26, 2009. Available online: http://ripostelaique.com/Comparer-l-antisemitisme-des/ (accessed February 5, 2018).

Cyrano. "Nous aimons la beauté démocratique." *Riposte Laïque*, November 2, 2009. Available online: http://ripostelaique.com/Nous-aimons-la-beaute-democratique/ (accessed February 8, 2018).

Cyrano. "Identité(s) nationale(s): la parole au(x) peuple(s)!" *Riposte Laïque*, November 9, 2009. Available online: http://ripostelaique.com/Identite-s-nationale-s-la-parole/ (accessed February 8, 2018).

Cyrano. "Pourquoi suis-je français?" *Riposte Laïque*, November 23, 2009. Available online: http://ripostelaique.com/POURQUOI-SUIS-JE-FRANCAIS/ (accessed February 8, 2018).

Cyrano. "Après la mission parlementaire, après la votation suisse, plus rien ne devra être comme avant." *Riposte Laïque*, December 7, 2009. Available online: http://ripostelaique.com/Apres-la-mission-parlementaire/ (accessed February 8, 2018).

Cyrano. "Nation, République, laïcité, voile intégral, prières dans la rue, identité nationale, votation suisse … La cohérence de RL." *Riposte Laïque*, December 14, 2009. Available online: http://ripostelaique.com/Nation-Republique-laicite-voile/ (accessed February 5, 2018).

Cyrano. "Oskar Freysinger a-t-il raison de dire que la France est foutue?" *Riposte Laïque*, December 21, 2009. Available online: http://ripostelaique.com/Oskar-Freysinger-a-t-il-raison-de/ (accessed February 5, 2018).

Cyrano. "Le maire de Trappes et son avocat menacent Riposte Laïque des foudres de la justice." *Riposte Laïque*, January 4, 2010. Available online: http://ripostelaique.com/Le-maire-de-Trappes-et-son-avocat/ (accessed February 5, 2018).

Cyrano. "En 2011, nombre de patriotes vont entrer en résistance contre l'islamisation de la France." *Riposte Laïque*, January 10, 2010. Available online: http://ripostelaique.com/En-2011-nombre-de-patriotes-vont/ (accessed February 5, 2018).

Cyrano. "L'enjeu du procès de Geert Wilders: la libre critique de l'islam." *Riposte Laïque*, January 22, 2010. Available online: http://ripostelaique.com/L-enjeu-du-proces-de-Geert-Wilders/ (accessed February 5, 2018).

Cyrano. "Blondel sur RFI, Ramadan sur France 24, l'islamophobie sur Beur FM: *Riposte Laïque* sur tous les fronts." *Riposte Laïque*, January 29, 2010. Available online: http://ripostelaique.com/Blondel-sur-RFI-Ramadan-sur-France/ (accessed February 8, 2018).

Cyrano. "Besancenot akbar!" *Riposte Laïque*, February 5, 2010. Available online: http://ripostelaique.com/Besancenot-akbar/ (accessed February 5, 2018).

Cyrano. "La colère d'un Français: c'est parti!" *Riposte Laïque*, February 8, 2010. Available online: http://ripostelaique.com/La-colere-d-un-Francais-c-est/ (accessed February 8, 2018).

Cyrano. "Le vrai clivage se situe entre ceux qui aiment la France, et ceux qui veulent qu'elle disparaisse." *Riposte Laïque*, February 12, 2010. Available online: http://ripostelaique.com/Le-vrai-clivage-se-situe-entre/ (accessed February 8, 2018).

Cyrano. "Quick halal: les Français ont tout compris, ce sera l'islam ou la République!" *Riposte Laïque*, February 24, 2010. Available online: http://ripostelaique.com/Quick-halal-les-Francais-ont-tout/ (accessed February 5, 2018).

Cyrano. "Caroline, pourquoi mentir aussi grossièrement pour salir RL?" *Riposte Laïque*, March 1, 2010. Available online: http://ripostelaique.com/Caroline-pourquoi-mentir-aussi/ (accessed February 5, 2018).

Cyrano. "Le voile islamique insulte la liberté de tous." *Riposte Laïque*, March 8, 2010. Available online: http://ripostelaique.com/Le-voile-islamique-insulte-la/ (accessed February 5, 2018).

Cyrano. "Le seul intérêt de ces élections régionales …" *Riposte Laïque*, March 12, 2010. Available online: http://ripostelaique.com/Le-seul-interet-de-ces-elections/ (accessed February 7, 2018).

Cyrano. "Refuser l'islamisation de 'Ma France'." *Riposte Laïque*, March 15, 2010. Available online: http://ripostelaique.com/Refuser-l-islamisation-de-Ma/ (accessed February 5, 2018).

Cyrano. "7 Français sur 10 ne veulent plus de Sarkozy-Aubry." *Riposte Laïque*, March 22, 2010. Available online: http://ripostelaique.com/7-Francais-sur-10-ne-veulent-plus/ (accessed February 8, 2018).

Cyrano. "'Peuple de France', une chanson qui résume le combat de Riposte Laïque." *Riposte Laïque*, March 31, 2010. Available online: http://ripostelaique.com/Peuple-de-France-une-chanson-qui/ (accessed February 5, 2018).

Cyrano. "Du terrorisme intellectuel de la bien-pensance aux intimidations physiques contre RL." *Riposte Laïque*, April 7, 2010. Available online: http://ripostelaique.com/Du-terrorisme-intellectuel-de-la/ (accessed February 5, 2018).

Cyrano. "Burqa, République, insécurité, Zemmour, immigration, laïcité 2010, avenir de RL: une vidéo pour débattre." *Riposte Laïque*, April 14, 2010. Available online: http://ripostelaique.com/Burqa-Republique-insecurite/ (accessed February 5, 2018).

Cyrano. "La France est en état de guerre civile, c'est un fait ..." *Riposte Laïque*, April 20, 2010. Available online: http://ripostelaique.com/La-France-est-en-etat-de-guerre/ (accessed February 5, 2018).

Cyrano. "Sortie du troisième livre de Riposte Laïque: '*Résistance Républicaine*.'" *Riposte Laïque*, April 24, 2010. Available online: http://ripostelaique.com/Sortie-du-troisieme-livre-de/ (accessed February 8, 2018).

Cyrano. "Assez d'impuissance face aux voyous racistes et aux fascistes islamistes!" *Riposte Laïque*, April 26, 2010. Available online: http://ripostelaique.com/Assez-d-impuissance-face-aux/ (accessed February 8, 2018).

Cyrano. "Deux nouveaux autocollants pour illustrer la résistance à l'agression islamiste." *Riposte Laïque*, May 3, 2010. Available online: http://ripostelaique.com/Deux-nouveaux-autocollants-pour/ (accessed February 5, 2018).

Cyrano. "Les autocollants de RL victimes provisoires de la pression islamiste." *Riposte Laïque*, May 10, 2010. Available online: http://ripostelaique.com/Les-autocollants-de-RL-victimes/ (accessed February 5, 2018).

Cyrano. "Bobos antiracistes bien-pensants, lisez bien les propos d'Houria Bouteldja ..." *Riposte Laïque*, May 17, 2010. Available online: http://ripostelaique.com/Bobos-antiracistes-bien-pensants/ (accessed February 5, 2018).

Cyrano. "Résistance Républicaine, c'est parti!" *Riposte Laïque*, June 7, 2010. Available online: http://ripostelaique.com/Resistance-Republicaine-c-est/ (accessed February 1, 2018).

Cyrano. "L'apéro géant saucisson pinard objet de toute la vindicte médiatique ..." *Riposte Laïque*, June 14, 2010. Available online: http://ripostelaique.com/L-apero-geant-saucisson-pinard/ (accessed February 8, 2018).

Cyrano. "Apéro géant et scandale Anelka-Ribery: ce que comprennent les Français ..." *Riposte Laïque*, June 21, 2010. Available online: http://ripostelaique.com/Apero-geant-et-scandale-Anelka/ (accessed February 5, 2018).

Cyrano. "Le peuple de France doit se préparer à un nouveau 1789." *Riposte Laïque*, June 28, 2010. Available online: http://ripostelaique.com/Le-peuple-de-France-doit-se/ (accessed February 5, 2018).

Cyrano. "Une troisième année qui a été décisive pour *Riposte Laïque*." *Riposte Laïque*, July 5, 2010. Available online: http://ripostelaique.com/Une-troisieme-annee-qui-a-ete/ (accessed February 8, 2018).

Cyrano. "Ils servent la soupe à la pire extrême droite, et ils se croient de gauche!" *Riposte Laïque*, July 12, 2010. Available online: http://ripostelaique.com/Ils-servent-la-soupe-a-la-pire/ (accessed February 5, 2018).

Cyrano. "Après Grenoble, cela peut-il continuer ainsi?" *Riposte Laïque*, July 19, 2010. Available online: http://ripostelaique.com/Apres-Grenoble-cela-peut-il/ (accessed February 5, 2018).

Cyrano. "Défendre la pensée juste et ne pas subir le politiquement correct." *Riposte Laïque*, July 26, 2010. Available online: http://ripostelaique.com/Defendre-la-pensee-juste-et-ne-pas/ (accessed February 6, 2018).

Cyrano. "Discours de Grenoble: encore du vent, ou la dernière cartouche de Sarkozy?" *Riposte Laïque*, August 2, 2010. Available online: http://ripostelaique.com/Discours-de-Grenoble-encore-du/ (accessed February 5, 2018).

Cyrano. "Halal, ramadan, émeutes: trois armes islamistes pour conquérir la France laïque." *Riposte Laïque*, August 9, 2010. Available online: http://ripostelaique.com/Halal-ramadan-emeutes-trois-armes/ (accessed February 5, 2018).

Cyrano. "La légitime révolte du peuple de France devant les multiples agressions que subit son pays." *Riposte Laïque*, August 17, 2010. Available online: http://ripostelaique.com/Une-accumulation-de-faits-qui-ne/ (accessed February 5, 2018).

Cyrano. "Insécurité, islam: honte aux dirigeants de cette 'gôche,' qui abandonnent le peuple et la République." *Riposte Laïque*, August 23, 2010. Available online: http://ripostelaique.com/Insecurite-islam-honte-aux/ (accessed February 5, 2018).

Cyrano. "Leur 4 septembre et le nôtre: deux conceptions inconciliables de la République." *Riposte Laïque*, August 30, 2010. Available online: http://ripostelaique.com/Leur-4-septembre-et-le-notre-deux/ (accessed February 8, 2018).

Cyrano. "L'ordre nouveau des islamogauchistes au service du fascisme vert." *Riposte Laïque*, September 6, 2010. Available online: http://ripostelaique.com/L-ordre-nouveau-des/ (accessed February 6, 2018).

Cyrano. "Coupables de trop aimer la France." *Riposte Laïque*, September 13, 2010. Available online: http://ripostelaique.com/Coupables-de-trop-aimer-la-France/ (accessed February 8, 2018).

Cyrano. "Les islamistes sortent du bois et annoncent la couleur: une France musulmane, soumise à la charia." *Riposte Laïque*, September 20, 2010. Available online: http://ripostelaique.com/Les-islamistes-sortent-du-bois-et/ (accessed February 5, 2018).

Cyrano. "Moussaoui, Techno Parade et Limoges: un silence politico-médiatique assourdissant!" *Riposte Laïque*, October 4, 2010. Available online: http://ripostelaique.com/Moussaoui-Techno-Parade-et-Limoges/ (accessed February 8, 2018).

Cyrano. "Pourra-t-on vaincre l'offensive islamiste par les seuls moyens démocratiques?" *Riposte Laïque*, October 11, 2010. Available online: http://ripostelaique.com/Pourra-t-on-vaincre-l-offensive (accessed February 5, 2018).

Cyrano. "Par quel miracle une jeune femme de 25 ans peut-elle encore aimer la France?" *Riposte Laïque*, October 18, 2010. Available online: http://ripostelaique.com/Par-quelle-miracle-une-jeune-femme/ (accessed February 5, 2018).

Cyrano, "La maison France est en feu: il est urgent de rassembler notre peuple autour de ses idéaux." *Riposte Laïque*, October 25, 2010. Available online: http://ripostelaique. com/La-maison-France-est-en-feu-il-est/ (accessed February 8, 2018).

Cyrano. "Ils livrent la République laïque à l'islam! Rassemblons-nous pour sauver la France." *Riposte Laïque*, November 1, 2010. Available online: http://ripostelaique. com/Ils-livrent-la-Republique-laique-a/ (accessed February 5, 2018).

Cyrano. "Causeur et *Riposte Laïque*: débattre entre Républicains, sans trop se chamailler ..." *Riposte Laïque*, November 8, 2010. Available online: http:// ripostelaique.com/Causeur-et-Riposte-Laique-debattre/ (accessed February 5, 2018).

Cyrano. "Vive les référendums suisses, nous aussi on veut voter ..." *Riposte Laïque*, November 29, 2010. Available online: http://ripostelaique.com/Vive-les-referendums-suisses-nous/ (accessed February 8, 2018).

Cyrano. "Des assises exceptionnelles, des intervenants formidables, un public en or ..." *Riposte Laïque*, December 19, 2010. Available online: http://ripostelaique.com/18-decembre-Un-nouvel-acte-de/ (accessed January 21, 2018).

Cyrano. "Assises sur l'islamisation: gros succès, 600,000 visiteurs en 2 jours, rendez-vous début 2011." *Riposte Laïque*, December 21, 2010. Available online: http:// ripostelaique.com/Assises-sur-l-islamisation-Plus/ (accessed January 21, 2018).

Cyrano. "BHL se ridiculise en voulant agresser Riposte Laïque." *Riposte Laïque*, December 27, 2010. Available online: http://ripostelaique.com/BHL-se-ridiculise-en-voulant/ (accessed February 5, 2018).

Cyrano. "Qui sont vraiment les 'nouveaux fachos'?" *Riposte Laïque*, January 17, 2011. Available online: http://ripostelaique.com/Qui-sont-vraiment-les-nouveaux/ (accessed February 8, 2018).

Cyrano. "Fourest-Tubiana veulent tuer *Riposte Laïque*, parce qu'ils détestent sa liberté d'expression." *Riposte Laïque*, January 31, 2011. Available online: http://ripostelaique. com/Fourest-Tubiana-veulent-tuer/ (accessed February 8, 2018).

Cyrano. "La LDH veut se faire Riposte Laïque devant les tribunaux!" *Riposte Laïque*, January 24, 2011. Available online: http://ripostelaique.com/La-LDH-veut-se-faire-Riposte/ (accessed February 6, 2018).

Cyrano. "Eric Zemmour condamné, Pascal Hilout convoqué par la police: où est la véritable extrême droite?" *Riposte Laïque*, February 26, 2011. Available online: http:// ripostelaique.com/eric-zemmour-condamne-pascal-hilout-convoque-par-la-police-cela-suffit-halte-au-fascisme-vive-la-liberte-dexpression/ (accessed February 5, 2018).

Cyrano. "Un islamo-collabo à la place d'une islamo-collabo, et Sarkozy-Fillon veulent en finir avec 1905!" *Riposte Laïque*, February 28, 2011. Available online: http:// ripostelaique.com/sarkozy-remplace-une-islamo-collabo-ump-par-un-islamo-collabo-ump/ (accessed February 5, 2018).

Cyrano. "Marine Le Pen en tête au premier tour: racisme ou insurrection démocratique des Français?" *Riposte Laïque*, March 7, 2011. Available online: http://ripostelaique. com/marine-le-pen-en-tete-au-premier-tour-racisme-des-francais-ou-insurrection-democratique/(accessed February 8, 2018).

Cyrano. "Les piliers du système perdent les pédales devant la progression de Marine Le Pen." *Riposte Laïque*, March 14, 2011. Available online: http://ripostelaique.com/les-piliers-du-systeme-perdent-les-pedales-devant-la-progression-de-marine-le-pen/ (accessed February 8, 2018).

Cyrano. "Et s'ils se rappelaient qu'ils sont élus pour protéger le peuple de France?" *Riposte Laïque*, March 21, 2011. Available online: http://ripostelaique.com/et-sils-se-rappelaient-quils-sont-elus-pour-proteger-le-peuple-de-france/ (accessed February 9, 2018).

Cyrano. "Nous confirmons que l'islam est incompatible avec la République laïque!" *Riposte Laïque*, March 28, 2011. Available online: http://ripostelaique.com/nous-confirmons-que-lislam-est-incompatible-avec-la-republique-laique/ (accessed February 5, 2018).

Cyrano. "Débat laïcité: une conférence de presse, de vraies solutions face à l'islamisation de la France." *Riposte Laïque*, April 5, 2011. Available online: http://ripostelaique.com/debat-laicite-une-conference-de-presse-de-vraies-solutions-face-a-lislamisation-de-la-france/ (accessed February 8, 2018).

Cyrano. "15 ans après, les chiens de garde nouveaux sont arrives." *Riposte Laïque*, April 18, 2011. Available online: http://ripostelaique.com/15-ans-apres-les-chiens-de-garde-nouveaux-sont-arrives/ (accessed February 6, 2018).

Cyrano. "Ni l'UMP ni le PS ne pourront arrêter la révolution sociale et identitaire en cours." *Riposte Laïque*, April 25, 2011. Available online: http://ripostelaique.com/ni-l'ump-ni-le-ps-ne-pourront-arreter-la-revolution-sociale-et-identitaire-en-cours/ (accessed February 8, 2018).

Cyrano. "Sous la pression de l'islam, l'incroyable acharnement judiciaire contre la liberté d'expression." *Riposte Laïque*, May 10, 2011. Available online: http://ripostelaique.com/sous-la-pression-de-lislam-lincroyable-acharnement-judiciaire-contre-la-liberte-dexpression/ (accessed February 8, 2018).

Cyrano. "DSK hors circuit, il va falloir en trouver un autre pour faire le sale boulot des mondialistes." *Riposte Laïque*, May 16, 2011. Available online: http://ripostelaique.com/dsk-hors-circuit-il-va-falloir-en-trouver-un-autre-pour-faire-le-sale-boulot-des-mondialistes/ (accessed February 8, 2018).

Cyrano. "Présidentielles: Le PS demande aux électeurs du FN et de l'UMP de choisir son candidat!" *Riposte Laïque*, May 30, 2011. Available online: http://ripostelaique.com/presidentielles-le-ps-demande-aux-electeurs-du-fn-et-de-lump-de-choisir-son-candidat/ (accessed February 7, 2018).

Cyrano. "Prières musulmanes: nous ne voulons pas que les rues de Paris ressemblent un jour à celles de Moscou." *Riposte Laïque*, June 13, 2011. Available online: http://ripostelaique.com/prieres-musulmanes-nous-ne-voulons-pas-que-les-rues-de-paris-ressemblent-un-jour-a-celles-de-moscou/ (accessed June 13, 2011).

Cyrano. "Les sales méthodes de Marianne pour salir notre initiative du 18 juin." *Riposte Laïque*, June 19, 2011. Available online: http://ripostelaique.com/les-sales-methodes-de-marianne-pour-salir-notre-initiative-du-18-juin/ (accessed February 8, 2018).

Cyrano. "Il faut l'unité des patriotes, face au bloc des mondialistes." *Riposte Laïque*, June 27, 2011. Available online: http://ripostelaique.com/il-faut-lunite-des-patriotes-face-au-bloc-des-mondialistes/ (accessed February 8, 2018).

Cyrano. "Martine Aubry, épouse Brochen, se plaint des 'rumeurs': Nous persistons et nous signons!" *Riposte Laïque*, July 11, 2011. Available online: http://ripostelaique.com/martine-aubry-epouse-brochen-se-plaint-des-rumeurs-nous-persistons-et-nous-signons/ (accessed February 5, 2018).

Cyrano. "Au bout de 2 mois l'imposteur normal 1er est déjà nu!" *Riposte Laïque*, July 16, 2012. Available online: http://ripostelaique.com/au-bout-de-2-mois-limposteur-normal-1er-est-deja-nu/ (accessed February 7, 2018).

Cyrano. "Lozès a osé: l'apéro saucisson-pinard coupable du drame d'Oslo!" *Riposte Laïque*, July 25, 2011. Available online: http://ripostelaique.com/lozes-a-ose-lapero-saucisson-pinard-coupable-du-drame-doslo/ (accessed February 6, 2018).

Cyrano. "Delanoë trahit la France laïque pour l'islam et son ramadan moyen-âgeux." *Riposte Laïque*, August 22, 2011. Available online: http://ripostelaique.com/delanoe-trahit-la-france-laique-pour-lislam-et-son-ramadan-moyen-ageux/ (accessed February 5, 2018).

Cyrano. "Accompagnatrices voilées, Saint-Gratien: la laïcité recule, sous la pression de l'islam." *Riposte Laïque*, August 29, 2011. Available online: http://ripostelaique.com/accompagnatrices-voilees-saint-gratien-la-laicite-recule-sous-la-pression-de-lislam/ (accessed February 5, 2018).

Cyrano. "La faute du bobo Jocelyn: un roman de politique-fiction signé Pierre Cassen et Christine Tasin." *Riposte Laïque*, September 26, 2011. Available online: http://ripostelaique.com/la-faute-du-bobo-jocelyn-un-roman-de-politique-fiction-signe-pierre-cassen-et-christine-tasin/ (accessed February 8, 2018).

Cyrano. "Une gauche qui méprise le peuple n'est plus la gauche." *Riposte Laïque*, October 3, 2011. Available online: http://ripostelaique.com/une-gauche-qui-meprise-le-peuple-nest-plus-la-gauche/ (accessed February 5, 2018).

Cyrano. "Une pétition qui marche, un journal qui fait causer." *Riposte Laïque*, November 5, 2011. Available online: http://ripostelaique.com/Une-petition-qui-marche-un-journal/ (accessed February 6, 2018).

Cyrano. "Pourquoi Riposte Laïque dérange-t-il autant?" *Riposte Laïque*, November 14, 2011. Available online: http://ripostelaique.com/pourquoi-riposte-laique-derange-t-il-autant/ (accessed February 5, 2018).

Cyrano. "Todd-Mélenchon-Fourest: vrais rebelles ou chiens de garde?" *Riposte Laïque*, November 21, 2011. Available online: http://ripostelaique.com/todd-melenchon-fourest-vrais-rebelles-ou-chiens-de-garde/ (accessed February 5, 2018).

Cyrano. "Barbarie islamiste ou amour de la vie: il faudra choisir, ce sera l'un ou l'autre ..." *Riposte Laïque*, November 28, 2011. Available online: http://ripostelaique.com/barbarie-islamiste-ou-amour-de-la-vie-il-faudra-choisir-ce-sera-lun-ou-lautre.../ (accessed February 8, 2018).

Cyrano. "En Iran, police des moeurs! En France, la police de la pensée!" *Riposte Laïque*, December 5, 2011. Available online: http://ripostelaique.com/en-iran-police-des-moeurs-en-france-police-de-la-pensee/ (accessed February 1, 2018).

Cyrano. "2012: Tous les soirs, à partir de 19 h 50, le Journal des Résistants, avec Christine Tasin." *Riposte Laïque*, December 26, 2011. Available online: http://ripostelaique.com/2012-tous-les-soirs-a-partir-de-19-h-50-le-journal-des-resistants-avec-christine-tasin/ (accessed February 8, 2018).

Cyrano. "Oseront-ils condamner Pascal et Pierre, après avoir acquitté Bouteldja?" *Riposte Laïque*, January 30, 2012. Available online: http://ripostelaique.com/oseront-ils-condamner-pascal-et-pierre-apres-avoir-acquitte-bouteldja/ (accessed February 8, 2018).

Cyrano. "Le seul intérêt de ces élections régionales …" *Riposte Laïque*, March 12, 2010. Available online: http://ripostelaique.com/Le-seul-interet-de-ces-elections/ (accessed February 7, 2018).

Cyrano. "Le vrai programme de François Hollande c'est Jacques Attali." *Riposte Laïque*, February 27, 2012. Available online: http://ripostelaique.com/le-vrai-programme-de-francois-hollande-cest-jacques-attali/ (accessed February 7, 2018).

Cyrano. "En finir avec la tyrannie post-soixante-huitarde et retrouver la vraie France." *Riposte Laïque*, March 5, 2012. Available online: http://ripostelaique.com/en-finir-avec-la-tyrannie-post-soixante-huitarde-et-retrouver-la-vraie-france/ (accessed February 5, 2018).

Cyrano. "Pour la liberté de diffuser 'Fitna'." *Riposte Laïque*, March 12, 2008. Available online: http://ripostelaique.com/Pour-la-liberte-de-diffuser-Fitna/ (accessed February 8, 2018).

Cyrano. "Comment protéger la France et les Français contre les fous d'Allah?" *Riposte Laïque*, April 2, 2012. Available online: http://ripostelaique.com/comment-proteger-la-france-et-les-francais-contre-les-fous-dallah/ (accessed February 8, 2018).

Cyrano. "Présidentielle: Cette exception française qui 'emmerde' Cohn-Bendit et les siens." *Riposte Laïque*, April 9, 2012. Available online: http://ripostelaique.com/presidentielle-cette-exception-francaise-qui-emmerde-cohn-bendit-et-les-siens/ (accessed February 5, 2018).

Cyrano. "La France est-elle foutue? Oui, sauf si …" *Riposte Laïque*, May 7, 2012. Available online: http://ripostelaique.com/la-france-est-elle-foutue-oui-sauf-si/(accessed February 5, 2018).

Cyrano. "Le président Hollande va-t-il devoir désavouer le socialiste Flamby?" *Riposte Laïque*, May 14, 2012. Available online: http://ripostelaique.com/le-president-hollande-va-t-il-devoir-desavouer-le-socialiste-flamby/ (accessed February 5, 2018).

Cyrano. "Pour faire voter les étrangers, Hollande-Ayrault devront en passer par le referendum." *Riposte Laïque*, June 18, 2012. Available online: http://ripostelaique.com/pour-faire-voter-les-etrangers-hollande-ayrault-devront-en-passer-par-le-referendum/ (accessed February 8, 2018).

Cyrano. "Les socialistes sont-ils des idiots utiles ou des traitres?" *Riposte Laïque*, July 30, 2012. Available online: http://ripostelaique.com/les-socialistes-sont-ils-des-idiots-utiles-de-lislam-ou-des-traitres-a-la-france-laique/ (accessed February 5, 2018).

Cyrano. "Valls livre délibérément la France aux jihadistes." *Riposte Laïque*, August 6, 2012. Available online: http://ripostelaique.com/valls-livre-deliberement-la-france-aux-jihadistes/ (accessed February 6, 2018).

Cyrano. "Après les JO du voile, place à la qatarisation du football … et de la politique francaise." *Riposte Laïque*, August 13, 2012. Available online: http://ripostelaique.com/apres-les-jo-du-voile-place-a-la-qatarisation-du-football-et-de-la-politique-francaise/ (accessed February 7, 2018).

Cyrano. "Nous aimons trop la liberté et la France des Lumières pour les abandonner à l'islam des ténèbres." *Riposte Laïque*, August 20, 2012. Available online: http://ripostelaique.com/nous-aimons-trop-la-liberte-et-la-france-des-lumieres-pour-les-abandonner-a-lislam-des-tenebres/ (accessed February 8, 2018).

Cyrano. "Jihad à Paris, Fourest agressée: Oriana Fallaci avait raison …" *Riposte Laïque*, September 17, 2012. Available online: http://ripostelaique.com/jihad-a-paris-fourest-agressee-oriana-fallaci-avait-raison/ (accessed February 5, 2018).

Cyrano. "Le 10 Novembre, tous à Paris contre le fascisme Islamiste." *Riposte Laïque*, September 24, 2012, Available online: http://ripostelaique.com/le-10-novembre-tous-a-paris-contre-le-fascisme-Islamiste.html. (accessed January 17, 2018).

Cyrano. "Ce que sera la France de Normal 1er en 2017 … s'il va au bout de son mandat." *Riposte Laïque*, October 1, 2012. Available online: http://ripostelaique.com/ce-que-sera-la-france-de-normal-1er-en-2017-sil-va-au-bout-de-son-mandat/ (accessed February 5, 2018).

Cyrano. "Après l'arrestation de futurs Merah, Valls peut-il interdire la manifestation du 10 novembre?" *Riposte Laïque*, October 8, 2012. Available online: http://ripostelaique.com/apres-larrestation-de-futurs-merah-valls-peut-il-interdire-la-manifestation-du-10-novembre/ (accessed February 5, 2018).

Cyrano. "Les fossiles de Génération Mitterrand veulent faire taire les jeunes de Génération Identitaire." *Riposte Laïque*, October 22, 2012. Available online: http://ripostelaique.com/les-fossiles-de-generation-mitterrand-veulent-faire-taire-les-jeunes-de-generation-identitaire/ (accessed February 5, 2018).

Cyrano. "Une première marche contre le fascisme islamiste qui en appelle d'autres …" *Riposte Laïque*, November 12, 2012. Available online: http://ripostelaique.com/une-premiere-marche-contre-le-fascisme-islamiste-qui-en-appelle-dautres/ (accessed February 5, 2018).

Cyrano. "L'alternative à l'UMPS ne peut qu'être islamophobe." *Riposte Laïque*, November 26, 2012. Available online: http://ripostelaique.com/lalternative-a-lumps-ne-peut-quetre-islamophobe/ (accessed February 5, 2018).

Cyrano. "La France subira obligatoirement des attentats-suicides musulmans." *Riposte Laïque*, December 3, 2012. Available online: http://ripostelaique.com/la-france-subira-obligatoirement-des-attentats-suicides-musulmans/ (accessed February 8, 2018).

Cyrano. "Au secours, Voltaire, ils sont devenus fous!" *Riposte Laïque*, December 8, 2012. Available online: http://ripostelaique.com/Au-secours-Voltaire-ils-sont/ (accessed February 6, 2018).

Cyrano. "Mariage homo: le bal des faux-culs socialistes." *Riposte Laïque*, January 7, 2013. Available online: http://ripostelaique.com/mariage-homo-les-faux-culs-socialistes/ (accessed February 6, 2018).

Cyrano. "Mariage homo, islam: la caste contre le people." *Riposte Laïque*, January 28, 2013. Available online: https://ripostelaique.com/mariage-homo-islam-la-caste-contre-le-peuple.html (accessed February 5, 2018).

Cyrano. "Reconquista ou Mort de l'Europe, de René Marchand: LE livre que nous attendions tous." *Riposte Laïque*, February 18, 2013. Available online: http://ripostelaique.com/reconquista-ou-mort-de-leurope-de-rene-marchand-le-livre-que-nous-attendions-tous/ (accessed February 8, 2018).

Cyrano. "Nous sommes gouvernés par les porteurs de valises du FLN et de l'islam." *Riposte Laïque*, March 18, 2013. Available online: http://ripostelaique.com/nous-sommes-gouvernes-par-les-porteurs-de-valises-du-fln-et-de-lislam/ (accessed February 8, 2018).

Cyrano. "L'actualité donne raison à Pierre et Pascal: que font-ils devant un tribunal?" *Riposte Laïque*, March 25, 2013. Available online: http://ripostelaique.com/lactualite-donne-raison-a-pierre-et-pascal-que-font-ils-devant-un-tribunal/ (accessed February 5, 2018).

Cyrano. "Médias et justice complices de Hollande et du changement de civilization." *Riposte Laïque*, May 6, 2013. Available online: http://ripostelaique.com/medias-et-justice-complices-de-hollande-et-du-changement-de-civilisation/ (accessed February 7, 2018).

Cyrano. "La dictature des juges Taubira contre la liberté d'expression." *Riposte Laïque*, May 13, 2013. Available online: http://ripostelaique.com/la-dictature-des-juges-taubira-contre-la-liberte-dexpression/ (accessed February 5, 2018).

Cyrano. "La société totalitaire que veulent mettre en place Hollande et sa clique." *Riposte Laïque*, July 1, 2013. Available online: http://ripostelaique.com/la-societe-totalitaire-que-veulent-mettre-en-place-hollande-et-sa-clique/ (accessed February 5, 2018).

Cyrano. "Dal-Bordeaux, antiracistes, Trappes: une même guerre contre la France." *Riposte Laïque*, July 22, 2013. Available online: http://ripostelaique.com/dal-bordeaux-antiracistes-bregignytrappes-une-meme-guerre-menee-contre-la-france/ (accessed February 7, 2018).

Cyrano. "Hollande et sa clique répriment les patriotes et bichonnent les islamo-racailles." *Riposte Laïque*, July 29, 2013. Available online: http://ripostelaique.com/hollande-et-sa-clique-repriment-les-patriotes-et-bichonnent-les-islamo-racailles/ (accessed February 8, 2018).

Cyrano. "Il faudra juger Hollande et sa clique pour haute trahison." *Riposte Laïque*, June 17, 2013. Available online: http://ripostelaique.com/il-faudra-juger-hollande-et-sa-clique-pour-haute-trahison (accessed February 8, 2018).

Cyrano. "Opération Pédalo et Islamectomie: Comment débarrasser la France de Hollande et de l'islam?" *Riposte Laïque*, August 19, 2013. Available online: http://ripostelaique.com/dans-deux-livres-de-riposte-laique-la-france-reussit-a-se-debarrasser-de-hollande-et-de-lislam/ (accessed February 8, 2018).

Cyrano. "L'armée dernier rempart de notre démocratie face aux barbares?" *Riposte Laïque*, August 26, 2013. Available online: http://ripostelaique.com/larmee-dernier-rempart-de-notre-democratie-face-aux-barbares/ (accessed February 5, 2018).

Cyrano. "Ils veulent nous tuer et accélérer la fin de la France." *Riposte Laïque*, September 2, 2013. Available online: http://ripostelaique.com/ils-veulent-nous-tuer-et-accelerer-la-fin-de-la-france/ (accessed February 8, 2018).

Cyrano. "14 septembre: Comment résister face à un gouvernement collabo?" *Riposte Laïque*, September 9, 2013. Available online: http://ripostelaique.com/14-septembre-comment-resister-face-a-un-gouvernement-collabo/ (accessed February 8, 2018).

Cyrano. "Une première vidéo qui montre la tension du débat Cassen-Ramadan." *Riposte Laïque*, October 7, 2013. Available online: http://ripostelaique.com/une-premiere-video-qui-montre-la-tension-du-debat-cassen-ramadan/ (accessed February 5, 2018).

Cyrano. "Pourquoi ont-ils si peur des référendums?" *Riposte Laïque*, October 14, 2013. Available online: http://ripostelaique.com/pourquoi-ont-ils-si-peur-des-referendums/ (accessed February 7, 2018).

Cyrano. "Les manipulations antiracistes de Hollande et sa clique ne marchent plus!" *Riposte Laïque*, December 2, 2013. Available online: http://ripostelaique.com/les-manipulations-antiracistes-de-hollande-et-sa-clique-ne-marchent-plus/ (accessed February 8, 2018).

Cyrano. "Fin de la France: le stupide Ayrault crache le morceau!" *Riposte Laïque*, December 16, 2013. Available online: http://ripostelaique.com/fin-de-la-france-le-stupide-ayrault-crache-le-morceau/ (accessed February 8, 2018).

Cyrano. "Pas de voile pour Marianne: le livre dont la France avait besoin." *Riposte Laïque*, January 6, 2014. Available online: http://ripostelaique.com/pas-de-voile-pour-marianne-le-livre-dont-la-france-avait-besoin/ (accessed February 8, 2018).

Cyrano. "Jour de colère: préserver l'unité des patriotes pour virer Hollande." *Riposte Laïque*, January 20, 2014. Available online: http://ripostelaique.com/jour-de-colere-preserver-lunite-des-patriotes-pour-virer-hollande/ (accessed February 5, 2018).

Cyrano. "Immigration-référendum: une manifestation qui fait parler." *Riposte Laïque*, March 10, 2014. Available online: http://ripostelaique.com/immigration-referendum-une-manifestation-qui-fait-deja-parler/ (accessed February 8, 2018).

Cyrano. "Hénin-Beaumont: quelle claque pour Ayrault et Mélenchon!" *Riposte Laïque*, March 24, 2014. Available online: http://ripostelaique.com/henin-beaumont-quelle-claque-pour-ayrault-et-melenchon/ (accessed February 7, 2018).

Cyrano. "Si la France n'éradique pas l'islam, elle deviendra musulmane." *Riposte Laïque*, April 21, 2014. Available online: http://ripostelaique.com/si-la-france-neradique-pas-lislam-elle-deviendra-musulmane/ (accessed February 5, 2018).

Cyrano. "Le vrai visage de Manuel Valls: un dangereux menteur mondialiste." *Riposte Laïque*, April 28, 2014. Available online: http://ripostelaique.com/le-vrai-visage-de-manuel-valls-un-dangereux-menteur-mondialiste/ (accessed February 7, 2018).

Cyrano. "25 mai: Peut-on se dire patriote et se planquer?" *Riposte Laïque*, May 5, 2014. http://ripostelaique.com/25-mai-peut-on-se-dire-patriote-et-se-planquer/ (accessed February 8, 2018).

Cyrano. "Copé-Mariani ou la couardise de l'UMP." *Riposte Laïque*, May 12, 2014. Available online: http://ripostelaique.com/cope-mariani-ou-la-couardise-de-lump/ (accessed February 5, 2018).

Cyrano. "Le 25 mai, châtiez dans les urnes les fossoyeurs de la France." *Riposte Laïque*, May 19, 2014. Available online: http://ripostelaique.com/le-25-mai-chatiez-dans-les-urnes-les-fossoyeurs-de-la-france/ (accessed February 6, 2018).

Cyrano. "Comment ce régime et ses journaleux préparent notre dissolution." *Riposte Laïque*, July 14, 2014. Available online: http://ripostelaique.com/comment-ce-regime-et-ses-journaleux-preparent-notre-dissolution/ (accessed February 8, 2018).

Cyrano. "Entre la France et l'islam, l'heure est venue de choisir son camp." *Riposte Laïque*, July 21, 2014. Available online: http://ripostelaique.com/entre-la-france-et-lislam-lheure-est-venue-de-choisir-son-camp/ (accessed February 5, 2018).

Cyrano. "Une France sans ramadan, ni supporteurs algériens ni adorateurs du Hamas …" *Riposte Laïque*, July 28, 2014. Available online: http://ripostelaique.com/une-france-sans-ramadan-ni-supporters-algeriens-ni-adorateurs-du-hamas/ (accessed February 8, 2018).

Cyrano. "Protéger la France de la nuisance d'avocats comme Guez Guez." *Riposte Laïque*, August 18, 2014. Available online: http://ripostelaique.com/proteger-la-france-de-la-nuisance-davocats-comme-guez-guez/ (accessed February 8, 2018).

Cyrano. "La Folle de Cayenne et la Parasite incompétente veulent tuer notre civilisation." *Riposte Laïque*, September 1, 2014. Available online: http://ripostelaique.com/la-folle-de-cayenne-et-la-parasite-incompetente-veulent-tuer-notre-civilisation/ (accessed February 5, 2018).

Cyrano. "Pour gagner cette guerre, il faudra éradiquer l'islam en France." *Riposte Laïque*, September 29, 2014. Available online: http://ripostelaique.com/pour-gagner-cette-guerre-il-faudra-eradiquer-lislam-en-france/ (accessed February 1, 2018).

Cyrano. "La guerre impitoyable de la gôche Hollande-Valls-Attali contre les Gaulois." *Riposte Laïque*, October 20, 2014. Available online: http://ripostelaique.com/la-guerre-impitoyable-de-la-goche-hollande-valls-attali-contre-les-gaulois/ (accessed February 5, 2018).

Cyrano. "Belkacem-djihadistes: même islam, même combat!" *Riposte Laïque*, October 27, 2014. Available online: http://ripostelaique.com/belkacem-djihadistes-meme-islam-meme-combat/ (accessed February 5, 2018).

Cyrano. "Le livre qui va faire causer: Musulmans, vous nous mentez, d'Hubert Lemaire." *Riposte Laïque*, December 1, 2014. Available online: http://ripostelaique.com/le-livre-qui-va-faire-causer-musulmans-vous-nous-mentez-dhubert-lemaire/ (accessed February 5, 2018).

Cyrano. "La collabosphère en mission contre la Résistance européenne." *Riposte Laïque*, December 15, 2014. Available online: http://ripostelaique.com/les-islamocollabos-en-premiere-ligne-contre-les-peuples-europeens/ (accessed February 5, 2018).

Cyrano. "Grâce à Mélenchon, il n'est plus tabou de parler de la remigration musulmanne." *Riposte Laïque*, December 22, 2014. Available online: https://ripostelaique.com/grace-a-melenchon-le-possible-retour-de-millions-de-musulmans-ne-sera-plus-un-sujet-tabou.html (accessed February 5, 2018).

Cyrano. "Face à la guerre islamique, que peuvent faire les Français?" *Riposte Laïque*, December 29, 2014. Available online: http://ripostelaique.com/face-a-la-guerre-islamique-que-peuvent-faire-les-francais/ (accessed February 8, 2018).

Cyrano. "Résistance européenne pour désislamiser nos pays." *Riposte Laïque*, January 19, 2015. Available online: http://ripostelaique.com/resistance-europeenne-pour-desislamiser-nos-pays/ (accessed February 5, 2018).

Cyrano, "Socialistes vous nous mentez, Musulmans vous nous mentez." *Riposte Laïque*, January 26, 2015. Available online: http://ripostelaique.com/socialistes-vous-nous-mentez-musulmans-vous-nous-mentez/ (accessed February 5, 2018).

Cyrano. "Le vrai péril fasciste, c'est l'islam, la clique Valls-Hollande et les collabos." *Riposte Laïque*, February 2, 2015. Available online: http://ripostelaique.com/le-vrai-peril-fasciste-cest-hollande-valls-lislam-et-les-collabos/ (accessed February 5, 2018).

Cyrano. "Islamophobie: Ils rêvent d'une loi contre des livres comme 'Reconquista ou Mort de l'Europe." *Riposte Laïque*, February 25, 2015. Available online: http://ripostelaique.com/islamophobie-ils-revent-dune-loi-contre-des-livres-comme-reconquista-ou-mort-de-leurope/ (accessed February 5, 2018).

Cyrano. "Islamistes et socialistes unis dans la destruction de la France." *Riposte Laïque*, April 27, 2015. Available online: http://ripostelaique.com/islamistes-et-socialistes-unis-dans-la-destruction-de-la-france.html (accessed February 8, 2018).

Cyrano. "Bien sûr qu'il y a bien trop de musulmans en France!" *Riposte Laïque*, May 11, 2015. Available online: http://ripostelaique.com/bien-sur-quil-y-a-bien-trop-de-musulmans-en-france.html (accessed February 5, 2018).

Cyrano. "Est-il vraiment incohérent de dire qu'il faut interdire l'islam en France?" *Riposte Laïque*, May 16, 2015. Available online: http://ripostelaique.com/est-il-vraiment-incoherent-de-dire-quil-faut-interdire-lislam-en-france.html (accessed February 8, 2018).

Cyrano. "Poitiers: Rencontres Charles Martel et Congrès des socialo-collabos." *Riposte Laïque*, June 1, 2015. Available online: https://ripostelaique.com/poitiers-rencontres-charles-martel-et-congres-des-socialo-collabos.html (accessed February 8, 2018).

Cyrano. "Comment réagira la France au prochain attentat islamique?" *Riposte Laïque*, June 8, 2015. Available online: http://ripostelaique.com/comment-reagira-la-france-au-prochain-attentat-islamique.html (accessed February 8, 2018).

Cyrano. "Larmes de Cazeneuve: qu'est-ce qu'ils doivent se marrer les égorgeurs!" *Riposte Laïque*, July 6, 2015. Available online: http://ripostelaique.com/larmes-de-cazeneuve-quest-ce-quils-doivent-se-marrer-les-egorgeurs.html (accessed February 7, 2018).

Cyrano. "Socialauds, vous paierez cher vos trahisons, et vos potes aussi!" *Riposte Laïque*, August 17, 2015. Available online: http://ripostelaique.com/socialauds-paierez-cher-vos-trahisons-vos-potes.html (accessed February 8, 2018).

Cyrano. "La prochaine étape des socialauds: contraindre les Français à loger les migrants." *Riposte Laïque*, September 6, 2015. Available online: http://ripostelaique.com/la-prochaine-etape-des-socialauds-contraindre-les-francais-a-loger-les-migrants.html (accessed February 6, 2018).

Cyrano. "Socialaud assassin, le peuple aura ta peau." *Riposte Laïque*, September 13, 2015. Available online: http://ripostelaique.com/socialaud-assassin-le-peuple-aura-ta-peau.html (February 5, 2018).

Cyrano. "Quoi qu'il arrive, merci au formidable Donald Trump!" *Riposte Laïque*, November 6, 2016. Available online: http://ripostelaique.com/quoi-quil-arrive-merci-au-formidable-donald-trump.html (accessed February 13, 2018).

Cyrano. "Donald Trump élu Président des Etats-Unis: Apéro saucisson-Champagne!" *Riposte Laïque*, November 9, 2016. Available online: http://ripostelaique.com/donald-trump-elu-president-des-etats-unis-apero-saucisson-champagne.html (accessed February 13, 2018).

D

Davies, Peter. *The Extreme Right in France, 1789 to the Present: From De Maistre to Le Pen*. London and New York: Routledge, 2002.

Dearden, Lizzie. "Nato accuses Sputnik News of distributing misinformation as part of 'Kremlin propaganda machine.'" *The Independent*, February 11, 2017. Available online: http://www.independent.co.uk/news/world/europe/sputnik-news-russian-government-owned-controlled-nato-accuses-kremlin-propaganda-machine-a7574721.html (accessed February 13, 2018).

Debray, Régis and Didier Leschi. *La Laïcité au Quotidien: Guide Pratique*. Paris: Éditions Gallimard, 2016.

De Boni, Marc. "Marion Maréchale-Le Pen valide la théorie du 'grand remplacement'." *Le Figaro*, February 4, 2015. Available online: http://www.lefigaro.fr/politique/le-scan/citations/2015/02/03/25002-20150203ARTFIG00176-marion-marechal-le-pen-valide-la-theorie-du-grand-remplacement.php (accessed December 13, 2017).

De Boni, Marc and E. Gallero. "Marine Le Pen désavoue Aymeric Chauprade après ses propos sur les musulmans." *Le Figaro*, January 19, 2015. Available online: http://www.lefigaro.fr/politique/le-scan/couacs/2015/01/19/25005-

20150119ARTFIG00131-marine-le-pen-desavoue-aymeric-chauprade-apres-ses-propos-sur-les-musulmans.php (accessed January 19, 2018).

De Gaulle, Charles. *Mémoires de Guerre Vol I*. Paris: Plon, 1954.

De Larquier, Ségolène. "Marine Le Pen en guerre contre l'islam radical." *Le Point*, January 8, 2015. http://www.lepoint.fr/politique/marine-le-pen-en-guerre-contre-l-islam-radical-08-01-2015-1894905_20.php (accessed January 18, 2018).

Debré, Jean-Louis. Rapport fait au nom de la Commission d'information sur la question du port des signes religieux à l'école. *Auditions* 1275, tome II, 2ème partie. Assemblée Nationale, Paris, December 4, 2003. Available online: http://www.assemblee-nationale.fr/12/rap-info/i1275-T2.asp (accessed January 21, 2018).

Dhollande-Monnier, Victor. "Avec la 'crise migratoire,' Marin le Pen craint 'le début de la fin du droit des femmes.'" *Europe 1*, January 12, 2016. Available online: http://lelab.europe1.fr/avec-la-crise-migratoire-marine-le-pen-craint-le-debut-de-la-fin-du-droit-des-femmes-2649923 (accessed December 27, 2017).

Dousset, Clément. "Michel Onfray, nouveau soldat contre l'islam et les musulmans." *Mediapart*, November 19, 2013. Available online: https://blogs.mediapart.fr/clement-dousset/blog/191113/michel-onfray-nouveau-soldat-contre-lislam-et-les-musulmans (accessed February 8, 2018).

Durand, Anne-Aël. "Ce que propose Marine Le Pen dans son programme." *Le Monde*, April 23, 2017. Available online: http://www.lemonde.fr/les-decodeurs/article/2017/04/23/ce-que-propose-marine-le-pen-dans-son-programme_5115963_4355770.html (accessed January 22, 2018).

Durand, Pascal and S. Sindaco, eds. *Le discours néo-réactionnaire*. Paris: CNRS Éditions, 2015.

Dupont-Aignan, Nicolas. "Débout la France. Le projet de Nicolas Dupont-Aignan pour l'élection présidentielle 2017." *Débout la France*, 2017. Available online: http://www.nda-2017.fr/themes/nda/file/projet-nda-20170324.pdf (accessed January 11, 2018).

E

Emon, Anver M., M. S. Ellis, and B. Glahn, eds. *Islamic Law and International Human Rights Law Searching for Common Ground?* Oxford: Oxford University Press, 2012.

F

Faye, Olivier. "Avec le SIEL, le Front National est en passe de perdre son seul allié." *Le Monde: Droite(s) Extrême(s)*, November 2, 2016. Available online: http://droites-extremes.blog.lemonde.fr/2016/11/02/avec-le-siel-le-front-national-est-en-passe-de-perdre-son-seul-allie/ (accessed January 13, 2018).

Faye, Olivier. "Marine Le Pen choque en déclarant que 'la France n'est pas responsable' de la rafle du Vél' d'Hiv." *Le Monde*, April 10, 2017. Available online: http://www.lemonde.fr/election-presidentielle-2017/article/2017/04/10/marine-le-pen-choque-en-declarant-que-la-france-n-est-pas-responsable-de-la-rafle-du-vel-d-hiv_5108622_4854003.html#I2cPIAMcE92xJm12.99 (accessed February 9, 2018).

Fassin, Didier. *Les Nouvelles Frontières de la Société Francaise*. Paris: La Découverte, 2010.

Fekete, Liz. *Europe's Fault Lines: Racism and the Rise of the Right*. London: Verso, 2018.

Felluga, Dino F. *Critical Theory: The Key Concepts*. London and New York: Routledge, 2015.

Fernando, Mayanthi L. *The Republic Unsettled. Muslim French and the Contradictions of Secularism*. Durham and London: Duke University Press, 2014.

Fielitz, Maik and L. L. Laloire, eds. *Trouble on the Far-Right: Contemporary Right-Wing Strategies and Practices in Europe*. Biefeld: Verlag, 2016.

Finkelkraut, Alain. *L'Identité Malheureuse*. Paris: Stock, 2013.

Finkelkraut, Alain. "C'est parce que j'ai déstabilisé l'édifice idéologique de la gauche avec mon livre que j'ai fait l'objet de tant de hargne." *Atlantico*, November 24, 2013. Available online: http://www.atlantico.fr/decryptage/finkielkraut-c-est-parce-que-j-ai-destabilise-edifice-ideologique-gauche-avec-livre-que-j-ai-fait-objet-tant-hargne-907138.html (accessed February 5, 2018).

Fitzgerald, Timothy. *Discourse on Civility and Barbarity*. Oxford and New York: Oxford University Press, 2008.

Foucault, Michel. *L'Archéologie du Savoir*. Paris: Gallimard, 1969.

Foucault, Michel. *Sécurité, Territoire, Population. Cours au Collège de France, 1977–1978*. Paris: Seuil-Gallimard, 2004.

France 2. A vous de juger [TV-program]. December 9, 2010.

France TV Info. "Marine Le Pen appelle ses partisans à utiliser les réseaux sociaux pour court-circuiter les medias." *France Télévisions*, May 1, 2016. Available online: https://www.francetvinfo.fr/politique/front-national/video-marine-le-pen-appelle-ses-partisans-a-utiliser-les-reseaux-sociaux-pour-court-circuiter-les-medias_1431019.html (accessed December 26, 2017).

France TV Info. "Appelez-le désormais François 'Le Rebelle' Fillon." *France Télévisions*, March 10, 2017. Available online: https://www.francetvinfo.fr/politique/francois-fillon/appelez-le-desormais-francois-le-rebelle-fillon_2090779.html (accessed December 26, 2017).

Fredrickson, George M. *Racism: A Short History*. Princeton: Princeton University Press, 2002.

Frison, Xavier. "Marine Le Pen se pose en gardienne des droits des femmes … mais ne veut pas s'en mêler." *Marianne*, October 16, 2016. Available online: https://www.marianne.net/politique/marine-le-pen-se-pose-en-gardienne-des-droits-des-femmes-mais-ne-veut-pas-s-en-meler (accessed December 27, 2017).

Front National. "Notre projet. Programme politique du Front National." 2015.

Front National. "Au nom du peuple: 144 engagements présidentielles: Marine 2017." 2017. Available online: http://www.frontnational.com/pdf/144-engagements.pdf (accessed December 27, 2017).

G

Gabizon, Cécilia. "La cour des comptes revoit sa copie sur la HALDE." *L'Express*, December 13, 2010. Available online: http://www.lefigaro.fr/conjoncture/2010/12/13/04016-20101213ARTFIG00622-la-cour-des-comptes-revoit-sa-copie-sur-la-halde.php (accessed December 26, 2017).

Gabon, Alain. "La République et ses voiles intégraux." *Contemporary French and Francophone Studies* **18**, no. 2 (2014): 133–141.

Galiero, Emmanuel. "Marine Le Pen se voit comme une «exception» de la présidentielle." *Le Figaro*, September 3, 2016. Available online: http://www.lefigaro.fr/politique/2016/09/03/01002-20160903ARTFIG00078-marine-le-pen-se-voit-comme-une-exception-de-la-presidentielle.php (accessed December 26, 2017).

Gallet, Ludwig. "Primaire à droite: *Riposte Laïque*, l'encombrant soutien de Franais Fillon." *L'Express*, November 25, 2016. Available online: https://www.lexpress.fr/actualite/politique/elections/primaire-a-droite-riposte-laique-l-encombrant-soutien-de-francois-fillon_1854040.html (accessed January 26, 2018).

Gaumer, Patrick. *Dictionnaire Mondial de la BD*. Paris: Larousse, 2010.

Geisser, Vincent. *La Nouvelle Islamophobie*. Paris: La Découverte, 2003.

Génération Identitaire. Available online: https://generationidentitaire.org/presentation/ (accessed January 18, 2018).

Génération Identitaire. Mission: Defend Europe. Available online: https://www.facebook.com/GenerationIdentitaire/videos/vb.203085803133570/1190224071088919/?type=2&theater (accessed January 19, 2018).

Génération Identitaire. @DefendEuropeID. *Twitter*. Available online: https://twitter.com/defendeuropeid (accessed January 19, 2018).

Génération Identitaire. "Defend Europe." *Magazine Identitaire*, **25**, Nov/Dec, 2017.

Gerbaudo, Paolo. *Tweets and Streets. Social Media and Contemporary Activism*. London: Pluto Press, 2012.

Gerin, André. Rapport d'information n°2262. Fait en application de l'article 145 du Règlement au nom de la mission d'information sur la pratique du port du voile intégral sur le territoire national. Paris: Assemblée Nationale, January 27, 2010. Available online: http://www.assemblee-nationale.fr/13/rap-info/i2262.asp (accessed January 21, 2018).

Goldberg, David T. *Are We All Post-Racial Yet?* Malden: Polity Press, 2015.

Goldberg, David T. *The Racial State*. Malden and Oxford: Blackwell Publishers, 2002.

Goldberg, David T. *The Threat of Race: Reflections of Racial Neoliberalism*. Malden, MA: Wiley-Blackwell, 2009.

Goodliffe, Gabriel. *The Resurgence of the Radical Right in France: From Boulangisme to the Front National*. Cambridge and New York: Cambridge University Press, 2012.

Gouëset, Catherine. "Comment la doite parlait du PACS il y a dix ans." *L'Express*, October 13, 2009. Available online: https://www.lexpress.fr/actualite/societe/comment-la-droite-parlait-du-pacs-il-y-a-dix-ans_794199.html (accessed December 10, 2017).

Greschter, Mireille. "Guillaume Faye explique la logique islamisatrice de la réforme Belkacem." *Riposte Laïque*, May 13, 2015. Available online: https://ripostelaique.com/guillaume-faye-explique-la-logique-islamistrice-de-la-reforme-belkacem.html (accessed December 26, 2017).

Green, Todd. *The Fear of Islam: An Introduction to Islamophobia in the West*. Minneapolis: Fortress Press, 2015.

Griffin, Roger. "Plus ça change! The Fascist Pedigree of the Nouvelle Droite." In *The Development of the Radical Right in France. From Boulanger to Le Pen*, edited by Edward J. Arnold, 217–252. London and New York: Palgrave Macmillan, 2000.

Griffin, Roger. "Introduction: God's counterfeiters? Investigating the triad of fascism, totalitarianism and (political) religion." *Totalitarian Movements and Political Religions* 5, no. 3 (2004): 291–325.

Griffin, Roger. "Interregnum or endgame? The radical right in the 'post-fascist' era." In *The Populist Radical Right: A Reader*, edited by Cas Mudde, 15–27. London and New York: Routledge, 2017.

Guiley, Ellen. *The Encyclopedia of Demons and Demonology*. New York: Facts on File, 2009.

H

Hajjat, Abdellali and M. Marwan. *Islamophobie*. Paris: La Découverte, 2013.

Halmos, Claude. "Contre les kalachnikovs: l'école." In *Nous Sommes Charlie*, 76–77. Paris: Livre de Poche, 2015.

Hameleers, Michael and D. Schmuck. "It's us against them: A comparative experiment on the effects of populist messages communicated via social media." *Information, Communication & Society* 20, no. 9 (2017): 1425–1444.

Harrison, Sarah and M. Bruter. *Mapping Extreme Right Ideology: An Empirical Geography of the European Extreme Right*. New York: Palgrave Macmillan, 2011.

Hausalter, Louis. "Le FN veut interdire kippa, voile et 'grande croix' dans la rue (et ne n'est pas nouveau)." *Marianne*, August 26, 2016. Available online: https://www.marianne.net/politique/le-fn-veut-interdire-kippa-voile-et-grande-croix-dans-la-rue-et-ce-nest-pas-nouveau (accessed January 19, 2018).

Hausalter, Louis. "L'islam compatible avec la République." *Marianne*, September 17, 2016. Available online: https://www.marianne.net/politique/lislam-compatible-avec-la-republique-la-phrase-de-marine-le-pen-qui-trouble-les-militants (accessed January 19, 2018).

Hausalter, Louis. "Immigration: Nicolas Dupont-Aignan s'inquiète d'un 'remplacement de population'." *Libération*, January 18, 2017. Available online: https://www. marianne.net/politique/immigration-nicolas-dupont-aignan-s-inquiete-d-un-remplacement-de-population (accessed January 11, 2018).

Hennette Vauchez, Stéphanie and V. Vincent. *L'Affaire Baby Loup ou la Nouvelle Laïcité*. Issy-les-Moulineaux: Lextenso Éditions, 2014.

Herreros, Romain. "C-Star: une ONG pro-réfugiés porte secours au bateau anti-migrants, qui refuse l'aid." *Huffington Poste*, August 11, 2017. Available online: http:// www.huffingtonpost.fr/2017/08/11/le-bateau-anti-migrants-c-star-secouru-par-une-ong-pro-refugies_a_23074496/ (accessed January 19, 2018).

Hogan, Jacqueline. *Gender, Race, and National Identity*. London and New York: Routledge, 2009.

Horatius. "Aymeric Chauprade: 'La France est en guerre avec des musulmans." *Fdsouche*, January 14, 2015. Available online: http://www.fdesouche.com/553557-aymeric-chauprade-france-en-guerre-musulmans# (accessed January 15, 2015).

Howarth, David and Yannis Stavrakakis. "Introducing discourse theory and political analysis." In *Discourse Theory and Political Analysis*, edited by David Howarth, A. J. Noval, and Y. Stavrakakis, 1–23. Manchester and New York: Manchester University Press, 2000.

Huffington Post. "Quatre skinheads renvoyés aux assises pour la mort de Clément Méric, l'intention de tuer pas retenue." *Huffington Post*, March 14, 2017. Available online: http://www.huffingtonpost.fr/2017/03/14/quatre-skinheads-renvoyes-aux-assises-pour-la-mort-de-clement-me_a_21886232/ (accessed January 11, 2018).

Huggler, Justin. "Dutch Pegida leader and expelled German deputy hunt migrants on Bulgarian border." *The Telegraph*, July 4, 2016. Available online: http://www. telegraph.co.uk/news/2016/07/04/pegida-pair-hunt-migrants-with-vigilantes-on-bulgarian-border/ (accessed January 22, 2018).

Hughey, Matthew. *Nationalists, White Bound: Antiracists and the Shared Meanings of Race*. Stanford, CA: Stanford University Press, 2012.

Huffington Post. "C Politique: L'essayiste Pascal Bruckner associe LGBT et pédophilie." *Huffington Post*, October 22, 2017. Available online: http://www.huffingtonpost. fr/2017/10/22/c-politique-lessayiste-pascal-bruckner-associe-lgbt-et-pedophile_a_23252007/ (accessed December 27, 2017).

I

Ifop. "L'image de l'islam en France." *Le Figaro*, 2012, p. 5. Available online: http://www. lefigaro.fr/assets/pdf/sondage-ipsos-islam-france.pdf (accessed January 11, 2018).

Igounet, Valérie. "Non au racisme anti-français." *France TV Info*, November 7, 2016. Available online: https://blog.francetvinfo.fr/derriere-le-front/2016/11/07/non-au-racisme-anti-francais.html (accessed December 11, 2017).

Igounet, Valérie. "On est chez nous!" *France TV Info*, February 19, 2017. Available online: https://blog.francetvinfo.fr/derriere-le-front/2017/02/19/on-est-chez-nous. html (accessed January 11, 2018).

Interview with Pierre Cassen and Christine Tasin, *Aix-en-Provence*, October 19, 2015.

J

Joahny, Stéphane. "L'enquête qui accuse Tariq Ramadan." *Le Journal du Dimanche*, February 3, 2018. Available online: http://www.lejdd.fr/societe/faits-divers/lenquete-qui-accuse-tariq-ramadan-3564416 (accessed February 5, 2018).

Johnson, Guillaume D., K. D. Thomas, and S. A. Grier. "When the burger becomes halal: A critical discourse analysis of privilege and marketplace inclusion." *Consumption Markets & Culture* **20**, no. 6 (2017): 497–522.

Jugement du May 3, 2017, 17e chambre correctionelle, n° du parquet 16204000172. *Tribunal de Grande Instance*. Paris, Mai 5, 2017.

Jugement du Octobre 1, 2017, 17e chambre correctionelle, n° du parquet 17010000380. *Tribunal de Grande Instance*. Paris, Octobre 5, 2017.

K

Kallis, Aristotle. "Breaking taboos and 'mainstreaming the Extreme'; The debates on restricting Islamic symbols in contemporary Europe." In *Right-Wing Populism in Europe*, edited by Ruth Wodak, M. KhosraviNik, and B. Mral, 55–70. New York and London: Bloomsbury, 2013.

Kemp, Anna. "Marianne d'aujourd'hui? The figure of the beurette in contemporary French feminist discourse." *Modern & Contemporary France* **17**, no. 1 (2009): 19–33.

Khosrokhavar, Farhad. *Radicalisation*. Paris: EMSH, 2014.

Kokoreff, Michel. *Sociologie des Émeutes*. Paris: Payot, 2008.

Kovacs, Stéphane. "Trois mois ferme pour du racisme anti-blanc." *Le Figaro*, April 1, 2016. Available online: http://www.lefigaro.fr/actualite-france/2016/04/01/01016-20160401ARTFIG00315-trois-mois-ferme-pour-du-racisme-anti-blanc.php (accessed December 13, 2017.)

Kristeva, Julia. *Powers of Horror: An Essay on Abjection*. New York: Columbia University Press, 1982.

Krämer, Benjamin. "Populist online practices: The function of the Internet in right-wing populism." *Information, Communication & Society* **20**, no. 9 (2017): 1293–1309.

Kundnani, Arun. *The Muslims Are Coming: Islamophobia: Extremism, and the Domestic War on Terror*. London and New York: Verso, 2014.

L

"La leçon de Trump selon Marine Le Pen: 'Ce que le peuple veut, le peuple peut.' *L'Express*. November 9, 2016. Available online: https://www.lexpress.fr/actualite/ politique/fn/la-lecon-de-trump-selon-marine-le-pen-ce-que-le-peuple-veut-le-peuple-peut_1849079.html (accessed December 26, 2017).

L'heure de vérité [TV-program]. "JM Le Pen: le 'Detail de l'Histoire'." Antenne 2, January 27, 1988. Available online: http://www.ina.fr/video/I00005274 (accessed February 8, 2018).

La Boétie. *Discours sur la Servitude Volontaire*. Paris: Éditions Mille et une Nuits, 1995.

Laborde, Cécile. *Critical Republicanism. The Hijab Controversy and Political Philosophy.* Oxford and New York: Oxford University Press, 2008.

Laclau, Ernesto. *On Populist Reason*. London: Verso, 1994.

Laclau, Ernesto. "Why constructing a people is the main task of radical politics." *Critical Inquiry* **32** (2006): 646–680.

Laclau, Ernesto and C. Mouffe. *Hegemony and Socialist Strategy*. London: Verso, 1985.

Larsson, Göran. "The fear of small numbers: Eurabia literature and censuses on religious belonging." *Journal of Muslims in Europe* **1** (2012): 142–165.

Le Blevennec, Nolwenn. "Sur Twitter, l'antisémite Jérôme Bourbon sort de l'ombre." *Le Nouvel Observateur*, February 24, 2016. Available online: http://tempsreel.nouvelobs. com/rue89/rue89-politique/20160224.RUE2270/sur-twitter-l-antisemite-jerome-bourbon-sort-de-l-ombre.html (accessed January 22, 2018).

Le Figaro. "Islam et Occupation: Marine Le Pen provoque un tollé." *Le Figaro* December 11, 2010. Available online: http://www.lefigaro.fr/politique/2010/12/11/01002-20101211ARTFIG00475-islam-et-occupation-la-provocation-de-marine-le-pen.php (accessed January 21, 2018).

Le Figaro. "320.000 enseignants formés à la laïcité dans les mois à venir." *Le Figaro* January 30, 2015. Available online: http://www.lefigaro.fr/actualite-france/2015/01/30/01016-20150130ARTFIG00138-320000-enseignants-formes-a-la-laicite-dans-les-mois-a-venir.php (accessed January 21, 2018).

Le Guevel, Elise. "Le double discours de Marine Le Pen sur la théorie du 'grand remplacement'." *France Info*, January 15, 2016. Available online: https://www. francetvinfo.fr/replay-magazine/france-2/envoye-special/video-envoye-special-le-double-discours-de-marine-le-pen-sur-la-theorie-du-grand-remplacement_1270287.html (accessed December 13, 2017).

"Nicolas Dupont-Aignan: son programme dans le detail." *Le Journal du Dimanche*, March 17, 2017. Available online: http://www.lejdd.fr/Politique/Nicolas-Dupont-Aignan-son-programme-dans-le-detail-854978 (accessed January 11, 2018).

"Emmanuel Macron: 'J'ai prouvé que j'avais une capacité de commandement'." *Le Journal du Dimanche*, March 19, 2017. Available online: http://www.lejdd. fr/Politique/Emmanuel-Macron-J-ai-prouve-que-j-avais-une-capacite-de-commandement-855152 (accessed December 15, 2017).

Le Monde. "Contre le terrorisme, la plus grande manifestation jamais recensée en France." *Le Monde*, January 11, 2015. Available online: http://www.lemonde. fr/societe/article/2015/01/11/la-france-dans-la-rue-pour-defendre-la-liberte_4553845_3224.html (accessed February 1, 2018).

"Manuel Valls: Oui, la France est en guerre contre le terrorisme." *Le Monde*, January 13, 2015. Available online: http://www.lemonde.fr/politique/article/2015/01/13/ manuel-valls-oui-la-france-est-en-guerre-contre-le-terrorisme_4555301_823448. html (accessed January 19, 2018).

"Présidentielle: au sein du gouvernement, qui soutient Hamon, qui soutient Macron?" *Le Monde,* March 23, 2017. Available online: http://www.lemonde.fr/election-presidentielle-2017/article/2017/03/23/presidentielle-au-sein-du-gouvernement-qui-soutient-hamon-qui-soutient-macron_5099784_4854003.html (accessed December 15, 2017).

"Une jeune Maghrébine sur une affiche de Le Pen." *Le Nouvel Observateur*, December 12, 2012. Available online: http://tempsreel.nouvelobs.com/politique/ elections-2007/20061211.OBS2440/une-jeune-maghrebine-sur-une-affiche-de-le-pen.html (accessed January 21, 2018).

"Valls plaide pour une formation 'obligatoire' des imams en France." *Le Nouvel Observateur.* March 3, 2015. Available online: https://tempsreel.nouvelobs.com/ attentats-charlie-hebdo-et-maintenant/20150303.OBS3743/valls-plaide-pour-une-formation-obligatoire-des-imams-en-france.html (accessed January 21, 2018).

"Marine Le Pen réussit son pari: 'Ce n'est qu'un début.' " *Le Parisien.* April 21, 2012. Available online: http://www.leparisien.fr/election-presidentielle-2012/ candidats/marine-le-pen-fait-le-meilleur-sccre-du-fn-a-une-presidentiel le-21-04-2012-1965686.php (accessed January 11, 2018).

"UMP: Copé, les pains au chocolat et le Ramadan." *Le Parisien.* October 26, 2012. Available online: http://www.leparisien.fr/politique/ump-cope-les-pains-au-chocolat-et-le-ramadan-06-10-2012-2209731.php (accessed February 5, 2018).

"Jean-Marie Le Pen repris par ses vieux demons." *Le Parisien* June 8, 2014. Available online: http://www.leparisien.fr/espace-premium/actu/jean-marie-le-pen-repris-par-ses-vieux-demons-08-06-2014-3905737.php (accessed December 27, 2017).

Le Pen, Marine. *À Contre Flots.* Paris: Éditions Jacques Granchier, 2006.

Le Pen, Marine. Discours de Marine Le Pen, Présidente du Front National, lors du Congrès de Tours janvier 15 et 16, 2011. *Front National*, January 16, 2011. Available online: http://www.frontnational.com/videos/congres-du-fn-a-tours-discours-d'investiture-de-marine-le-pen/ (accessed January 21, 2018).

Le Pen, Marine. @MLP_Officiel, Twitter, November 19, 2014: Available online: https://twitter.com/mlp_officiel/status/535332620218171392 (accessed December 26, 2017).

Le Pen, Marine. "Déclaration de Marine Le Pen suite aux attentats de Charlie Hebdo." Youtube: Front National, January 7, 2015. Available online: https://www.youtube. com/watch?v=RwbS_6GR7U4&bpctr=1516290030 (accessed January 18, 2018).

Le Pen, Marine. "CP 002580—Nanterre." *Front National*, June 19, 2015. Available online: http://www.frontnational.com/pdf/statuts2.pdf (accessed January 11, 2018).

Le Pen, Marine. "Conference de presse: La France au défi terroriste." *Front National*, April 10, 2017. Available online: http://www.frontnational.com/videos/conference-presidentielle-n5-la-france-face-au-defi-terroriste/ (accessed January 19, 2018).

"Maintenant, le Front National cible les élites." *Le Parisien,* October 2, 2015. Available online; http://www.leparisien.fr/politique/maintenant-le-front-national-cible-les-elites-02-10-2015-5147247.php (accessed December 26, 2017).

Lejeune, Yves. "Le vrai visage de Manuel Valls. Entretien avec Emmanuel Ratier." *Novopresse*, April 28, 2014. Available online: https://fr.novopress.info/164634/vrai-visage-manuel-valls-entretien-emmanuel-ratier/ (accessed December 27, 2017).

Lentin, Alana. "Post-race, post politics: The paradoxical rise of culture after multiculturalism." *Ethnic and Racial Studies* 37, no. 8 (2014): 1268–1285.

Liberation. "Quand le FN faisait grand bruit." *Libération*. September 9, 2012. Available online: http://www.liberation.fr/france/2012/09/09/quand-le-fn-faisait-grand-bruit_845032 (accessed December 26, 2017).

Liogier, Raphael. *Une Laïcité 'Légitime.' La France et ses Religions d'État*. Paris: Médicis Entrelas, 2006.

Liogier, Raphael. *Le Mythe de l'Islamsation: Essai sur une Obsession Collective*. Paris: Points, 2016.

Loi du 29 juillet 1881 sur la liberté de la presse. *Legifrance*, January 29, 2017. Available online: https://www.legifrance.gouv.fr/affichTexte.do?cidTexte=LEGITE XT000006070722 (accessed January 22, 2018).

Loi n° 2001-434 du 21 mai 2001 tendant à la reconnaissance de la traite et de l'esclavage en tant que crime contre l'humanité. *JORF*, n°0119, May 23, 2001. Available online: https://www.legifrance.gouv.fr/affichTexte.do?cidTexte=JORFTEXT000000405369&c ategorieLien=id (accessed December 26, 2017).

Lusher, Adam. "George Soros: The billionaire investor who became the favourite target of conspiracy theories and antisemitic hatred." *The Independent*, February 8, 2018. Available online: http://www.independent.co.uk/news/uk/politics/geore-soros-brexit-antisemitism-jew-conspiracy-theories-telegraph-story-plot-hungary-broke-bank-of-a8201651.html (accessed February 14, 2018).

M

Macfie, Alexander L., ed. *Orientalism: A Reader*. Edinburgh: Edinburgh University Press, 2000.

Mauriac, Laurent. "Indignation après l'occupation de la mosquée de Poitiers." *Rue 89: Nouvel Observateur*, October 21, 2012. Available online: https://www.nouvelobs.com/rue89/rue89-nos-vies-connectees/20121021.RUE3312/indignation-apres-l-occupation-de-la-mosquee-de-poitiers.html (accessed January 19, 2018).

Mammone, Andrea, E. Godin, and B. Jenkins, *Varieties of Right-Wing Extremism in Europe*. Oxon and New York: Routledge, 2013.

Marchand, René. *Reconquista ou Mort de l'Europe. L'Enjeu de la Guerre Islamique. Pour une Stratégie de Contre-Offensive*. Éditions Riposte Laïque, 2013.

Marcus, Jonathan. *The National Front and French Politics: The Resistable Rise of Jean-Marie Le Pen*. Hampshire and London: Macmillan, 1995.

Martin, Claude. "The PACS and marriage and cohabitation in France." *International Journal of Law. Policy and the Family* **14**, no. 3 (2001): 135–158.

Mastnak, Tomaz. "Western hostility toward Muslims: A history of the present." In *Western Hostility toward Muslims: A History of the Present*, edited by Andrew Shyrock, 29–52. Bloomington and Indianapolis: Indiana University Press.

Matar, Nabil. "Britons and Muslims in the early modern period: From prejudice to (a theory of) toleration." *Patterns of Prejudice* **43**, no. 3–4 (2009): 213–231.

Mathoux, Hadrien. "Droits de LGBT: Marine Le Pen prépare discrètement la grande regression." *Marianne*, April 28, 2017. Available online: https://www.marianne.net/politique/droits-des-lgbt-marine-le-pen-prepare-discretement-la-grande-regression (accessed December 27, 2017).

McAuley, James. "French Muslims enraged by passage of Macron's version of Patriot Act." *The Washington Post*, October 3, 2017. https://www.washingtonpost.com/world/europe/with-french-patriot-act-macron-enrages-french-muslims/2017/10/03/998a0af4-a841-11e7-9a98-07140d2eed02_story.html?utm_term=.c034c0d15491 (accessed December 15, 2017).

McCarthy, John D. and N. Z. Mayer. "Resource mobilization and social movements: A partial theory." *American Journal of Sociology* **82**, no. 6 (1977): 1212–1241.

McClintock, Anne. *Imperial Leather*. London and New York: Routledge, 1995.

Mélenchon, Jean-Luc. *Qu'Ils s'en Aillent Tous!* Paris: Flammarion, 2010.

Meer, Nasar. "Racialization and religion: Race, culture and difference in the study of antisemitism and Islamophobia." *Ethnic and Racial Studies* **36**, no. 3 (2013): 385–398.

Mestre, Abel and C. Monnot. "Les 'assises sur l'islamisation': pas d'interdiction, mais …" *Le Monde Blogs: Droite(s) Extrême(s)*. December 16, 2010. Available online: http://droitesextremes.blog.lemonde.fr/2010/12/16/les-assises-sur-lislamisation-pas-dinterdiction-mais (accessed January 21, 2018).

Ministère de l'Éducation Nationale, de l'Enseignement Supérieur et de la Recherche, *Grande Mobilisation de l'École pour les Valeurs de la République* Paris: La Rèpublique Française. Available online: http://www.education.gouv.fr/cid85644/onze-mesures-pour-un-grande-mobilisation-de-l-ecole-pour-les-valeurs-de-la-republique.html (accessed January 21, 2018).

Miqueu, Christophe and P. Gros. *Comprendre la laïcité*. Paris: Max Milo Éditions, 2017.

Moffit, Benjamin. *The Global Rise of Populism: Performance, Political Style, and Representation*. Stanford, CA: Stanford University Press, 2016.

Mouloud, Laurent. "Affaire Sniper. Le mauvais cible de Sarkozy." *L'Humanité*, November 11, 2003. Available online: http://www.humanite.fr/node/486757 (accessed January 27, 2015).

Mudde, Cas. *Radical Right Parties in Europe*. Cambridge: Cambridge University Press, 2007.

Mudde, Cas, ed. *The Populist Radical Right: A Reader*. London and New York: Routledge, 2017.

Mudde, Cas. "What the stunning success of AFD means for Germany and Europe." *The Guardian*, September 24, 2017. Available online: https://www.theguardian.com/commentisfree/2017/sep/24/germany-elections-afd-europe-immigration-merkel-radical-right (accessed February 13, 2018).

Müller, Jan-Werner. *What is Populism?* Philadelphia: University of Pennsylvania Press, 2016.

N

Nilsson, Per-Erik. "Who is Madame M? Staking out the borders of secular France." In *Religion as a Category of Government and Sovereignty*, edited by Timothy Fitzgerald, Trevor Stack, and Naomi Goldenberg, 21–37. Leiden: Brill, 2015.

Nilsson, Per-Erik. "'Secular retaliation': A case study of integralist populism, anti-muslim discourse, and (il)liberal discourse on secularism in contemporary France." *Politics, Religion & Ideology* **16**, no. 1 (2015): 87–106.

Nilsson, Per-Erik. *Unveiling the French Republic*. Leiden: Brill, 2017.

Noiriel, Gérard. *Immigration, Antisémitisme et Racisme (XIXe-XXe siècle): Discours Publics, Humiliations Privées*. Paris: Fayard, 2007.

O

Obertone, Laurent. *La France Orange Mécanique*. Paris: Ring, 2013.

Ollivier, Enora and M. Rescan. "Radicalisation: 'Le rôle des mosquées est très effacé dans les nouvelles formes du djihadisme'." *Le Monde*, November 26, 2015. Available online: http://www.lemonde.fr/attaques-a-paris/article/2015/11/26/radicalisation-le-role-des-mosquees-est-tres-efface-dans-les-nouvelles-formes-du-djihadisme_4818497_4809495.html (accessed December 13, 2017).

Onfray, Michel. *Rendre la Raison Populaire*. Paris: Éditions Autrement, 2013.

Ory, Pascal. "François Fillon un candidat 'antisystème' … pur produit du serial." *Le Monde*, November 22, 2016. Available online: http://www.lemonde.fr/idees/article/2016/11/22/francois-fillon-un-candidat-antisysteme-pur-produit-du-serail_5035725_3232.html (accessed December 26, 2017).

Ouchikh, Karim. "Avec le SIEL, j'apporte mon soutien à Marine Le Pen aux présidentielles et aux candidats de mon parti aux législatives." *SIEL*, February 26, 2017. Available online: http://www.siel-souverainete.fr/actualites/communiques/803-avec-le-siel-j-apporte-mon-soutien-a-marine-le-pen-aux-presidentielles-et-aux-candidats-de-mon-parti-aux-legislatives.html (accessed January 13, 2018).

P

Paligot, Carole Reynaud. *La République Raciale 1860–1930*. Paris: Presses Universitaires de France, 2009.

Panizza, Francisco. "Introduction." In *In Populism and the Mirror of Democracy*, edited by Francisco Panizza. London: Verso, 2005.

Parti Plus. "Présentation du Parti Plus." PartiPlus: Youtube, April 30, 2013. Available online: https://www.youtube.com/watch?v=gbSgFEcrT6k (accessed February 13, 2018).

Passmore, Kevin. *From Liberalism to Fascism: The Right in a French Province*. Cambridge: Cambridge University Press, 1997.

Paxton, Robert. *Vichy France: Old Guard and New Order, 1940–1944*. New York: Columbia University Press, [1972] 2001.

Paxton, Robert. *The Anatomy of Fascism*. New York: Alfred A. Knopf, 2004.

Pech, Marie-Estelle. "Éducation: les 10 principales mesures sur la laïcité." *Le Figaro*, January 22, 2015. Available online: http://www.lefigaro.fr/actualite-france/2015/01/22/01016-20150122ARTFIG00193-education-les-10-principales-mesures-sur-la-laicite.php (accessed January 21, 2018).

Pecnard, Jules. "Présidentielle: la chute de François Fillon dans les sondages." *L'Express*, February 10, 2017. Available online: https://www.lexpress.fr/actualite/politique/elections/presidentielle-la-chute-de-francois-fillon-dans-les-sondages-en-deux-graphiques_1878117.html (accessed December 26, 2017).

Pelinka, Anton. "Right-wing populism: Concept and typology." In *Right-Wing Populism in Europe*, edited by Ruth Wodak, M. KhosraviNik, and B. Mral, 3–22. New York and London: Bloomsbury, 2013.

Peña-Ruiz, Henri. *Dictionnaire Amoureux de la Laïcité*. Paris: Plon, 2014.

Pézerat, Thibaut. "Le directeur des jeunes du FN favorable à une interdiction de la 'propagande gay' comme en Russie." *Europe 1*, January 8, 2014. Available online: http://lelab.europe1.fr/le-president-des-jeunes-du-fn-favorable-a-une-loi-similaire-a-l-interdiction-de-la-propagande-gay-en-russie-12386 (accessed December 27, 2017).

Philips, Susan A. *Wallbangin'. Graffiti and Gangs in L.A.* Chicago and London: University of Chicago Press, 1999.

Politi, Caroline. "Menu sans porc à la cantine: la fausse polémique de Marine Le Pen." *L'Express*, April 7, 2014. Available online: https://www.lexpress.fr/actualite/societe/menu-sans-porc-a-la-cantine-la-fausse-polemique-de-marine-le-pen_1506856.html (accessed February 5, 2018).

Postill, John. "Digital Politics and Political Engagement." In *Digital Anthropology*, edited by Heather A. Horst and D. Miller, 165–184. London and New York: Berg, 2012.

R

R. V. "Vidéo. Des journalistes de 'Quotidien' violemment expulsés lors d'une visite de Marine Le Pen." *Sud Ouest*, February 1, 2017. Available online: http://www.sudouest.fr/2017/02/01/video-des-journalistes-de-quotidien-violemment-expulses-lors-d-une-visite-de-marine-le-pen-3158730-5208.php (accessed December 26, 2017).

Radio Télévision Suisse. "L'UDC valaisan Jean-Luc Addor condamné pour discrimination raciale." August 17, 2017. Available online: https://www.rts.ch/info/regions/valais/8848544-l-udc-valaisan-jean-luc-addor-condamne-pour-discrimination-raciale.html (accessed February 13, 2018).

Ratier, Emmanuel. *Le Vrai Visage de Manuel Valls*. Paris: Éditions Facta, 2014.

Rigouste, Mathieu. *L'Ennemi Intérieur: La Généalogie Coloniale et Militaire de l'Ordre Sécuritaire dans la France Contemporaine*. Paris: La Découverte, 2009.

Riposte Laïque. "Peuple de France." Youtube: *Riposte Laïque*, November 9, 2010. Available online: https://www.youtube.com/watch?v=9hJBtGhgkJc (accessed February 8, 2018).

Riposte Laïque. "Macron: Le candidat des musulmans veut islamiser la France." YouTube: *Riposte Laïque*, May 2, 2017. Available online: https://www.youtube.com/watch?time_continue=17&v=FaAc7W5vWkY.

Robin, Jean. "Lille: Piscines pour femmes musulmanes ou pour femmes obèses?" *Fdsouche*, April 25, 2012. Available online: http://www.fdesouche.com/296712-lille-piscines-pour-femmes-musulmanes-ou-pour-femmes-obeses-video (accessed December 26, 2017).

Robin, Jean. *La Nouvelle Extreme-Droite*. Paris: Xenia Éditions, 2010.

Rochefort, Florence, ed. *Le Pouvoir du Genre. Laïcités et Religions 1905–2005*. Toulouse: PUM, 2007.

Rousseau, Noémie. "À Hayange, nous festoyons comme les Francais." *Libération*, September 6, 2015. Available online: http://www.liberation.fr/societe/2015/09/06/a-hayange-nous-festoyons-comme-les-francais_1376925 (accessed January 12, 2018).

Roy, Olivier. *Saving the People: How Populists Hijack Religion*. London: C. Hurst & Co. Publishers, 2016.

Rydgren, Jens. *The Populist Challenge: Political Protest and Ethno-Nationalist Mobilization in France*. Oxford and New York: Berghahn Books, 2003.

Rydgren, Jens. *The Oxford Handbook of the Radical Right*. Oxford and New York: Oxford University Press, 2018.

S

Said, Edward. *Orientalism*. New York: Vintage Books, 1979.

Santucci, Antonio. *Antonio Gramsci*. New York: Monthly Review Press, 2010.

Sarkozy, Nicolas. Discours du Président de la République, 12 Juillet. Remise collective de décorations Palais de l'Élysée. *Palais de l'Élysée*, Paris, July 12, 2007.

Sarkozy, Nicolas. "Allocution devant le Conseil consultatif Riyad (Arabie Saoudite)." *Palais de l'Elysée*, Paris, January 14, 2008.

Scott, Joan W. *The Politics of the Veil*. Princeton: Princeton University Press, 2007.

Scott, Joan W. *The Fantasy of Feminist History*. Durham and London: Duke University Press, 2011.

Scrinzi, Francesca. "A 'new' National Front? Gender, religion, secularism, and the French Populist Radical Right." In *Gender and Far Right Politics in Europe*, edited by Michaela Köttig, R. Bitzan, and A. Petö, 127–140. Cham: Palgrave Macmillan, 2017.

Shields, Jim G. *The Extreme Right in France: From Pétain to Le Pen*. London and New York: Routledge, 2007.

Selby, Jennifer. *Questioning French Secularism. Gender Politics and Islam in a French Suburb*. New York: Palgrave McMillan, 2012.

Selby, Jennifer A. "Un/veiling women's bodies: Secularism and sexuality in full-face veil prohibitions in France and Québec." *Studies in Religion/Sciences Religieuses* **43**, no. 3 (2014): 439–466.

Shaheen, Jack. *Guilty: Hollywood's Verdict on Arabs after 9/11*. Northampton: Olive Branch Press, 2008.

Silverman, Max. *Deconstructing the Nation*. London and New York: Routledge, 1992.

SOS Homophobie. "Rapport sur l'homophobie 2017: Lutte contre la lesbophobie, la gayophobie, la biophpobie et la transphobie." *SOS Homophobie*, 2017. Available online: https://www.sos-homophobie.org/sites/default/files/rapport_annuel_2017. pdf (accessed December 27, 2017).

Soyer, François. "Faith, culture and fear: comparing Islamophobia in early modern Spain and twenty-first-century Europe." *Ethnic and Racial Studies* **36**, no. 3 (2013): 399–416.

Stavrakakis, Yannis and A. Jäger. "Accomplishments and limitations of the 'new' mainstream in contemporary populism studies." *European Journal of Social Theory* (2017): 1–19.

Sternhell, Zeev. *Neither Right nor Left: Fascist Ideology in France*. Princeton: Princeton University Press, [1983] 1986.

Stier, Sebastian, L. Posch, A. Bleier, and M. Strohmaierm. "When populists become popular: comparing Facebook use by the right-wing movement Pegida and German political parties." *Information, Communication & Society* **20**, no. 9 (2017): 1365–1388.

Stockemer, Daniel. *Continuity and Change under Jean-Marie Le Pen and Marine Le Pen*. Cham: Springer International Publishing, 2017.

T

Taras, Raymond. *Xenophobia and Islamophobia in Europe*. Edinburgh: Edinburgh University Press, 2012.

Tasin, Christine. "Je ne suis pas Charlie, je suis Charles Martel." *Résistance Républicaine*, January 9, 2015. Available online: http://resistancerepublicaine.eu/2015/01/09/je-ne-suis-pas-charlie-je-suis-charles-martel/ (accessed January 12, 2018).

Tasin, Christine and René d'Armor. *Les Assasins Obéissent au Coran*. Paris: Résistance Républicaine, 2016.

TF1/Public Sénat. *Primaire de Droite* [TV program]. October 16, 2016.

TF 1. *Débat présidentiel* TF1. *Débat Présidentiel* [TV show]. March 20, 2017.

Teitelbaum, Benjamin. *Lions of the North. Sounds of the New Nordic Radical Nationalism*. Oxford: Oxford University Press, 2017.

Tévanian, Pierre. "A conservative revolution within secularism." *Les Mots sont Importants*, March 15, 2014. Available online: http://lmsi.net/A-Conservative-Revolution-within (accessed January 1, 2015).

TF1. *Journal télévisé de 20h* [TV program]. March 15, 2007. 20.00.

Tincq, Henri. "Liberté, égalité, fraternité, laïcité. Mais quelle laïcité?" *Slate*, January 13, 2015. Available online: http://www.slate.fr/story/96767/liberte-egalite-fraternite-laicite (accessed February 1, 2018).

Torfing, Jacob. "Discourse Theory: Achievements, Arguments, and Challenges." In *Discourse Theory in European Politics Identity: Policy and Governance*, edited by David Howarth and J. Torfing, 1–32. Hampshire and New York: Palgrave Macmillan, 2005.

Tremblay, Pierre. "À Caen, François Fillon dénonce pour la première fois le 'racisme anti-Français.'" *Huffington Post*, March 17, 2017. Available online: http://www.huffingtonpost.fr/2017/03/16/a-caen-francois-fillon-denonce-pour-la-premiere-fois-le-racism_a_21898525/ (accessed December 13, 2017).

Trump, Donald. "Inaugural Address." *The White House*, January 20, 2017. Available online: https://www.whitehouse.gov/briefings-statements/the-inaugural-address/ (accessed January 31, 2018).

Tyrer, David. *The Politics of Islamophobia: Race, Power, and Fantasy*. London: Pluto Books, 2013.

V

Vaillant, Gaël. "Martine Aubry veut en finir avec la polemique de la piscine réservée aux femmes." *Le Journal du Dimanche*, March 27, 2012. Available online: http://www.lejdd.fr/Politique/Actualite/Martine-Aubry-veut-en-finir-avec-la-polemique-de-la-piscine-reservee-aux-femmes-497816 (accessed December 26, 2017).

Valério, Ivan. "Pour Marine Le Pen, la théorie du 'grand remplacement' relève du 'complotisme.'" *Le Figaro*, November 2, 2014. Available online: http://www.lefigaro

fr/politique/le-scan/citations/2014/11/02/25002-20141102ARTFIG00145-pour-marine-le-pen-la-theorie-du-grand-remplacement-releve-du-complotisme.php (accessed December 13, 2017).

Varadarajan, Tunku. "Prophet of decline." *The Wall Street Journal*, June 23, 2005. Available online: https://www.wsj.com/articles/SB111948571453267105 (accessed December 12, 2017).

Vardon, Philippe. "Avant-propos: La première ligne." In *Génération Identitaire: Une Declaration de Guerre contre les soixante Huitards*, edited by Markus Willinger, 7–10. London: Arktos Media, 2014.

Véliocas, Joachim. *Ces Maires qui Courtisent l'Islamisme*. Paris: Tatamis, 2010.

Veron, Michel. "A Lille, Aubry a-t-elle vraiment réservé des créneaux de piscine à des musulmanes?" *L'Express*, March 20, 2012. Available online: https://www.lexpress.fr/actualite/politique/aubry-a-t-elle-vraiment-reservee-des-creneaux-de-piscine-a-des-musulmanes_1098551.html

Vigoureux, Caroline. "Copé et 'l'empiétement sémantique' sur le FN." *Le Journal du Dimanche*, September 26, 2012. Available online: http://www.lejdd.fr/Politique/Actualite/Racisme-anti-blanc-Cope-reprend-une-expression-du-FN-interview-560852 (accessed December 11, 2017).

W

Wahnich, Sophie. *L'Impossible Citoyen: l'Étranger dans le Discours de la Révolution Française*. Paris: Albin Michel, 2010.

Waters, Sarah. "New social movements in France: Une nouvelle vague citoyenne?" *Modern & Contemporary France* **6**, no. 4 (1998): 493–504.

Weaver, Simon. "A rhetorical discourse analysis of online anti-Muslim and anti-Semitic jokes." *Ethnic and Racial Studies* **36**, no. 3 (2013): 483–499.

Weil, Patrick. *Qu'est-ce qu'un Français? Histoire de la nationalité française depuis la Révolution*. Paris: Folio, 2005.

Weil, Patrick, ed. *Politiques de la Laïcité au XXe Siècle*. Paris: PUF, 2007.

Wieviorka, Michel. "After new social movements." *Social Movement Studies: Journal of Social, Cultural and Political Protest* **4**, no. 1 (2005): 1–19.

Winock, Michel. *Nationalism, Antisemitism, and Fascism in France*. Stanford: Stanford University Press, [1982] 2000.

Wodak, Ruth, M. KhosraviNik, and B. Mral, eds. *Right-Wing Populism in Europe: Politics and Discourse*. London and New York: Bloomsbury, 2013.

Wodak, Ruth and M. KhosraviNik. "Dynamics of discourse and politics in right-wing populism in Europe and beyond: An introduction." In *Right-Wing Populism in Europe. Politics and Discourse*, edited by Ruth Wodak, M. KhosraviNik, and B. Mral, xvii–xxviii. London, New Delhi, New York, and Sydney: Bloomsbury, 2013.

Y

Ye'Or, Bat. *Eurabia: The Euro-Arab Axis*. Teaneck, NJ: Fairleigh Dickinson, 2005.

Yilmaz, Ferruh. *How the Workers Became Muslims: Immigration, Culture, and Hegemonic Transformations in Europe*. Ann Arbor: The University of Michigan Press, 2016.

Yuval-Davis, Nira and F. Anthias, eds. *Racialized Boundaries. Race, Nation, Gender, Colour and Class and the Anti-Racist Struggle*. London and New York: Routledge, 1992.

Z

Zempi, Irene and I. Awan. *Islamophobia: Lived Experiences of Online and Offline Victimisation*. Bristol: Policy Press, 2017.

Zúquete, José Pedro. "The European extreme-right and Islam: New directions?" *Journal of Political Ideologies* **13**, no. 3 (2008): 321–344, p. 323.

Index